GOVERNANCE, INSTITUTIONAL CHANGE AND REGIONAL DEVELOPMENT

Governance, Institutional Change and Regional Development

Edited by
MIKE DANSON, *University of Paisley*
HENRIK HALKIER, *Aalborg University*
GRETA CAMERON, *University of Paisley*

Routledge
Taylor & Francis Group
LONDON AND NEW YORK

First published 2000 by Ashgate Publishing

Reissued 2018 by Routledge
2 Park Square, Milton Park, Abingdon, Oxon OX14 4RN
711 Third Avenue, New York, NY 10017, USA

Routledge is an imprint of the Taylor & Francis Group, an informa business

A Library of Congress record exists under LC control number: 99075457

ISBN 13: 978-1-138-63759-7 (hbk)
ISBN 13: 978-1-138-63758-0 (pbk)
ISBN 13: 978-1-315-20519-9 (ebk)

Contents

Tables

Figures

Contributors

Oddbjørn Bukve, Sogn og Fjordane College, Norway
Greta Cameron, University of Paisley, Scotland
Charlotte Damborg, Aalborg University, Denmark
Mike Danson, University of Paisley, Scotland
Ruth Downes, University of Strathclyde, Scotland
Peter Garside, Kingston University, England
Henrik Halkier, Aalborg University, Denmark
Christian Jensen, Gothenburg University, Sweden
Thomas Jud, Joanneum Research, Austria
Grigoris Kafkalas, Aristotle University of Thessaloniki, Greece
Svante Leijon, Gothenburg University, Sweden
Michael Steiner, University of Graz, Austria
Elisavet Thoidou, Aristotle University of Thessaloniki, Greece
Cecilia Wong, University of Manchester, England

PART I

INTRODUCTION

1 Regional Governance, Institutional Change and Regional Development

MIKE DANSON, HENRIK HALKIER AND GRETA CAMERON

Europe is currently experiencing two parallel developments: the increasing political importance of the regional level and the proliferation of regionally-based initiatives in economic promotion and development. Both have important consequences for the distribution of the institutionalised capacity which has been established to take and influence decisions with regard to the long-term future and development of a particular locality: in short, for the patterns of regional governance. This volume highlights the prominent role given to institution-building and institutional change in regional development within the EU towards the end of the millennium. Although institutions, networks and partnerships rather than policies often seem to be the answer to regional problems, they have also been stimulated by the general acknowledgement across the social sciences of the importance of institutional issues. Reflecting this, within the UK the establishment of the Scottish Parliament, Welsh and Northern Ireland Assemblies, and the imminent arrival of regional development agencies on the already crowded economic development landscape of England emphasise the need to put these initiatives into some context and, given the primary role of the EU in shaping that landscape, to draw on experience from across Europe. It is widely recognised and stressed in the publications of the European Commission and of the UNIDO that institutions and governance are the critical factors in the determination of the potential and success of Europe's regions. A comparative analysis of developments across Europe, therefore, is a key dimension to this book.

Much of the analysis of the trend towards decentralisation, albeit that devolution has been uneven across Europe, has often primarily been undertaken from the perspective that equates this with an increase in democracy. This approach has seen the national level as an inherently centralising force, which only reluctantly is giving way to the rising tide of regionalism, with its demands for enhanced levels of self-determination. While this is, undoubtedly, in many cases an important part of the story, there is, however, also another side to the trends towards decentralisation. In particular, central government can be accused of relieving itself of responsibility for policy areas that have become a liability. This can arise because the centre lacks the resources to manage them effectively, because the economic burden can be off-loaded by passing them onto lower tiers of government, or because the political burden of being responsible for unsuccessful policies is deemed to be high.

In this summary introduction, the rationale for this volume is advanced against this background, explaining why it is an opportune moment to address the main themes of governance and institutional change in exploring regional development. By definition, therefore, it argues that it is necessary to use a wider range of theoretical approaches to the analysis of recent changes in the economic performances and structures of areas, in contrast to the normal practice. An aim of this chapter is to offer an insight into the relevant literature on developments in institutional and governance theory, and to set the scene for the rest of the book. The chapter identifies and interprets the issues and different perspectives brought to recent debates by a range of disciplines, including economics, organisational development, politics and geography. The structure of the different sections on 'partnership and regional development', 'networking and regional governance' and 'regional development and multi-level governance' are described in brief. The main conclusions drawn by the editors from the papers reproduced here and accessed at several workshops over the last few years are presented at the end of the book.

Two aspects are central to the discussions presented here:

- the question of governance - how does the ongoing process of institution-building affect the ways in which the regions and localities are governed, including questions of democracy, participation, regional self-determination, public-private partnerships and accountability;
- the consequences of new modes of governance and institutional change for regional development strategies and policies, particularly in the context of large-scale industrial restructuring and city-region and urban regeneration.

In addressing the emerging issues of regional governance and institutional capacity this book reflects the growing intellectual interest in regional development, institutional and evolutionary economics, fiscal federalism, and the devolution of powers down from the level of the nation state. For instance, recent publications edited by Amin and Thrift (1994), Heinelt and Smith (1996), Hooghe (1996), Newlands and McCarthy (1999), Danson, Hill and Lloyd (1997) and the reference work by Wannop (1994) address various aspects of these themes.

This volume is based on the research of a network of experts across Europe who are involved in the analysis of institutions, governance and regional development. Many of the authors contributed to our previous edited book on 'Regional Development Agencies in Europe' (Halkier, Danson and Damborg 1998) which provided a comprehensive and scientific approach to the analysis of the development agency as semi-autonomous institutions. This new book complements and builds upon the conclusions of that publication. Other authors have been commissioned specially to contribute papers on particular experiences with certain models of sub-national structures or with the need to come to terms with the wider forces of globalisation, flexibility and the rise of European Union institutions.

A critical conclusion of the earlier book was that regional development agencies (RDAs) are beginning to evolve into organisations which do not aim to deliver economic development services directly as much as to co-ordinate these activities. Acting as catalysts in this way, they progress the concept of such agencies beyond simple bodies engaged in development themselves towards working in partnership with other players in the regional economy.

Reflecting the traditional form of these agencies, much analysis to date on their role and that of European and regional partnerships within different environments has focused on their policies, programmes and performances, utilising traditional economic evaluation techniques. Their evolution into and the establishment of new forms of development institutions suggest that new theoretical approaches and assessments are required. Significant as these institutions are in the delivery of regional economic strategies across the developed world, witnessed by the imminent introduction of RDAs to the English regions, there is a clear need to consider their position within the overall structures of governance. It is important to analyse how areas are administered as well as governed, therefore, in considering regional economic development structures and strategies.

In the background studies for this volume and in the editing of papers from a broad network of researchers, it has been clearly apparent that a range of methodologies have been applied to the study of governance and institutional change by the contributing authors. Indeed, without recourse to a range of disciplines, it would not have been possible to gain an understanding of the matrix of forms and structures implemented across Europe. The theoretical bases to the analyses of the case study areas and the variety of institutional frameworks have been essential in the attempts to compare and contrast these different experiences. A corollary, of course, is that no one discipline or approach has been adopted universally to explain the development of governance and institutions within or between countries.

In the following section, a number of theoretical approaches are applied which owe their origins to American studies. Although some of these translate well to the European environment, including the organisational theories of, for instance, DiMaggio and Powell (1983), others are less able to travel successfully. A good example of this latter problem is demonstrated by Cecilia Wong in chapter 4 who shows that urban regime theory is strong on predictions that do not do particularly well having crossed the Atlantic. Others have used developments of institutionalism/network theory, combining aspects of organisational theory with traditional themes in political science to examine the evolution of partnerships of organisations and authorities. The increasing concern and associated literature on competitiveness of small and medium enterprises and the promotion of intelligent regions in the (re-)generation of the economies of particular areas is applied herein by a number of authors. They therefore place institutional thickness and capacity at the heart of the analysis of the economic development process, reflecting the preoccupation of a sizable paradigm in the 1980s (Macleod 1996).

In discussing multilevel governance, a growth industry in its own right within political science, the 'actor-centred' approach that specifies the role of particular individuals and institutions in the decision making process (Marks *et al.* 1996, p.346) has been adopted in explaining some of the developments within Europe. By way of contrast, at the national level, the 'power-dependence' approach has been applied to aid understanding of the relationship between central government and sub-central public bodies (Rhodes 1988). To an extent, the 'policy network' approach addressed below in the final section goes some way to highlighting the associations between these two theories in its recognition of the importance of a multitude of actors exchanging information, expertise and other resources at both the national and European levels.

Across the sections and chapters here, it is possible to identify some common features in the application of frameworks for analyses. These reflect the disciplinary backgrounds of the authors but also the obvious need to adopt multi-disciplinary approaches to examine such complex issues as regional governance and institutions in a rapidly changing political and economic environment. There is a focus, therefore, on relations of power, the exchange of resources, and the willingness to accept that institutional and organisational features influence policy and have their own generic dynamics.

This volume discusses questions related to the relationship between governance, institutional change and regional development under three main headings, providing the basic structure of the book:

- on a micro-level the relationship between individual development bodies and their environment is explored under the heading of 'Partnership and regional development'. Building strong relationships with private sector firms and organisations has been seen as a priority for public and semi-public development agencies, and the actual experience in European regions, both the difficulties and the successes, needs to be subjected to critical and theoretically informed analysis;

- on a meso-level the role of development agencies in the political make-up of their region is examined under the heading 'Networking and regional governance'. The increasing reliance on individual agencies or networks of development bodies raises important questions about the relationship between functional efficiency and democratic legitimacy, not least when the European dimension in the form of Structural Funds programmes is involved;
- on a macro-level the relationship between regionally-based initiatives and the emerging European system of governance in Western Europe is discussed under the heading of 'Regional development and multi-level governance'. The last few decades have seen a decreasing role for the traditional regional subsidy programmes of central government and a veritable explosion of bottom-up development bodies and initiatives, and through the Structural Funds these two levels have been linked together in an intricate pattern spanning across Europe. In the search for knowledge about the new developments on the regional and European levels, the transformed role of central government has been somewhat overlooked and therefore considering the relationship between the regional, national and European levels of governance is very much a worthwhile task.

Each section is introduced with a presentation of the themes, theories and findings developed in the following chapters, with an overall introduction and conclusion to make a coherent volume and set of arguments.

Despite the breadth of contrasting theoretical approaches in this book, there does appear to be some consensus identifying where experiences and practices are transportable and where developments are regional specific. This suggests that the EU and national developments are creating the need for an evolving research agenda for regional commentators. Undoubtedly, with the apparently contradictory movements towards both greater powers for supra-national bodies such as the European Union on the one hand, and enhanced devolution to sub-national levels on the other, the theme of this volume will become ever more crucial. In this environment, a better understanding of the underpinnings of successful regional governance structures and regional institutions will be an essential feature in determining the sustainable development of communities across Europe.

References

Amin, A. and Thrift, N. (eds) (1994) *Globalization, Institutions and Regional Development in Europe*. Oxford: Oxford UP.

Danson, M., Hill, S. and Lloyd, G. (eds) (1997) *Regional Governance and Economic Development*. European Research in Regional Science 7. London: Pion.

DiMaggio, P.J and Powell, W. (1983) 'The iron cage revisited: institutional isomorphism and collective rationality in organizational fields.' *American Sociological Review 48*, 147-60.

Halkier, H., Danson, M. and Damborg, C. (eds) (1998) *Regional Development Agencies in Europe*. London: Jessica Kingsley Publishers.

Heinelt, H. and Smith, R. (eds) (1996) *Policy Networks and European Structural Funds*. Aldershot: Ashgate.

Hooghe, L (ed.) (1996) *Cohesion Policy and European Integration. Building Multi-level Governance*. Oxford: Oxford UP.

Macleod, G. (1996) 'The cult of enterprise in a networked, learning region? Governing business and skills in lowland Scotland.' *Regional Studies 30*, 749-756.

Marks, G., Hooghe, L. and Kermit, B. (1996) 'European integration from the 1980s: state-centric v. multi-level governance.' *Journal of Common Market Studies 34*, 3, 341-78.

Newlands, D. and McCarthy, J. (eds) (1999) *Governing Scotland: Problems and Prospects. The Economic Impact of the Scottish Parliament*. Aldershot: Ashgate.

Rhodes, R.A.W. (1988) *Beyond Westminster and Whitehall - The Sub-central Governments of Britain*. London: Unwin Hyman.

Wannop, U. (1994) *The Regional Imperative: Regional Planning and Governance in Britain, Europe and the US*. London: Jessica Kingsley Publishers.

PART II

PARTNERSHIP AND REGIONAL DEVELOPMENT

In the 1990s development of a particular region is no longer the responsibility of just one organisation, be it central government or a regionally-based development agency. Instead a range of organisations have become involved: some of them local, some regional, and others again acting on behalf of national or European institutions. Most of these agencies will be working together on a more or less regular and formalised basis, and many of them will be involved in partnership-arrangements with private sector organisations and actors. In short, the days where regional development was about one agency deciding the appropriate strategies and doing the implementation would seem to have gone for good. Today regional development bodies would appear to be essentially networked organisations, achieving their objectives by working in partnership with other public and private actors.

Against this background it is hardly surprising that partnership has become one of buzz-words of regional development, a good thing in itself that any self-respecting development agency would adopt as an integral part of its mode of operation. That the star of partnership has risen fast may, however, simply be a consequence of this particular type of institutional arrangement having become ubiquitous, and its mantra-like status may obscure the fact that operating through partnership may not only generate benefits but could also involve disadvantages. A more balanced view is, in other words, called for. Just looking at the possible reasons for engaging in partnership arrangements would seem to suggest the need for caution. Building consensus and pooling resources in order to ensure coordinated efforts and efficient implementation will in many cases entail very real advantages, and may well be an important part of the real reasoning behind the growth of the networked development agency. But at the same time it is also clear that the current popularity of partnership arrangements is rooted in the specific historical circumstances of the last decade. The decline of central government regional subsidies that fuelled the growth of bottom-up initiatives into an uneven web of regional and local development organisations, and the 1988 reforms of the Structural Funds made partnership a general requirement in European regional programmes. Add to this public sector bodies with limited resources constantly searching for ways of enhancing their capacity to promote development, and the well-publicised experience of very particular localities like the so-called Third Italy where consensual networking appeared to be the secret behind a thriving regional economy - and partnership could easily be construed as the new panacea. The motives of a development agency for linking up with other public and private bodies could in other words be a combination of push and pull factors: on the one hand the search for functional advantages, on the other hand a constant quest for additional resources from other public and private actors.

The chapters in this section focus primarily on two aspects of partnership. Firstly, the question of the motives and interests of the partners involved. These could be expected to differ between e.g. public and private actors and various tiers of government, and diverging economic interests, different time perspectives, incompatible strategies, and territorial politics could well make it difficult to attain the potential benefits of collaboration. Secondly, once partnership arrangements have been established, the question of their consequences for the participating organisations arises. The short-term effect is, hopefully, access to additional resources, but how will the institutionalised links influence the strategies and modus operandi of the participating organisations in the medium to long term?

In Chapter 2 Greta Cameron and Mike Danson set the scene by looking at partnership from the perspective of organisational theory, using Scotland as a case study and exploring especially its consequences for development bodies and the ways it may challenge traditional perceptions of the advantages of both regional development agencies and networking. In Chapter 3 Thomas Jud and Michael Steiner analyse the process of consensus building and strategy development in the Austrian region of

Styria, highlighting the importance of communicative aspects of regional development activities. Chapter 4 by Cecilia Wong explores the workings of partnerships in two English regions by analysing the views of development practitioners in the organisations involved, thereby questioning some of the central assumptions of urban regime theory about the role of private and public actors in partnerships.

2 The European Partnership Model and the Changing Role of Regional Development Agencies: A Regional Development and Organisation Perspective

GRETA CAMERON AND MIKE DANSON

Introduction

Partnerships between the European Union (EU) and the member states, public, private, voluntary and community sectors are seen to be the order of the day, and indeed these are often prerequisites stipulated by the European Commission (EC) and national governments (especially the UK) before any financial assistance can be granted for regional development (Boland 1996, p.299).

The aim of this chapter is to consider the partnership model for regional development and how its adoption can result in changes in the role of such institutions as regional development agencies (RDAs). Using the Scottish experience as an example, the chapter examines how networking within a partnership could impact on these institutions and proposes a framework for analysing such developments. The main focus, therefore, is on whether the partnership model developed in the Strathclyde region of Scotland is unproblematic in practice and so whether it can be transferred uncritically throughout the EU to promote regional development. In particular the chapter, in addressing the extent to which the considered success of this approach can be replicated elsewhere, recognises the dependency on specific historical, political, economic, cultural and organisational factors. Therefore, any implications of changing the operational environment and modes of working of the RDAs should be considered within these contexts. The development and importance of networks and inter-firm linkages between local economic agents for the internal organisation of regional institutions, and for regional development agencies especially, is analysed using organisational theory. A key question is whether the partnership model is appropriate for every area in the EU assisted through the Structural Funds, and so whether the current imposition of a partnership approach to delivering the single programming documents (SPDs) or community support frameworks (CSFs) is justifiable, given the potential disruption to the organisations themselves. As it is anticipated that the different infrastructures in regions suggest different abilities to benefit from this approach, some tentative conclusions are drawn on the suitability of enforcing a partnership model where the instruments and institutions do not exist to realise the gains of this delivery mechanism.

European Community Regional Policy Development

There was no collective regional policy in the EU until 1975 when the European Regional Development Fund (ERDF) was established to assist depressed areas by providing grants for investment and interest rebates on other Community loans for industrial, craft service and infrastructure projects. The ERDF underwent major reform in 1979, 1984 and again in 1988. The change in 1979 saw funding becoming more selective and by 1984 rather than supporting individual projects the emphasis moved towards funding Community Programme Contracts between the EU and member states. At this time the EU moved towards encouraging indigenous development by giving increased assistance to small and medium enterprises (SMEs) and indigenous firms in depressed areas. The Community also increased its assistance to urban areas through an expansion of the programme of Integrated Development Operations (IDOs) (Armstrong and Taylor 1993). The fundamental changes made in the 1988 reforms showed a clear commitment to partnership between the EU, member states, local and regional authorities in tackling regional difficulties. These reforms led to greater decentralisation of decision making to regional and local authorities, more consistency between the policies of national, regional and local agencies through regional partnership arrangements, and a shift towards funding multi-annual, region wide negotiated programmes.

The concept of regional partnership became central to the planning and implementation of structural fund programmes, as is clear from the way its broad functions have been defined: 'The partnership shall cover the preparation and financing as well as the ex ante appraisal, monitoring and ex post evaluation of operations' (CEC 1993, p.48-9).

The commitment to partnership influenced the 1988 reforms in two ways. First, regional planning was strengthened through the method of single programming document proposals for the use of structural funds. Second, there was an increased focus on programme rather than project assistance (Roberts and Hart 1996).

Regional Policy within Scotland

Scotland differs from other European regions in several ways which may have impacted on the success of the partnership model to date. According to Danson *et al.* (1997) there are three differences in the Scottish case. First, the responsibility of the 'Implementing Authority' has been devolved to the Scottish Office rather than being overseen by a department of central government in the capital. This relative autonomy has facilitated better relationships with local and regional organisations and given the regional partnerships more scope to develop their own momentum and operating procedures. Second, powerful regional authorities have been evident, especially in the form of Strathclyde which was created in 1975 (as coincidentally was the European Regional Development Fund). In addition to this, Strathclyde Regional Council and the City of Glasgow Council were also proactive in the formation of alliances with other European regions to promote common interests and to lobby for appropriate policy reforms as well as being represented on the main bodies in structural fund negotiations. In other words Scotland has been actively involved in accessing the structural funds and negotiating their position and as such has built up a great level of experience and knowledge in this arena over the past twenty two years of European regional development funding. Finally, the historical tradition of partnerships for urban and regional development within Scotland and in particular within Strathclyde Region, which includes Glasgow, has been evident since the 1970s when the Glasgow East Area Renewal scheme (GEAR) was created to be followed by Task Forces, Area Initiatives, etc. (see Moore and Booth 1986; Morison 1987), and then by the National Programme of Community Interest (NPCI). These initiatives were the first of their kind in Scotland, where decisions on projects for the City were taken locally by a partnership comprising the key agencies for regional development, including the Regional Council, the Scottish Office and the European Community.

The concept of a more decentralised decision making partnership for regional development was extended in 1988 when Strathclyde secured an Integrated Development Operation (IDO). This was the first European funded integrated Objective 2 economic development programme approved for a five year period in the UK. A novel feature of the IDO was the creation of a separate secretariat or 'Executive' to manage the programme within the region. The IDO enabled decentralised decision making on policy issues as well as on project applications by a Committee. The Committee consisted of agencies with a role in the economic development of the region and was chaired by the Scottish Office.

An indicator of the IDO's success is considered to be the fact that a further three independent executives were introduced in Scotland to manage the 1994-99 programmes in the Highlands and Islands, Eastern Scotland and Dumfries and Galloway.

Strathclyde continued to receive structural Objective 2 funding in the form of the 1994-1999 Operational Programme which continued to be managed by the 'Executive'. Following the reorganisation of local government in 1996 the Programme Executive was made a company limited by guarantee and is now known as The West of Scotland European Partnership. Since the creation of the IDO, membership of the Committees and their advisory groups has been widened to reflect an expanding partnership and to include independent technical experts.

The long history of collaborative working (Moore and Booth 1986; Morison 1987) and the formalised structure of the European Partnership which necessitated the formation of relationships between agencies, politicians and organisations within Scotland, may lead to the realisation of the benefits of the networking paradigm. However the following discussion on the difficulties which may arise from an organisation's environment must also be considered in the debate for the most effective, efficient, equitable and economic delivery of regional policy.

The Role of RDAs

The increased interest in economic development partnerships has been argued to be part of stimulating greater 'bottom up' development, or developing indigenous potential, compared with some former policies that tended to be more dominated by 'top down' concerns (see for example,

Stöhr 1989) and an important part in this process has been played by semi-autonomous regional development agencies (RDAs). Such institutions have existed in a number of European countries since the 1950s, but in the academic literature their increasing importance has been reflected mainly in case-studies of individual organisations (Halkier and Danson 1997). Of interest with regard to the imposition of the partnership model for access to the ERDF is the changing role of the RDAs *vis-à-vis* the other organisations in the regional development field.

A model RDA as defined by Halkier and Danson (1997, p.245) is a body which complies with the following three criteria: first, organisationally it is in a semi-autonomous position *vis-à-vis* its sponsoring political authority. Second, it supports mainly indigenous firms by means of 'soft' policy instruments. Finally, it is a multifunctional and integrated agency, the level of which may be determined by the range of policy instruments it uses.

Advantages of RDAs

RDAs are set up as a method of reducing the level of localised market failure in accordance with and in support of the government's macro-economic regional policy instruments and objectives. The political economy argument in support of development agencies - as the most effective tool for addressing such local market failures as risk aversion in the financial sector, poor market information, externalities in the provision of infrastructure and training, and problems associated with rapid growth and technological change (Danson, Lloyd and Newlands 1993) - rests on several advantages over other methods of policy implementation which have been promoted in the post-war period.

Able to intervene and interact with the economy at the most appropriate jurisdictional level (Armstrong 1997), the potential advantages of regional agencies are that they bring substantial resources to bear on problems of local economic development; they combine area and sectoral strategies as opportunities arise; they offer comprehensive business services; and they are one step removed from government and can thus develop a degree of operational freedom and credibility which regional departments of government may lack. Furthermore, potential leverage of significant private funds may be a strong advantage that a regional development agency has over central government. In addition a number of responsibilities which may be split between different departments or quasi-government agencies - such as the provision of sites, attraction of industry, environmental improvement, sector strategy, and urban development - could be located within a single organisation and so realise synergy (Moore and Booth 1986, p.119). In the words of the Trade and Industry Committee, LECs (the local enterprise companies for the Scottish regions) are 'able to deliver national schemes and programmes flexibly, in response to local needs and circumstances' (Trade and Industry Committee 1995).

Conclusion

Within the regional economic development structure of the late 20th century, there would appear to be a dominant partnership model approach which stresses the possibility of realising synergies and capturing positive externalities through formal networking. Within this environment, the institutional form established to address regional market failure, the regional development agency, is being encouraged to relate more closely to the other economic actors in regeneration and restructuring. Some have argued that this points them towards a role as a facilitator, enabler or catalyst in the regional economy (Morgan 1998), rather than the multifunctional all-embracing organisation of the 1970s.

There would appear to be an essential transmogrification implied in the incorporation of the RDA into such partnerships. Whether there are conflicts and disadvantages to these developments does not appear to have been addressed in the literature. For instance, in considering the Scottish experience, it has been suggested that the advantages of partnership include:

- increasingly innovative policies and better operational decisions arising from dialogue and interaction among organisations with different responsibilities and perspectives on problems;
- increased continuity and consistency in policy within individual organisations as a result of the building of trust and understanding with others;
- resolution of conflict and disagreement through widespread consultation and involvement in decision making;
- coordination and integration of disparate actions and aggregation of separate budgets, to enhance policy impacts;
- high level of strategic planning and decision making through shared agreement reached on essential needs and priorites. (Danson *et al.* 1997).

To assess these claims, and especially the second advantage, it is necessary to introduce a theoretical framework appropriate to the analysis of organisations working in partnership and through networks.

Networks and Partnerships

Traditional research in organisational theory has tended to concentrate on intra-firm rather than inter-firm relationships; however, with the increased interest in networking (Nohria and Eccles 1992) and indeed partnership, it has been necessary to consider the relationships between organisations in a more structured way. In addition, the impact that the external (networking) environment may have on the structure, culture and functioning of the individual organisation should have increasing importance as decentralised decision making, indigenous development and collaborative working in regional economic development become more common (Cooke and Morgan 1993; Garmise and Rees 1997; Mackintosh 1992).

The Importance of Local Networks

A basic assumption of the relationships formed to provide a network is that the organisations are mutually dependent upon resources controlled by each other, and that there are benefits to be gained by pooling their resources. Thus in network forms of resource allocation, organisations do not operate on an individual basis but relative to all the organisations in their network (Nohria and Eccles 1992; Cooke and Morgan 1993). In many ways the analysis of cartels and oligopolistic behaviour is analogous to this.

Networks are the intricate links based on trust and reciprocal patterns of communication and exchange between producers and clients that are necessary to ensure an economic capability and responsiveness (Grabher 1993). The ideal networks would enhance market allocation decisions: and in economic terms they would facilitate the externalities of decisions becoming internalised to the members. Networks mean that key agents have to work more closely together to fulfill the needs of those included in, and affected by, the network.

Networks established to deliver economic services are fundamentally local affairs (Bennett and McCoshan 1993). They depend upon the way in which businesses are served by local community and business leaders and elites, the way in which local networks perform, and in how participation takes place at a local level. However, the character of local networks, their leadership and elites, are also fundamentally determined by the economic structure and layout of their economies, which in turn depends on the relation of the local economy to the national and global economic system. As a result, different types of area possess very different types of networks of relationships. For example, there are strong contrasts between older and newer industrial areas, between areas concentrated on urban settlements and those in more dispersed urban or rural areas.

The contrasts of networks between areas create very different possibilities for development. In some areas networks allow a strong positive lead to be taken which allows the rapid economic change and adjustment on which service quality is founded (Ricard 1997). In other areas, the absence of an effective network, or a network tuned to bygone circumstances, can be a strong inhibition to economic growth. Local networks thus can be strong supply side factors that raise or lower the economic growth potential for different parts of the country (Bennett and McCoshan 1993; Doeringer, Terkla and Topakian 1987).

From Networks to Partnerships

Networks are the essential means for linking one group of agents to others whom they effect and are the mechanism for the exchange of information and services in support of business development. Beyond simple networks, partnerships require the commitment of the agents to work fully together. This means:

- accepting long term structures that work towards sustained commitment to change and achievement of quality;
- accepting an active commitment to changing the internal operations of each agent, and helping other agents also to change to achieve an improved system overall. (WMEB Consultants 1995).

Hence networking alone is largely passive, whereas partnerships require active participation (Mackintosh 1992). Partnerships are based on firm agreements by agents to work together. They extend far beyond network flows of information, to offer a system that ensures that the problem, or the client, is fully addressed. Partnerships can range from agreements between actors to work together towards a common end, to agreements which form a legal contract through which specific targets for performance are defined by the contracting parties. Over this range of possibilities the parties may act as relatively equal partners, but frequently the partnership is not equal: it is more important to one party than to others, or performance is mandated or coerced by one party on another (frequently through financial powers).

Networking and Partnerships in the European Context

The European Commission is considered to be one of the main driving forces in the development of partnership, and therefore in networking behaviour, with the aim of achieving the goal of European integration and cohesion (Bennett and Krebs 1994). As a means of encouraging this behaviour many of their initiatives and programmes have a pre-requisite that the organisations must be involved in a partnership or network (Cooke and Morgan 1993). As highlighted earlier, this is evident in the arrangements for regional policy funding and for accessing structural funds. The aim of those arrangements is to harness the energy, skills and resources of the key actors in the regional development environment and to develop and implement solutions to increase cohesion across the European Union. Given the pre-eminent position of the Strathclyde model in the evolution of this partnership form of delivering structural funds in the EU (Danson *et al.* 1997), Figure 2.1 outlines the structure and functions of the West of Scotland Partnership.

The Partners: Strathclyde European Partnership Around 180 public agencies involved in economic regeneration have accessed the structural funds and are therefore included in the partnership. These organisations are referred to as partners and are involved in the locally based decision making process outlined in the accompanying diagram. Proposals flow up from the partner organisations, through the Advisory Groups to the Programme Committee. Over 120 representatives from 65 agencies make up the committees. Strathclyde European Partnership is supported by a full time programme Executive - SEP Limited - based locally, and it is responsible for the day-to-day management of the various European Programmes being applied in the area. SEP Limited provides the link between the local partners, the European Commission and The Scottish Office. SEP Limited is a company limited by guarantee formed by the twelve local government Councils, Scottish Enterprise, five local enterprise companies, and the Further Education College Partnership for the region. The partners contribute 50 per cent of the management costs of the Programme and the European Commission contributes the other 50 per cent. The partners categorised by sectoral / interest groups are:

- European Commission DGXVI and DGV
- The Scottish Office and central Government agencies
- Local Authorities
- Scottish Enterprise and the Local Enterprise Companies
- Universities and Further Education Colleges
- Enterprise Trusts and Economic Initiatives
- Area Tourist Boards
- National and regional bodies involved in economic development
- Eligible voluntary bodies and charitable organisations involved in economic development

The SEP is a broadly based structure, therefore, with all the major and significant economic development actors incorporated into the Partnership. To a greater or lesser extent, each of these organisations influences and is influenced by the culture, mores and philosophies of the other partners, beyond their operational forms and modes of working.

The danger always exists that such network development and so partnerships may become dysfunctional. Just as the forces which encouraged collaborative working started, so they can be discontinued by the key persons or organisations losing faith in the merits of joint working arrangements. At the network level if those that discontinue their involvement are the main power and resource providers (as the network will usually be formed for access to increased or better resources e.g. finance, information, goods) the network may stagnate and the partnership fail (Soeters 1993).

Regional Development and Organisational Theory

Cooke and Morgan's study (1993) examined network forms of organisation, assessing their significance in the field of regional development. Their criticism was that to date 'organisational theory pays insufficient attention to network relations between firms and public or quasi-public intermediary agencies' (Cooke and Morgan 1993, p.543). On

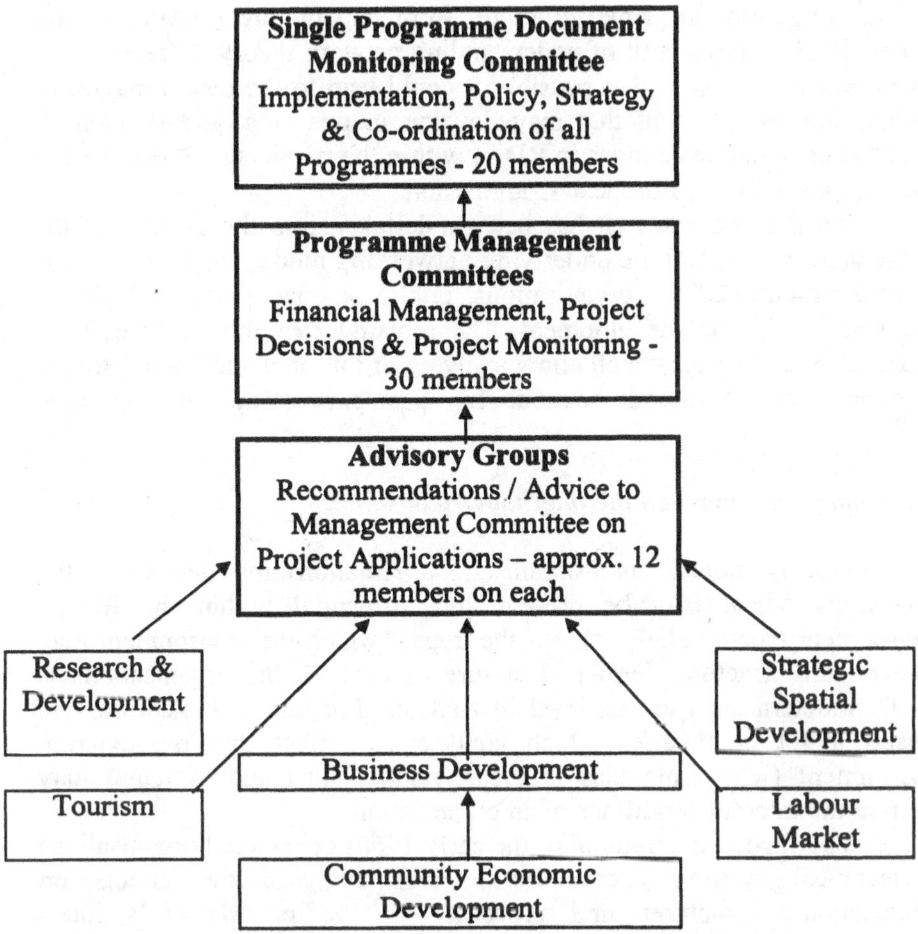

Figure 2.1 Committee Structure 1997-1999: Strathclyde European Partnership

their particular criticism, it will be argued that it is important to consider not only the networks within the regional development environment but also the impact that the networks have on each organisation's internal environment. Therefore it is necessary to centre on regional development, and to apply the organisational theoretical view of institutions. Regardless of the type of network (including level of trust, power relationships etc.) or environment (political, technological etc.), it can be argued that organisations sharing and facing the same external environment, over time, will converge on the same structure, form and culture (DiMaggio and Powell 1983). The benefit of understanding network theory in the regional development context is that possibly it could lead to the determination of the internal environment that may develop in this area, and so identify potential or probable changes in RDAs within the partnership model that is being imposed by the European Commission.

To date no research has been undertaken into the effect that the partnership model, and the underlying networking model, may have on the internal structure of the organisations, public or quasi-public, which are involved in regional development. The remainder of the paper outlines organisational theories which allow analyses of this area and applies this to the experience in Scotland, the model European partnership area (Danson *et al.* 1997).

Environmental Impact on the Internal Organisation

As previously noted, inter-organisational relationships determine the institutions which may be present and influential within the RDA's environment (spatial analysis), but the impact which the environment may have on the structure, form and culture of each of the organisations is wholly indeterminant at this level of analysis. For this, it is necessary to consult a set of theories which analyse the effect that the external environment (which includes linkages, relationships and systems) may exert on the internal conditions of an organisation.

The favoured paradigm of the early 1960s considered organisations as technical systems (Scott 1991). This analysed the effects on organisational structures and processes of the organisation's interdependence with its environment in terms of resource inputs and outputs, known as the 'input-throughput-output' paradigm. The problem with this set of theories was they only considered technical aspects, where structures and processes were shaped purely by the technical rationality of the organisations, and not by the social context and the interdependence of organisations and their environments. Any apparent departure from rationality was assessed by looking inside the organisation (at power and social structures) rather than at the social structures in the organisation's external environment.

Following from these technical models, the population ecology model (Hannan and Freeman 1977) considered more fully the effects of the environment on the organisation's internal functioning, with its main focus being on organisations competing for their survival. It differed from traditional explanations of organisational change in several ways. Instead of looking at the internal organisation to determine the cause of change it focused on the nature and distribution of resources in the external environment as the central force in change. The theory also took into account the historical context within which organisations emerge, paying particular attention to the economic and political conditions. However, there are several difficulties with the population ecology model which may suggest that it is inappropriate for the analysis of the external environment of the RDAs and the impact on their internal organisation. For example, Hatch (1997, p.83) argues:

> When competitiveness is compromised by the existence of enormously powerful organizations or barriers to entry or exit, the population ecology model loses much of its explanatory power.

The involvement of the government and the European Commission through finance and legislation, and the legal barriers for entry and exit in the regional development sector, can be considered as significant limitations on the applicability of this theory. Furthermore, these theories have been applied to account for the diversity in the types and structures of organisations whereas this paper argues for the possibility of homogeneity in culture, structure and form between organisations working within the same external environment.

Institutionalisation Theory

Akin to the population ecology model, much of modern organisational theory posits a diverse and differentiated world of organisations and seeks to explain variation among organisations in structure and behaviour (Woodward 1965; Child and Kieser 1981). However, of more interest for the continuing and changing role of the RDA is the homogeneity of organisational forms and practices rather than the variation in the organisational field.

DiMaggio and Powell (1983) agreed that in the initial stages of their life cycles, organisational fields display considerable diversity in their approach and form. However, they further noted that once a field had become well established, as indeed we may consider the regional development organisational field within Strathclyde and the West of

Scotland, there is an inexorable push towards homogenisation. Institutionalisation theory, which looks first to the social interdependence of organisations and then focuses on 'isomorphism within the institutional environment' (Zucker 1987, p.443), whereby organisations adopt patterns which are externally defined as appropriate to their environments and that are reinforced by the social relationships of other actors in their environment, explains the process.

Organisational Fields For institutional theorists, the appropriate level of analysis for the environment is neither the whole society nor the individual organisation but an intermediate level. The most accepted term for this level is the 'organisational field' defined by DiMaggio and Powell (1983, p.148) as:

> those organisations that, in the aggregate, constitute a recognised area of institutional life: key suppliers, resource and product consumers, regulatory agencies and other organisations that produce similar services or products.

The considered virtue of this level of analysis is that it directs attention to all the relevant actors in the environment of an organisation. According to DiMaggio and Powell the organisational field is a social structure in that it involves mutual awareness of the activities that the organisations have in common. In other terms they are aware of all the actors in their particular environment (Westney 1988).

The organisational field analysis comprehends the importance of both connectedness (Laumann *et al.* 1978) and structural equivalence (White *et al.* 1976). Connectedness and structural equivalence respectively are: the existence of transactions tying organisations to one another either formally or informally, and the similarity of position in the network (DiMaggio and Powell 1983). That is, this level of analysis takes account of the network of relations within which they interact. DiMaggio and Powell (1983, p.148) called attention to the increasing 'structuration' of inter-organisational relations and organisational fields which they believed led to the emergence of homogenisation of organisational forms, culture and output. The process of defining an 'institution' or the structuration of an organisational field was determined by DiMaggio (DiMaggio and Powell 1983, p.148), whereby four aspects of the environment should be considered:

an increase in the extent of interaction among organizations in the field; the emergence of sharply defined interorganizational structures of domination and patterns of coalition; an increase in the information load with which organizations in a field must contend; and the development of a mutual awareness among participants in a set of organizations that they are involved in a common enterprise.

DiMaggio proposed that once disparate organisations in the same line of business are structured into an actual field by competition, the government, or the professions, powerful forces emerge that lead them to become more similar to one another. Thus the question arises: if the field of regional development is highly structured, which method of delivery of regional policy is the most effective, efficient, equitable and economic. Furthermore, should the model of partnership be encouraged throughout the other assisted areas of the European Union if it causes homogeneity of structure, culture and outputs rather than heterogeneity, innovation and an obvious role for each organisation in the field?

By contrast, Scott and Meyer (1983) argued that, under some conditions, more highly structured organisational environments may create an increasing diversity of form. For example, they suggested that where environments lack centralised control or authority the organisational forms will move towards being homogenous through imitation, competition or pressure. However, they proposed that in highly centralised decision making areas, where authority was powerful, the decision makers may create a variety of highly specialised organisational forms, and thus by design homogenisation will not occur.

One of the limitations involved in using this theory lies in defining the boundaries of the organisational field. There are four main choices regarding boundaries identified by Scott (1991, p.174):

- defining the degree of connection and influence which is required to include an organisational actor within the functional field;
- choosing the level for the 'similarity' of services or products;
- making the assumptions where large or multi-functional organisations operate in the field;
- accounting for bound cultural patterns, which are generally less visible, being more subtle and invasive than structural links.

Boundaries are set according to the similarity of service, critical exchange partners, sources of funding, regulatory groups, professional or trade associations, and any other influential sources. Local and non-local, vertical and horizontal linkages, cultural and political influences as well as technical relationships are included in 'any other influential sources' (Scott 1991). In the case of the Strathclyde European Partnership, the boundaries would be defined as any organisation accessing the partnership either through funds or in a legal or advisory capacity (as described in the formal structures outlined earlier).

Isomorphism The concept of isomorphism was described by Hawley as a 'constraining process that forces one unit in a population to resemble other units that face the same set of environmental conditions' (DiMaggio and Powell 1983, p.149). In other words over time a process of homogenisation occurs.

DiMaggio and Powell (1983), following Meyer and Fennel, considered two types of isomorphism: competitive and institutional. Competitive isomorphism assumes a system rationality that emphasises market competition, niche change and fitness measures. Such a view is useful where there is free and open competition in a field. However in the network / partnership model it does not present an adequate analysis as the basic assumption is that the relationships are based on leadership, not competition, and therefore an environment of open competition is not provided. For these cases DiMaggio and Powell developed an institutional view of isomorphism which had been introduced by Kanter.

There are three mechanisms of institutional isomorphic change depicted by DiMaggio and Powell (1983, p.150):

i) Coercive Isomorphism

This occcurs where organisational patterns are imposed on organisations by a more powerful authority, usually the Government. It results from both formal and informal pressures exerted on an organisation by other members of the organisational field, upon which the organisation depends and by cultural expectations in the society in which the organisation functions.

Pfeffer and Salancik (1978) considered how organisations faced with unmanageable interdependence seek to use the greater power of the larger social system and its government to eliminate difficulties or provide for needs. They noted two different characteristics of environments which had been set up by the Government. First, that political decision makers do not always directly experience the consequences of their actions and second, political decisions are often applied across whole classes of organisations thus decision making is less flexible and less adaptive.

Meyer and Rowan (1977) examined the nature of change as states and large organisations expanded their dominance and found that as the level of dominance rises the organisational structures increasingly reflected the rules institutionalised and legitimised by and within the state. As a result institutions are increasingly homogenous within given organisational fields and increasingly organised around rituals of conformity to wider institutions. Any expansion of the government's control supports the homogeneity of organisational fields through direct authority relationships.

ii) Mimetic Isomorphism

This is where organisations respond to the uncertainty in their environment by modelling themselves on the organisations that are perceived to be successful in their type of environment. This can be achieved indirectly through employee transfer or turnover, or explicitly by organisations such as consulting firms or industry trade associations. In this way models of structure, for example, can be implemented by mimetic process rather than by rational decision making by the organisation, for example, on the efficiency of such a structure.

iii) Normative Isomorphism

Larson (1977) and Collins (1979), interpret professionalism as the collective struggle of members of an occupation to define the conditions and methods of their work, to control 'the production of producers' (Larson 1977) and to establish a cognitive base and legitimation for their occupational autonomy.

Perrow (1974) asserted that the normative pressures of professional behaviour mechanisms created a group of almost interchangeable individuals who occupy similar positions across a range of organisations. Therefore because the group is so similar in its characteristics and direction it may dominate any possible variations in tradition and control that might have shaped organisational behaviour.

Two aspects of professionalism that may lead to isomorphism are, first, the increasingly formalised educational structures determining a cognitive base and, second, the large number of organisational networks which bridge organisations and lead to a rapid diffusion of new models. Other important factors may contribute to normative isomorphism. These could include a specific labour market for an organisational field and the existence of common career paths and titles: namely structural homogenisation and status competition where organisations attempt to provide the equivalent services and benefits as others in the field.

This pressure is felt where 'appropriate' organisational patterns are championed by professional organisations.

It is apparent from the theories discussed here that there are parallels elsewhere in the market economy of organisations becoming more like each other through partnerships and networking. Whether the form, nature, structures and operations of the European Partnership model have been constructed in such a way to promote such evolutions is of concern if these consequential changes in the development agencies, for instance, were to be to the disadvantage of the regional economy. It is to an examination of these potential changes that we now turn.

Predictions from Organisational Theory

It is not intended to test the Strathclyde European Partnership nor the various development bodies, and the regional development agency for Scotland, Scottish Enterprise, in particular, against the organisational theories described above. Rather the aim of this paper is to identify where the theory may suggest potential disadvantages for the efficient and effective working of the development agencies when they become incorporated into partnerships and networking strategies. By the very fact that the mechanisms of isomorphic change can be determined, it is possible to go further and suggest hypotheses which may predict the changes within the field of regional development within Strathclyde. These hypotheses can then be examined through the collection of data on the characteristics of the relevant organisations and analysed both cross-sectionally and, preferably, over time. The full operationalisation of the testing of these hypotheses is a significant part of a larger research programme which is contributing to the PhD of Greta Cameron, one of the authors of this chapter.

DiMaggio and Powell (1983) suggested several hypotheses for the determination of the level of homogenisation of structure, process and behaviour in an organisational field. They categorised the hypotheses by the three previously identified isomorphic pressures to change and further grouped them as organisational level or organisational field predictors. The predictors require that indicators be determined for each category and group. However, as the focus of this paper is on the level of isomorphic pressure to change - on one particular organisation in the field of regional development and not on the whole set - the organisational field level predictors will be not be detailed at this stage. So, the given organisational level predictors outlined below may be used for the analysis of particular regional development agencies within Strathclyde and, at this stage, the associated indicators are not relevant.

The organisational level predictors are:

i) Coercive Isomorphism

a) An organisation will become increasingly similar in structure, climate and behavioural focus to another organisation where its dependence on a particular organisation is highest.
b) The higher the level of centralisation of resources an organisation has, the more it will change isomorphically as this level of dependency increases.
c) The greater the level of legislative and financial power asserted by a member of an organisational field the more it will change isomorphically as the level of dependency increases.

The levels of dependency of Scottish Enterprise on other organisations in the field may be considered by setting indicators for those areas of most importance to the organisation. This would allow the position of Scottish Enterprise to be identified. Following this the level of isomorphic change and level of institutionalisation in individual organisations may be determined:

ii) Mimetic Isomorphism

a) The more uncertain the operating environment the more an organisation will model itself on others whom it deems successful.
b) The more ambiguous the goals of an organisation the more liable it is to model itself on another organisation it perceives as successful.
c) The more an organisation has to increase its area of expertise the more liable it is to follow the strategy for internal growth and

development of another organisation which it perceives as successful.

In order to consider the role of the regional development agencies in Strathclyde in the partnership, the type of operating environment which each organisation in the field perceives is important will need to be identified and analysed. Similarly, the views of the RDAs on which organisations they perceive to be most successful will be relevant. It would be significant if they were all modelling themselves on the same organisation, whether or not it was within the partnership, and whether they introduced such cultures and forms of operating into other non-Strathclyde European Partnership activities.

iii) Normative Isomorphism

a) The higher the level of dependence in an organisation on academic credentials for choosing staff the greater the level of isomorphism.
b) The greater the participation of the staff in professional and trade associations the greater the influence of normative isomorphic pressure.
c) The more the screening and recruitment procedures are determined by outside consultants the greater the pressure of isomorphic change.

Given the relative isolation of the Scottish local economic development community, and the attempts to introduce postgraduate qualifications accessible by staff of the Scottish Enterprise Network, local authorities, and other agencies, an internal labour market might be identified, within the particular field. A degree of mobility between the members of the Strathclyde European Partnership, where workers take their cultures and ideas between organisations, would be indicative of potential isomorphic change.

The organisational level predictors are useful in the determination of the level of pressure of isomorphic change exerted on Strathclyde RDAs. Additionally, this chapter is considering the impact that the model of partnership has had on this organisational field and in particular on the role of these local agencies. Thus a key question remains, could the partnership model lead to, or exacerbate, the isomorphic pressures of change and the level of institutionalisation in the organisation and its field?

To undertake this analysis requires further consideration of the model of partnership and the resultant advantages and disadvantages that are proposed for this model of economic regional development.

Conclusion

Disadvantages of Partnership

It would appear that at least two of the points identified as advantages of partnership above may be applied to highlight the existence of isomorphism, using the very nature of the model of partnership to demonstrate these potential disadvantages.

To reiterate, the benefits claimed by some commentators of partnership have been identified as:

- increasingly innovative policies and better operational decisions arising from dialogue and interaction among organisations with different responsibilities and perspectives on problems;
- *increased continuity and consistency in policy within individual organisations as a result of the building of trust and understanding with others;*
- resolution of conflict and disagreement through widespread consultation and involvement in decision making;
- coordination and integration of disparate actions and aggregation of separate budgets, to enhance policy impacts;
- high level of strategic planning and decision making through shared agreement reached on essential needs and priorites. (Danson *et al.* 1997; *emphasis added*).

These, however, now could be reinterpreted as disadvantages when taking account of the organisational level predictors for isomorphic change. For example:

- A tendency to generalised, 'lowest common denominator' policies and difficulties in acting strategically, where each institution has to compromise their unique approach to the solutions of regional problems in favour of what is acceptable to the other partners, would suggest coercive, isomorphic pressure is present.

- There may be inefficient, time consuming procedures as a result of the extensive communication, deliberation and pressure to reach consensus. This may be for reasons of transparency and accountability, even if only to the other institutions in the partnership, while committee structures may have been established to build trust and so co-operation. Due to the fact that pressure to reach consensus is apparent, this would suggest the likelihood of coercive, isomorphic change.
- There may be a *confusion of roles, responsibilities and accountability as a result of the obscure, shared process of decision-making* (see (b) above). Apparent democratic committee structures in a partnership will lessen the freedom of action of the individual partners and so their abilities to pursue the independent strategies imposed on them by their founders and sponsors. Any resultant confusion of roles etc. can lead to mimetic isomorphism; however, if the emphasis is on reducing the freedom of action it may be that coercive isomorphic change is the strongest pressure. Both forces may be identified within one organisational structure.
- There is may be a concealment of divergent interests and unequal power relationships between partners, despite the installed committee and programme structures demonstrating manifest consensus and cohesion. This can lead to some partners remaining more equal than others, with a greater capability to meet the criteria for matchable funding, to access the powerful sponsors of the partnership, and to apply technical competencies, allowing a greater real control over the resources and agenda of the partnership than is apparent from the documentation. In this case, concealment and unequal power again imply the ability for coercive isomorphic pressure to become commonplace.
- The operating environment can become highly politicised, with short-term considerations the norm. Therefore, uncertainty for those organisations involved in local economic development at times may be significant. Within this type of environment, mimetic forces would be expected to be seen where their strategic processes.
- The rise in courses which are pertinent to those working in local economic development suggest that professionalism within this environment is increasing. This may demonstrate normative isomorphic pressure of change.

A critical question for this field of study is whether the process of partnership is encouraging the transmogrification of the traditional RDAs into merely the catalysts, co-ordinators and animateurs of regional economic development. If they are losing the essence of their original rationale: to be integrated and coherent institutions able to act semi-autonomously in regeneration, then the definition of Halkier and Danson (1997) of a model agency becomes problematic. And, more significantly perhaps, it suggests that the form of the RDA which has been promoted as the exemplar through the last two decades may well be being developed into a much closer instrument of government - national or European - than has been considered desirable to date. If RDAs are witnessing an erosion of their semi-autonomous position vis-à-vis their sponsoring political authorities, with the EC and other partners constraining their freedom of action; a limitation on their support for indigenous firms by means of 'soft' policy instruments, because of changed priorities and higher binding regulations; and the loss of some of their range of functions and degree of integration to other partners, then the traditional RDA may have been a short lived form of institution.

These changes may appear rational and consistent with the objectives of the partnership model and of the Structural Funds, but they do raise questions of whether synergies and independence are being foresaken in favour of apparent accountability and organisational targeting across institutions. So, a research agenda is suggested which addresses these propositions by returning to the rationale for the establishment of regional development agencies as argued by such as Danson, Lloyd and Newlands (1993) and Halkier and Danson (1997) and considering these hypothesised developments against them.

These commentators claimed that they are not only 'the "manageable" bottom up alternative, avoiding the bewildering maze of local initiatives' but they also allow 'for flexibility and receptiveness to the specific problems of indigenous industry within the region. At the same time, a position outside the mainstream government *apparatus* appears to make it possible to pursue public policies without evoking the ghosts of *interventionism or state dirigisme*, and so to make it easier to adopt a *long-term perspective*, while the *distance from government* frequently generates an operating environment more closely attuned to the needs of enterprise' (Halkier and Danson 1995, p.1, *emphasis added*). In other words, the perceived advantages of RDAs as a form of regional policy delivery institution may well be compromised by the increasing moves to partnership and formal networking. Whether these costs are worth bearing will depend on the benefits realised and the synergies released by the European Partnership model. We would argue that a detailed analysis of this is necessary and current research on this will be reported in future publications.

The questions which may arise at this point are first, whether the RDAs organisational field is highly organised and structured and second, if so, and in accordance with Scott and Meyer's proposals, have the Government and European Commision taken steps to ensure that homogenisation does not occur (i.e. is there legal clarification of the roles of those involved in regional development) through the increased need to raise finance by interaction in partnerships (inducement to participate)? Third, could partnerships and networking in the field of regional development lead to an increase in isomorphic pressures and therefore speed up the process of homogenisation? Finally, was homogenisation present previous to the inducement of working in partnership and, if so, can the degree of institutionalisation be determined in this field and compared to other areas which are now beginning this process?

References

Armstrong, H. (1997) 'Regional-level jurisdictions and economic regeneration initiatives'. In M. Danson, S. Hill and G. Lloyd (eds) *Regional Governance and Economic Development.* European Research in Regional Science 7. London: Pion, 26-46.

Armstrong, H. and Taylor, J. (1993) *Regional Economics and Policy.* 2nd edition. Hemel Hempstead: Harvester Wheatsheaf.

Bennett, R.J. and Krebs, G. (1994) 'Local economic development partnerships: an analysis of policy networks in EC LEDA local employment development strategies. *Regional Studies 28*, 2, 119-141.

Bennett, R.J. and McCoshan, A. (1993) *Enterprise and Human Resource Development: Local Capacity Building.* London: Paul Chapman Publishing.

Boland, P. (1996) 'Regional development strategies in Europe.' In J. Alden and P. Boland (eds) *Regional Development Strategies: A European Perspective.* London: Jessica Kingsley Publishers, 296-304.

CEC (1993) *Community Structural Funds 1994-1999 Revised Regulations and Comments.* Commission of the European Communities: Brussels.

Child, J. and Kieser, A. (1981) 'Development of organizations over time.' In P.C. Nystrom and W.H. Starbuck (eds) *Handbook of Organizational Design.* Oxford: Oxford University Press, 28-64.

Collins, R. (1979) *The Credential Society.* New York: Academic Press.

Cooke, P. and Morgan, K. (1993) 'The network paradigm: new departures in corporate and regional development.' *Environment and Planning D: Society and Space 11*, 543-564.

Danson, M., Fairley, J., Lloyd, M.G., Turok, I. (1997) *The Governance of the European Structural Funds: The Experience of the Scottish Regional Partnerships.* Paper 10, Scotland Europa Centre, Brussels.

Danson, M., Lloyd, M.G. and Newlands, D. (1993) 'The role of regional development agencies.' In R.T. Harrison and M. Hart (eds) *Spatial Policy in a Divided Nation* London: Jessica Kingsley Publishers, 162-175.

DiMaggio, P.J. and Powell, W. (1983) 'The iron cage revisited: institutional isomorphism and collective rationality in organizational fields.' *American Sociological Review 48*, 147-60.

Doeringer, P., Terkla, D. and Topakian, G. (1987) *Invisible Factors in Local Economic Development.* New York: Oxford University Press.

Garmise, S. and Rees, G. (1997) 'The role of institutional networks in local economic development: a new model of governance?' *Local Economy 12*, 2, 104-118.

Grabher, G. (ed) (1993) *The Embedded Firm, On the Socioeconomics of Industrial Networks.* London: Routledge.

Halkier, H. and Danson, M. (1995) 'Regional development agencies in Western Europe: a survey of key characteristics and trends.' *European Studies Working Paper 7*, University of Paisley.

Halkier, H. and Danson, M. (1997) 'Regional development agencies in Western Europe: a survey of key characteristics and trends.' *European Urban and Regional Studies 4*, 3, 241-254.

Hannan, M.T. and Freeman, J.H. (1977) 'The population ecology of organizations.' *American Journal of Sociology 82*, 929-64.

Hatch, M.J. (1997) *Organization Theory: Modern Symbolic and Postmodern Perspectives.* Oxford: Oxford University Press.

Larson, M.S. (1977) *The Rise of Professionalism: A Sociological Analysis.* University of California Press.

Laumann, E.O., Galaskiewicz, J. and Marsden, P. (1978) 'Community structure as interorganizational linkage.' *Annual Review of Sociology 4*, 455-84.

Mackintosh, M. (1992) Partnership: issues of policy and negotiation.' *Local Economy* 7, 3, 210-224.

Meyer, J.W. and Rowan, B. (1977) 'Institutionalized organizations: formal structure as myth and ceremony.' *American Journal of Sociology 83*, 340-63.

Moore, C. and Booth, S. (1986) 'Unlocking enterprise: the search for synergy.' In W.F. Lever and C. Moore *The City in Transition, Policies and Agencies for the Economic Regeneration of Clydeside.* Oxford: Clarendon Press, 107-119.

Morgan, K. (1998) 'Institutions, innovation and regional renewal - the development agency as animateur.' In H. Halkier, M. Danson and C. Damborg (eds) *Regional Development Agencies in Europe.* London: Jessica Kingsley Publishers, 229-252.

Morison, H. (1987) *The Regeneration of Local Economies.* Oxford: Clarendon Press.

Nohria, N. and Eccles, R.G. (eds) (1992) *Networks and Organisations: Structure, Form and Action.* Boston: Harvard Business School Press.

Perrow, C. (1974) 'Is Business Really Changing?' *Organizational Dynamics*, Summer, 31-44.

Pfeffer, J. and Salancik, G.R. (1978) *The External Control of Organisations: A Resource Dependence Perspective.* New York: Harper & Row.

Ricard, J. (1997) 'Brittany: endogenous development and socio-political networks.' *Regions*, April, 31-36.

Roberts, P. and Hart, T. (1996) *Regional Strategy and Partnership in European Programmes: Experience in Four UK Regions*. York: York Publishing Services.

Scott, W.R. (1991) 'Unpacking institutional arguments.' In W. Powell and P. DiMaggio (eds) *The New Institutionalism in Organizational Analysis*. Chicago: The University of Chicago Press., 164-182.

Scott, W.R. and Meyer, J.W. (1983) 'The organization of societal sectors.' In J.W. Meyer and W.R. Scott (eds) *Organizational Environments: Ritual and Rationality*. Beverly Hills: Sage, 129-153.

Soeters, J.L. (1993) 'Managing Euregional networks.' *Organization Studies 4*, 639-656.

Stöhr, W. (1989) 'Regional policy at the crossroads: an overview.' In *Regional Policy at the Crossroads: European Perspectives*. L. Albrechts, F. Moulaert, P. Roberts and E. Swyngedouw (eds). London: Jessica Kingsley Publishers, 191-197.

Trade and Industry Committee (1995) *Regional Policy 1994-1995*. 4th Report. London: HMSO.

Westney, D.E. (1988) 'Isomorphism, institutionalization and the multinational enterprise.' Paper presented at the Academy of International Business Annual Meeting, San Diego, California.

White, H.C., Scott, A.; Boorman, S.A. and Breiger, R.L. (1976) 'Social structure from multiple networks, I: blockmodels of roles and positions.' *American Journal of Sociology 81*, 730-80.

WMEB Consultants (1995) *Local Economic Development Learning Pack*. Birmingham: WMEB.

Woodward, J. (1965) *Industrial Organization Theory and Practice*. London: Oxford University Press.

Zucker, L.G. (1987) Institutional theories of organizations.' *Annual Review of Sociology 13*, 443-64.

3 Developing a Culture of Collaboration: Concepts and Experiences in a Regional Context

THOMAS JUD AND MICHAEL STEINER

Introduction

Within the last twenty years regional policy has undergone some profound changes. Up to the late 1970s it was still firmly embedded in a general fiscal policy scheme and mostly exercised and executed at a national level. In the early 1980s new approaches both on a theoretical and on a policy making level slowly took shape: concepts such as innovation orientation, and reliance on the endogenous potential emerged while a bottom-up perspective appeared. At the same time, emphasis was placed on new factors of regional development: the importance of small- and medium-sized firms, the development of infrastructure, and the existence of a service sector. These 'objective' factors had to be supplemented by 'subjective' ones: entrepreneurial behaviour, technological know-how, managerial capabilities, and qualification and education of the workforce.

In the late 1980s and early 1990s these approaches were enriched by the concepts of networking, embeddedness and alliances. In contrast to a narrowly defined 'endogenous approach' accentuating the importance of the utilisation of local resources, a stronger integration of these potentials in transregional, national and international networks was asked for. The process of internationalisation was regarded as a gradual learning process and as a strategic task requiring permanent efforts; it presupposes a continual adjustment of the specific forms of co-operation with other firms. Regional policy also had to take into account the change in the organisational form of industrial and service enterprises, of the mostly immaterial character of infrastructure, and of the tacit character of large parts of technological and organisational knowledge.

All these insights have called for a 're-engineering' of regional policy and thus have changed its character: it is confronted with a larger degree of uncertainty with strong non-deterministic elements, it involves more actors on different levels and from diverse institutions, and it incorporates more and more knowledge elements. Information exchange, enforcement of communication processes and co-operation therefore become important elements of regional policy and necessitate a more experimental approach. Regional policy design becomes more and more a concept in progress, a process of 'learning in developing the results'.

In the following we will present an example of such an approach: the elaboration and step-wise implementation of a technology policy concept for the province of Styria in Austria. During three years of work, the Institute of Technology and Regional Policy - InTeReg developed a Technology Policy Concept for Styria on behalf of the regional government of Styria. Comprehensive empirical work was carried out to analyse technological and economic strengths and weaknesses of the region and to serve as a basis for a set of promotional measures and initiatives developed to improve regional economic competitiveness within national and international contexts. In this process an experimental approach was used which combined scientific methods with strong communicational elements. These elements were necessary to ensure a better acceptance of the measures by the actors involved and to build a collaborative framework for the process of their implementation.

The paper describes the rationale behind this specific approach, used to elaborate the regional technology policy concept and the various effects it is having on Styrian regional technology policy in general as well as on the collaborative behaviour of regional actors in the economic, the administrative and the political sphere. First we outline Styria's economic background. Second we briefly present the empirical basis and the strategic orientation of the technology policy concept and give some concrete examples of collaborative projects conducted and new organisational frameworks established. Finally we discuss how the implementation is influenced by an experimental approach and can be understood as a process of 'learning in developing the results'.

Regional Economic Background: Styria is a Heterogeneous Region with an Improving Economic Performance

Styria is one of the nine provinces of the Federal Republic of Austria situated in the south- eastern part of the country, bordering on Slovenia and close to Hungary. It has a population of around 1.2 million, an area of 16,000 km² and a 12 per cent share of the Austrian GNP. Following Palme (1989) it can be classified into four different types of regions according to the profitability of firms (indicated by labour costs in relation to net production value), accessibility (indicated by size of firms), resource endowment (indicated by the number of white collar workers in an industry in relation to total employment in an industry and wage rate) and the dominating economic sectors within these areas (indicated by employment in capital intensive or labour intensive industries in relation to total employment).[1]

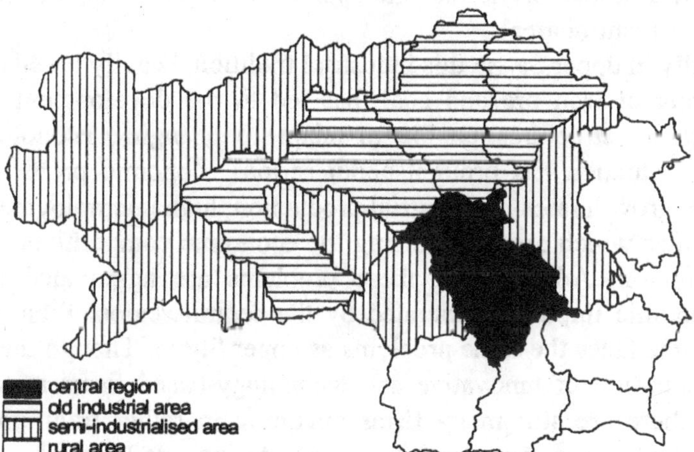

Figure 3.1 Regional classification of Styria

[1] To determine indicator values, economic data at the level of Styrian districts were used by Palme.

These four areas are characterised by:

> *central area*: high accessibility, good resource endowment, a balanced mix of economic branches and high profitability.
> *old industrial area (upper Styria)*: a predominance of capital intensive branches, poor resource endowment and rather low profitability.
> *semi-industrialised area*: a mix of branches similar to the central region producing low-value products, low accessibility, weak resource endowment but profitability similar to the central region (low wage rate and a relatively high net production value).
> *rural area*: a predominance of labour intensive branches, poor resource endowment, low accessibility and low profitability.

Styria's regional economy is strongly dominated by the manufacturing sector, which represents 21 per cent of the GDP. This can be traced to a long industrial tradition in the two most important economic areas within Styria: upper Styria and the capital of Styria, Graz, with its surrounding areas (central area).

Especially in upper Styria this industrial tradition, heavily based on the manufacturing of iron ore and coal, has led to the development of inflexible economic structures unable to adapt to changing economic conditions. This situation has brought about serious economic problems indicated by low growth rates in industrial production, high unemployment and migration rates which are jeopardising the economic competitiveness of the whole region. Additionally, these problems are aggravated by insufficient economic impulses generated by the central region. First, in some respects Graz faces the same problems as upper Styria. Though there is a high concentration of innovative and technology-based firms in the central region, there are still many firms operating in rather traditional branches (e.g. textiles, paper, leather manufacturing etc.) which are confronted with stagnating markets. Second, Graz does not function as a service centre for Styria. Firms in the service sector are too small in size and too few in number to 'export' their services proactively to the rest of Styria. Third, Graz has not been able to take full advantage of the liberalisation of the eastern countries until now, mainly because of its poorly developed transport infrastructure (Gruber *et al.* 1996; Jud and

Piber 1996). In addition Styria's rural areas have not only suffered from poor resource endowment and low accessibility, but their economic problems have been aggravated by the fact that these areas are located near the former eastern European countries, the frontier to developed western market economies.

During the last ten years a number of studies (Tichy *et al.* 1982; Steiner 1984; Geldner 1989; Steiner and Tichy 1990; Tichy 1990; Clement *et al.* 1995; Gruber *et al.* 1996) have analysed the economic situation of Styria and its regional subparts in different contexts in order to elaborate adequate strategies and initiatives for the protection of its long term competitiveness. Strongly simplified, the recommendations of these works can be summarised as follows:

- improve technology transfer in all of its possible forms[2] to generate innovative impulses for the regional economy and to promote innovative activities within productive entities in Styria (firms, research, transfer, advisory institutions etc.);
- restructure nationalised industry to make it more flexible with respect to a changing economic environment;
- integrate the rural and the peripheral areas into transregional networks and promote cross border co-operation.

Based on these proposals, big nationalised firms have been reorganised and divided into smaller parts, while new application-oriented research institutions have been established, and technology parks founded. A technology transfer and advisory service infrastructure has been built up and a regional development agency (RDA) has been established to support innovative economic activities financially and with different kinds of soft measures (e.g. advisory services, information services etc.). Altogether these initiatives seem to have prompted a slow change in the economic situation of Styria: employment in the private sector has increased, Styrians show more entrepreneurial spirit, indicated by the increasing

2 Transfer of technical, organisational, managerial know how etc. by educational measures, incentives for establishing firms and for firm foundations, establishment of research institutions, supply of advisory services etc.

number of firms being founded (see e.g. Steiner *et al.* 1993) and innovative activity has been increased (see e.g. Steiner *et al.* 1996).

Elaborating a Technology Policy Concept for Styria

With these developments in mind the regional government of Styria together with other regional actors in 1993 decided to develop a 'regional technology policy concept' in order to drive improvements and to increase economic competitiveness of the region. Three different tasks had to be fulfilled by this concept at the outset.

First, innovative activities in Styrian firms had to be further increased. Measures guided by a technology policy concept needed to be able to stimulate propensity of firms to develop and commercialise new products and production processes, to improve relationships between Styrian science and research centres and regional economic actors, to reduce barriers to innovation and to accelerate the diffusion of new technologies within the economy.

Second, the national and international integration of the Styrian economy needed to be reinforced by stimulating transregional and border-crossing co-operation and by improving the access of Styrian firms to nationally and internationally based knowledge and technology transfer networks.

Third, diverse soft and financial measures supplied by different Styrian institutions had to be co-ordinated with each other and supplemented by new instruments to reduce redundancies and raise effectiveness. In addition, the policies and instruments used needed to be reconciled with initiatives and support schemes in the wider national and European context.

Using an Experimental Approach: Communication Matters

In order to convert these three central tasks into a technology policy concept for Styria an experimental approach was used combining scientific methods with strong communicational elements. Major regional actors were involved in the process of designing appropriate measures and initiatives for Styria in order to build a collaborative framework for their realisation.

This experimental approach has some similarities with the 'Government Technology Foresight Exercises' used by many industrialised countries[3] to plan for future technological developments and their economic and social consequences. These second generation Foresight Exercises can be distinguished from their predecessors - the deterministic forecasting studies of the 1970s - by the enormous importance laid on information exchange and communicational processes between the experts involved (see e.g. Tichy 1997). They focus on the process of 'learning in developing the results' in the same way as the Styrian technology policy concept in order to make the following implementation of measures and initiatives based on these results more effective.

As a first step to elaborate the Styrian concept a research plan was developed with four distinct working phases: First, relevant theoretical and empirical works in the field of regional and technology policy were examined to determine their significance for Styria.

Second, numerous empirical investigations of the economic and technological situation of Styria were conducted in order to gain information about strengths and weaknesses of the region.

Based on the empirical results, four main strategies and eight different measures and initiatives were formulated.

In the last phase, a series of workshops with major economic and political decision-makers and representatives of different interest groups was organised to discuss the measures and strategies proposed and to reconcile them with the notions and suggestions of the participants. These workshops helped to design and formulate an effective set of innovation policies which fit the needs of Styrian businesses and at the same time took the various political restrictions into account. They also helped to generate the collaborative framework necessary to spur innovative behaviour and economic development in Styria.

[3] Government Technology Foresight Exercises were conducted for example in Germany (1993, 1995, 1997), the Netherlands (1991), France (1994), Australia (1994), Great Britain (1995) etc. (see Tichy 1997).

After developing the research plan a project review group was established consisting of experts in different fields as well as political decision makers at both the national and the regional levels. They oversaw the project during all four work phases and took on two distinct functions.

Even if empirical investigations are based on sound theoretical considerations, the gathering of 'decentrally' distributed information remains a complex procedure characterised by many uncertainties. The researcher cannot ensure that he has taken into account all the aspects relevant for answering the research questions at stake, and of course this is especially important if appropriate strategies and policies which should be based upon empirical facts have to be designed. One way to reduce these kinds of uncertainties is to pool the knowledge and know-how of various experts and to make it accessible. The review group was meant to be such a pool of knowledge employed to accompany and to guide the project.

Beside their ability to function as information and know-how suppliers, many of the members of the group were public administrators and therefore had major influence on the realisation and funding of public measures to support innovative activities in general. So the presentation of the results to the review group at the end of each working phase and the following discussions should have brought about the political consensus and the impetus necessary to implement the strategies and measures worked out in the course of the project.

Establishing a project review group and organising numerous workshops with major regional actors introduced those elements into the process which fostered the exchange of information and spurred communication processes and should eventually lead to an improved implementation of the concept.

In Search of Appropriate Policies: Networking Spurs Innovative Behaviour

The empirical investigations, based on new trends in regional policy theory which in turn focus on the innovation and collaborative behaviour of firms, were comprehensive and diversified. They consisted of four parts:

- Competitive and technological clusters: Using the results of different empirical studies about competitive and technological clusters in Austria the specific Styrian situation was investigated.

- Co-operative strategies and innovative activities of Styrian firms: In addition to these literature-based inquiry, a Styrian-wide survey was conducted to shed light on the innovative and the collaborative behaviour of Styrian firms. The survey was supplemented by regionally disaggregating the results of an Austrian-wide innovation survey conducted in 1990.
- Technological infrastructure of Styria: By means of brochures, booklets, journals, diverse statistical data together with telephone interviews, the supply of technological services and the collaborative behaviour of Styrian research centres, universities, technology-transfer institutions etc. were recorded and analysed.
- New technology-based firms (NTBFs): The potential and the obstacles for young entrepreneurs to start-up and develop a new technology-based firm were observed and analysed.

Simply stated, the empirical work delivered two main results which are relevant in the context of this paper.

The interrelations of Styrian firms in terms of input-output relations, licensing activities and information exchange is rather strong. For about 57 per cent of the firms Styria is an important market for their products and about 75 per cent use other Styrian firms as suppliers. More than 40 per cent of the firms have informal contacts to Styrian partners and nearly 25 per cent have licensing agreements with other firms in the region. Altogether three different types of clusters could be identified within Styria with varying degrees of interrelations between the firms: traditional industrial clusters, growing young economic sectors and weakly developed sectors. Examples of strongly interrelated productive networks are the materials cluster in upper Styria, the automotive cluster in the central region and to a lesser extent the eco-cluster in Graz (environmental technology cluster). But in spite of their strong relationships Styrian firms do not collaborate proactively in the form of strategic alliances in order to conduct complex research projects, to jointly develop composed goods or to build up mutual distribution systems to stimulate exports.

During the last decade various different institutions have been established to propel the innovative activities of Styrian firms and the economic growth of the region as mentioned above. In 1994 Styria had 13 industrial and technology parks, two different institutions allocating public money by means of various distinct support schemes for innovation, three universities, one research centre, 16 R&D laboratories and institutes in different fields, four technology transfer institutions and a few additional bodies engaged in related fields. It is not astonishing that so many different institutions without any authority co-ordinating them produced considerable redundancies in their supply of services. In addition money and resources available to support innovation was widely dispersed and could not be directed to specific targets thus diminishing the effectiveness of all the efforts to strengthen innovation and economic growth.

Based on these findings two main principles and several different strategies were developed and discussed with the review group in order to solve the three main tasks of the technology policy concept described above:

- Political activities should be directed towards strengthening and improving the economic performance of Styrian clusters by means of:
    - supporting collaborative behaviour of Styrian firms
    - accelerating the diffusion and absorbtion of innovations
    - upgrading the quality of Styrian products and services and the human capital of Styrian firms.
- Activities and services supplied by existing public and semi-public institutions in Styria should be co-ordinated in order to reduce redundancies and increase effectiveness by means of:
    - a specific model designed to institutionalise collaboration between the different bodies.

After the first presentation, members of the review group generally agreed with the strategies proposed. The reasons behind this quick success were twofold. On the one hand representatives of the administrative body were aware of the redundancies in the supply of supporting services and the need for increased co-ordination. On the other hand our proposals were strategic in nature having no immediate consequences for the prevailing behaviour of decision makers. Delivering strategic proposals, however, led to an extended discussion about the orientation and the value of our work. Some of the members of the review group involved in managing support programs for Styrian firms expected to receive 'how to do' advice instead of rough guidelines. During a time-consuming discussion the value and the meaning of a strategic perspective directed towards elaborating a policy concept guiding policy-makers for the next five to ten years had to be clarified.

Based on the principles and strategies agreed on by the review group, measures and initiatives had to be elaborated that were not only effective but also had a realistic chance of being implemented. But there is a trade off. If policies are designed by means of pure desk work they can take all theoretical and empirical findings of previous research into account in order to be effective. The resulting proposals, however, run the risk of not being implemented or not being accepted by firms.

Decision makers implementing proposals are interested in programs and initiatives which are easy to administer and not too different from the activities they usually perform. In addition they prefer measures delivering results which improve values of the performance indicators used to assess their activities like additional employment, number of successful projects supported etc. Evidently, there is no reason why effective policies should match the first criterion but there are good reasons why they could get in conflict with the second one. Often performance indicators are very simple, designed more to produce figures than accurate data which in turn could cause an adverse selection of activities to be promoted. If for example the number of successful innovation projects supported is a decisive indicator to assess the working of a promotion agency, the agency might prefer to promote low risk projects of firms which would have been conducted anyway. In contrast, effective support schemes would aim at high risk projects not being pursued by profit driven firms on their own which produce positive externalities and thus social benefits over and above expected private profits.

Private firms prefer support schemes which fit well into their usual line of business because this provide them with additional funding for projects and activities they would have performed anyway. Thus in some sense the interests of promotion agencies and profit driven firms tend to be compatible with each other but may get in conflict with the goals of effective policies (see e.g. Yager and Schmidt 1997).

Surely this does not totally remove the scope for policy initiatives but it sets up the trade-off mentioned above and creates incentives for firms as well as managers of support initiatives to get involved in the process of designing policies and to resist policy proposals elaborated without their participation. In the course of developing the technology policy concept we used a twofold approach to cope with these problems.

To be effective, measures were elaborated by desk work based on our empirical and theoretical findings, but measures and initiatives proposed followed particular guidelines in order to reduce the risk of being rejected. First, they were based on international experience with policies already successfully applied. This should help to prevent potential opponents from rejecting proposals on grounds of being untested and experimental. Second, they were designed to supplement, consolidate and improve the supply of support services already available in Styria. This should leave decision-makers with instruments they are familiar with and allow a more effective implementation and handling of policy instruments. Third, they were meant to be realised by existing institutions without the need to set up new promotion agencies. This should prevent decision makers from being afraid of new competing institutions. Together with the German Fraunhofer Institute of Systems and Innovation Research, which brought additional know-how and international experience to the process, first drafts of proposals were developed.

To gain support from private and public stakeholders not involved in the process of policy design, remaining concerns had to be resolved and awkward aspects reconciled. In line with this mission, proposed measures and initiatives were presented and discussed with the review group, with representatives of Styrian firms (e.g. representatives of leading firms in Styria, technology-based entrepreneurs, consultants etc.) and various Styrian institutions (e.g. representatives of science and research institutions, universities, the chamber of commerce, the chamber of employees etc.). It took eight workshops and presentations and an additional five meetings with selected stakeholders before all the necessary adaptations had been made and draft proposals could be put into final form. During all these communication processes we did not have to deal with significant resistance of the actors involved caused for example by their competition for funding sources. This may be explained by stakeholders interpreting the process of implementation following our work as being decisive for the final shaping of policies and hence their access to support. Probably they felt the strategic direction to be right and saw enough scope to get involved in pinning down support schemes and

Table 3.1 Technology policy concept for Styria - strategies and instruments

Strategies/Instruments supporting collaborative behaviour of firms	*Goals*	*Type of Support*
Umbrella projects	Co-operation Initiative Elimination of co-operation and innovation risks	Co-operation events Subsidies to project costs Project management
Soft cluster support	Elimination of information handicaps/barriers, co-operation risks and organisation barriers	Arrangement of co-operation by means of information and advisory services and training
So-called 'AN-Institutes' (e.g. University Institutes)	Active technology transfer Elimination of innovation risks	Initial financial support Expansion and financial participation of research institutions
Accelerating diffusion and absorption of innovations		
Information initiative	Elimination of information deficiencies	Free supply of information Active distribution of information Initial consultations at low costs
Demonstration centres	Elimination of technology-specific Information and quality deficiencies	Demonstration of techniques Initial consultation at low costs Education and training
Upgrading quality of products & services and human capital of firms		
Qualification offensive	Meet qualification demands	Extension of specialised higher education Integration of learning and working Enforcement of external training
Innovation assistance	Elimination of qualification barriers in SMEs	Contribution to salaries Acquisition and preliminary selection of applicants Advisory services, education
Co-ordinating activities and services supplied by existing public institutions		
Regional co-operation model	Improvement in efficiency of technology-political instruments	Co-ordination and further development of existing institutions and their services offered Institutional framework for co-operation of regional 'actors'

shaping the actual practice of their future management. The results of the policy designing process are summarised in Table 3.1.

Introducing Policies in Line with the Proposals

The technology policy concept for Styria, containing the results of the empirical investigations together with the long term strategies proposed and the catalogue of measures and initiatives to be realised in the short and medium term, was finalised in autumn 1995 and published in early spring 1996 (Steiner *et al.* 1996). The first initiatives by Styrian institutions to implement some of the strategies and measures proposed had already started several months before the project was finished. Currently many activities and projects focusing mainly on improving the collaborative behaviour of both public and semi-public institutions and Styrian firms themselves are well underway:

- A technology transfer and co-ordination network has been established between different public and semi-public suppliers of innovation related services.
- By means of various soft and financial measures the Styrian Regional Development agency (Steirische Wirtschaftsförderungs-gesellschaft - SFG) tries to intensify network relationships and collaboration within the Styrian automotive cluster.
- Currently similar initiatives are being prepared by SFG and a technology transfer institution in upper Styria to support the Styrian environmental technologies cluster (eco-cluster) and the materials cluster in upper Styria.
- In November 1996 the Styrian regional government together with DG XVI of the European Commission and Joanneum Research organised an international conference on competence clusters in order to spur the international exchange of best practice policies and experiences with cluster support programmes and to present respective Styrian initiatives.
- Different Styrian institutions have launched projects and programmes to accelerate knowledge and technology transfer within the region.
- Recently a support scheme has been developed called 'Innovators for SMEs'. The programme creates incentives for SMEs to employ graduates of universities and Fachhochschulen in order to improve their propensity to innovate and collaborate with other firms. The scheme will be launched in the near future.

- The Styrian AMS (labour market service institution) is strongly engaged in developing qualification and training programmes for employees which are in line with firms' needs for innovation and in order to improve their proactive long term labour market policy.

In the following, two of the activities mentioned above are described in more detail in order to illustrate Styrian efforts to improve the regional culture of collaboration.

Increasing the Effects of Innovation Policies: The Styrian Technology Partners

The idea of establishing a technology transfer and co-ordination network emerged out of the problems faced handling the so-called 'Active Technology Transfer Programme' launched by the Economic Development Department of the Graz City Council and the Graz University of Technology. Initially, representatives of all regional transfer agencies and respective public bodies were invited to join a loose informal 'technology transfer club' to exchange experiences and to present their services to the other members. Eventually the club covered a wide range of bodies considering employees' as well as employers' views: the Styrian regional development agency SFG, the Styrian research centre Joanneum Research, the regional chamber of commerce (technology and trade fairs department), the regional EU Innovation Relay Centre, the industrial liaison departments of Styrian Universities, technology transfer centres, science parks, the federation of industrialists, training institutions of the chamber of labour and local and regional authorities administering diverse financial support schemes.

Some of the members of the club were part of the review group for the technology policy concept and most of them attended one or more of the workshops held to communicate the results of the project. So they were confronted not only with the experiences made during the club meetings but also with the empirical investigations conducted in the course of the project showing redundancies and deficiencies in the Styrian innovation support system and the proposals worked out to offer solutions for the current problems in the form of a Regional Co-operation Model. This initiated diverse discussions which eventually led to a new state in the development process of the network.

The different members of the 'technology transfer club' agreed to develop and establish a joint information system called 'Technologiepartner Steiermark' (TPS) in order to better co-ordinate their activities and to improve transparency of and access to the supply of services for Styrian firms. The new system is an open Internet-based 'One-Stop-Shop'. Styrian firms can send requests in terms of technology, training, funding and other support to the Internet home page of TPS. All requests are categorised according to the services offered by the different members of TPS and immediately distributed to the individual members with appropriate expertise. Co-ordination of requests and management of the Internet server is the responsibility of SFG. All requests are logged and accumulated in a growing project database which also gives interesting insights to the regional 'innovation climate'.

The advantages of this system are many: Any request of a regional business is dealt with by the 'multiplied intelligence' of an interdisciplinary group of public or semi-public business service providers. Solutions can be delivered quickly and with high quality. Thus the system can be seen as a major advance in supporting regional innovative activity and the collaborative behaviour of firms. In addition it offers the opportunity for regional agencies to 'listen to the market', to constantly review their services, co-ordinate measures and policies and to implement the strategies and measures proposed by the technology policy concept for Styria.

Improving Strategic Collaboration Between Firms: The Styrian Automotive Cluster

The Styrian automotive cluster consists of three core firms producing automobiles and diverse components, different research centres within and outside of the university and numerous small- and medium-sized subcontractors for the national and international automobile producing industry which is highly concentrated in the central area of Styria. Though studies elaborated some years ago identified considerable potential for growth, international developments put pressure on the Styrian automotive industry to intensify collaborative R&D activities, to produce high quality components just in time, to become more flexible and adaptable, and to introduce international quality management standards.

In reaction to the numerous discussions about appropriate cluster support policies during the elaboration of the technology policy concept, the Styrian regional development agency SFG decided to start an initiative combining elements proposed by the concept with instruments and measures developed in other countries, for example by the Welsh Development Agency in Great Britain.

Though the Styrian Cluster support initiative, which aims at improving collaborative relations between different 'members' of the cluster, is currently in an initial stage of development, some of the procedures and instruments used can already be described.

The programme is promoted by the SFG which covers running costs and has appointed a key account manager for the programme who is supported by a German consultant. The starting point of this undertaking was a survey of the needs and wants of major firms within the cluster, especially of the three core firms. The results were presented and discussed during a workshop with the surveyed firms and numerous smaller businesses which were interested and willing to collaborate. Subsequently, various smaller workshops were organised to exchange information and transfer know-how about current themes (e.g. about the importance of total quality management systems). At the same time the programme management collected various proposals for potential collaborative projects between different groups within the cluster. In spring 1997 seven different meetings were held to make proposed projects more concrete and to establish new strategic partnerships between firms or to intensify existing ones. The meetings were centred around the following topics:

- collaborative development and marketing of a new oil pump
- collaborative procurement of various resources
- joint participation in international fairs and exhibitions
- introducing joint environmental standards for production.

For the near future, the programme management plans to develop a database which contains information about products, services and related issues of all the institutions and firms involved in the Styrian automotive cluster.

It is much too early to give a meaningful evaluation of the overall project. But it should be noted that Styrian firms in the automotive industry are highly interested in the programme launched and managed by SFG. This can be seen in their participation in the diverse workshops and meetings organised.

Summary and Conclusions: Learning by Developing Results Collaboratively

Styria is a very heterogeneous region which can be classified in four different types of subregions with different economic performance figures: the central area, the old industrial area, the semi-industrial area and the rural area. Numerous studies were carried out during the last decade inquiring into the economic situation of Styria and formulating strategies in order to improve regional long term competitiveness. The various proposals put forward focus on improving technology transfer and promoting innovative activities of Styrian firms and subsequently various policies have been introduced to realise these strategies which have eventually led to an improvement in the economic situation of Styria but have nonetheless left several problems unsolved.

With these developments in mind the Styrian regional government commissioned the Styrian research centre Joanneum Research to elaborate a technology policy concept for Styria in order to speed up the slowly moving improvements and deal with the problems still unsolved: Innovative activities of Styrian firms should be increased further, the national and international integration of the regional economy should be reinforced and the activities of different public and semi-public institutions supporting Styrian firms should be co-ordinated.

To meet these objectives an experimental approach was used by the project team similar to the procedures employed by the 'Government Technology Foresight Exercises' conducted by many industrialised countries during the last years. Scientific methods analysing the economic and technological situation of Styria were combined with communication and information procedures to involve major regional actors in the process of designing appropriate measures and initiatives for Styria. The focus was laid on 'learning in developing the results' in order to build up a collaborative framework for their realisation.

A research plan was developed and followed step by step from first empirical investigations to formulating appropriate measures. This scientific procedure was guided and accompanied by a project review group consisting of experts in different fields and political decision makers at regional and national levels. Establishing this group helped to pool the knowledge of influential decision makers and to make it accessible for the project team in order to deal with unavoidable uncertainties of empirical investigations. In addition it helped bring about the political consensus and the impetus necessary to implement strategies and measures proposed. To elaborate measures and initiatives which are effective and executable, a twofold approach was used. Policy proposals were developed by desk work in order adjust them to the empirical findings. In addition they were based on international experience with policies already successfully applied and took into account the institutions and the supply of support services already available in Styria. Finally numerous workshops with representatives of interest groups, different regional institutions and selected Styrian firms were held in order to discuss the policies proposed within a wider scope and to reconcile them with the various suggestions put forward.

The technology policy concept for Styria, which mainly focuses on increasing innovative activities of regional economic actors by means of improving their collaborative behaviour, was finalised in autumn 1995 and published in early spring 1996. The first initiatives in line with the concept have been initiated even before the project was finished and have multiplied since then.

Additional research efforts would be necessary to verify the contribution of the experimental approach in terms of propelling the implementation of strategies and measures proposed. Yet the authors are convinced that its actual influence was quite large. Continuous presentations of the project results and the intensive exchange of information with numerous regional actors clarified the ideas and concepts developed and used in the course of the project and created a climate of collaboration between private, public and semi-public institutions involved. Though the implementation of a comprehensive, future-oriented regional technology policy is currently at its very beginning, the numerous activities undertaken during the last one and a half years are likely to accelerate the changes towards increased innovative activities and economic growth that are currently under way.

References

Clement, W., Fabris, W., Hohl, N., Mazdra, M. and Schick, M. (1995) *Wirtschaftsleitbild Steiermark.* IWI - Studien, Band XXV.

Geldner, N. (1989) 'Das altern von wirtschaftsregionen. In *WIFO Monatsberichte 5,* 89, 364-356.

Gruber, M., Hartmann, C. and Schrittwieser, W. (1996) 'Glück im Winkel oder Zentrum Südost.' *Raum 21,* 96, 8-10.

Gruber, M., Hartmann, C., Schr ttwieser, W., and Steiner, M. (1996) *Wirtschaftsleitbild Graz.* Studie im Auftrag des Magistrates Graz.

Jud, T., and Piber, H. (1996) 'Der steirische KFZ-Cluster - chancen und risiken für Graz.' *Raum 21,* 96, 11-13.

Palme, G. (1989) 'Entwicklungsstand der industrieregionen Osterreichs.' *WIFO Monatsberichte 89,* 5, 331-345.

Steiner, M. (1984) *Alte Industriegebiete - theoretische Ansatze und wirtschaftspolitische Folgerungen.* Dissertation, Uni Graz.

Steiner, M. and Tichy, G. (1990) *Die Internationalisierung der steirischen Wirtschaft.* Studie im Auftrag des Amtes der Steiermärkischen Landesregierung, Graz.

Steiner, M., Sturn, D., and Wendner, R. (1993) *Wirtschaftspark Obersteiermark.* Joanneum Research, Graz.

Steiner, M., Jud, T., Pöschl, A. and Sturn D. (1996) *Technologiepolitisches Konzept Steiermark.* Leykam, Graz.

Tichy, G., Osterreichisches Institut fur Raumplanung (OIR), Osterreichisches Wirtschaftsforschungsinstitut (WIFO) (1982) *Regionalstudie Obersteiermark.* Bericht der Gutachter, Wien.

Tichy, G. (1990) *Das steirische Grenzland - Vergangenheit, Gegenwart und Zukunft.* Studie im Auftrag des Amtes der Steiermärkischen Landesregierung, Graz.

Tichy, G., (1997) 'Technologieprognosen und technologiepolitik.' *Wirtschaft und Gesellschaft 23,* 2, 193-209.

Yager, L. and Schmidt, R. (1997) *The Advanced Technology Program.* Washington, D.C. The AEI Press.

4 Local Development Networks in England

CECILIA WONG

Introduction

The increasing attention given to local economic development (LED) in recent years is due to the widely acknowledged problems of long term economic decline and unemployment in Western countries, and the exhaustion of markets for traditional, massively produced, commodities (Blakely 1994; Stöhr 1990). The increasing threat of international competition for capital investment and market share in the accelerated process of global restructuring has produced dramatic shifts in the location of economic growth (Amin and Thrift 1994; Dicken 1992; Mair 1993). The spatial inequality of development has stimulated local actors to rediscover place identities and to react by formulating economic and marketing strategies to enhance the competitive advantage of the locality in the national and world economy (Levy 1990; Kearns and Philo 1993). In Britain, the rapid proliferation of local economic initiatives and development agencies has been partly due to the failure of traditional regional and industrial policy to alleviate economic decline and unemployment problems (Roberts *et al.* 1990). The rise of the so-called 'new localism' is also due to an increasing awareness among local actors of their role in shaping the development of the local economy.

From the mid-1980s, central government was increasingly criticised for a lack of strategy on local development and failing to coordinate its own programmes (Audit Commission 1989; Coopers and Lybrand Deloitte *et al.* 1991; Robson *et al.* 1994). In response to these criticisms, the conservative government introduced some dramatic alterations to the administrative structures and funding mechanisms of local development in April 1994. The former regional offices of four Government Departments: Environment, Transport, Trade and Industry, and Education and Employment, were combined to form the new

Government Offices for the Regions in order to strengthen the co-ordination of government programmes and policies. Meanwhile, the funding regimes of the Government also went through a fundamental change, with the introduction of the Single Regeneration Budget (DoE 1995) which continues to provide funding for existing programmes such as City Challenge and Urban Development Corporations during their lifetime, and incorporates a Challenge Fund element to elicit bids for funds from competing coalitions of local regeneration agencies. It is interesting to find that the emphasis is now put on *partnerships*, *competitiveness* and *good value for money* which drifts away from the earlier approach of a centrally determined overview of social and economic needs. The status quo of different organisations in local areas has also been disturbed by the Department of Trade and Industry's Business Link (BL) initiative. BL was introduced in 1993 with the intention to create partnerships of Training and Enterprise Councils, local authorities, enterprise agencies and Chambers of Commerce and other private organisations to create a one stop shop for all business support services.

The sea-change in the funding and administrative framework has inevitably created some extra incentives as well as pressures on local actors to form alliances to bid for discretionary challenge funds, and to adjust their own previously-held positions. It is the context of these turbulent changes and conflicts that provides the central thesis of this chapter which explores the complex interplay between public and the private sector organisations in the local development policy networks.

Regime Analysis

The involvement of local stakeholders in policy-making has led to the birth of modern partnerships literature (e.g. Bennett and Krebs 1991; Stone *et al.* 1991; Stoker 1995). Regime analysis (Elkin 1987; Harding 1994; Stone 1989; Stoker and Mossberger 1994) has served as a paradigm for understanding urban politics and the variety of responses to economic restructuring in recent years. Regime formation is the 'informal arrangements by which public bodies and private interests function together in order to be able to make and carry out governing decisions' (Stone 1989, p.6). Due to limited state capacity, this new form of decision-making necessitates cooperation and coordination of public and business resources in order to meet the demand of local policy agenda. The notion that a regime is pragmatically evolved around resource mobilisation is clearly articulated by Stone *et al.* (1991). There is also an assumption that a clear vision exists among the participants to achieve some common goals such as project realisation or image building in the regime. Regimes can sustain and survive in the highly complex and fragmented political environment because the actors have a common purpose to act (Stoker and Mossberger 1994). The process of cooperation and consensus building is motivated by different mechanisms such as the desire for growth (Ward 1996), the local dependency of business (Stoker and Mossberger 1994) and the availability of selective material incentives (Eisenschitz and Gough 1993).

The concept of strong business participation in urban coalition building very much originated from empirical studies of American cities. This trans-Atlantic import of regime theory to Britain cities has, however, been found problematic (e.g. Strange 1997; Ward 1996). First of all, regime theory fails to address the structural positions of different partners (Ward 1996) and assumes that there is a fixed set of institutional characteristics (Harding 1994). The assumption of a dominant role for the business community in setting local development agendas is very much based on the experience in US cities. As Strange (1997) finds out, the business community in the UK is much less well-organised at the local level. Similarly, the formation of regimes in the UK is not necessary related to the benefit seeking motives of partners. Instead, it is very much due to the financial curtailment imposed by the Whitehall on local government, and the pre-requisite of having an input from the private sector when submitting funding bids (Eisenschitz and Gough 1993; Harding 1990). Another major criticism of regime theory is its emphasis on the management of local interests and conflicts, and that it pays little attention to the relationship between local development and higher spatial levels of intervention from national government and supra-national institute like the European Union (Harding 1994; Keating 1991; Stoker and Mossberger 1994). Finally, regime theory has been criticised as offering limited explanatory power (Ward 1996). Regime analyses tend to focus on identifying the defining characteristics of regimes from empirical case studies in order to provide taxonomic classifications (for example, Stone and Sanders 1987; Stone *et al.* 1991; Stoker and Mossberger 1994). Although such case studies can illustrate alternative forms of regime formation, the resulting typologies are often descriptive and theoretically weak.

As Bulmer argues (1979), if social theory is divorced from the empirical realm and compartmentalised into its own world, it provides very little guidance to research. The problems encountered in the empirical testing of regime theory in the UK case studies give two clear signals. Firstly, there is a need to take into account the negative evidence presented to reformulate some of the propositions to facilitate further investigation. Secondly, due to the very general sense of direction provided by regime theory to guide empirical research (Stoker 1995), its theoretical development has to be more closely interwoven with empirical data (see Bulmer 1979). These two pointers provide a reference frame to guide the conceptual and methodological approach used in this study. By taking into account the propositions and the critics of regime theory, four research questions are addressed here to examine the relationships between key actors in LED networks:

- to find out whether the assumption that some common goals exist among different agencies prevail, and the compatibility of different agencies' LED objectives is interpreted in the light of their structural positions and institutional characteristics;
- to find out the key mechanisms which motivate key actors to form partnerships, to assess the importance of 'public', 'private' and 'other external' resources in fostering partnerships, and to explore the conflict and balance of these partnerships;
- to set the scene against the context of higher spatial policy intervention from central government and the European Union, and to examine the relationships between actors in different spatial scales; and
- to examine the role played by LED professionals in establishing local development networks.

Methodologies

The lack of clear conceptual specifications from regime theory calls for the adoption of a more rigorous empirical approach in this study. First, instead of studying a particular locality (e.g. Haughton and Williams 1996; Martin and Oztel 1996; Roberts *et al.* 1990) or concentrating on a particular organisation sector (e.g. Bennett *et al.* 1994; Hart *et al.* 1996; Sellgren 1990; Strange 1997), this research provides a cross-sectional snapshot of the views of LED professionals in two English regions; the analysis is interpreted in the light of their organisational setting and geographical circumstances.

Second, because the partnership ethos has extended beyond the urban frontier in Britain, this study concentrates on LED rather than being tightly bounded by the spatial focus of urban areas or city development. Empirical findings were yielded from two case study areas, the North West (including the North West and Merseyside Government Offices) and the Eastern Region. Most urban areas in the North West, especially the Merseyside and Greater Manchester conurbations, have suffered from serious industrial decline and unemployment problems in the last few decades. In contrast, the Eastern Region has very different socio-economic conditions and experience as it is the fastest growing region in Britain, with the lowest unemployment rate and an increasing share of national GDP. Its economic buoyancy is related to a concentration of hi-tech industries and service sectors. It is chosen because its LED agenda has been under-researched, and it provides a robust comparison to the North West which will lead to a more rigorous interpretation of the findings.

Finally, a triangulation of quantitative and qualitative techniques was used on a complementary basis to generate multiple-sourced information. The main purpose of this study is to apply the method of *Verstehen* (which was defined by Max Weber (1964, p.29) as the interpretative understanding of social behaviour by penetrating the subjective meanings that actors attach to their own behaviour and to the behaviour of others) to achieve a sympathetic understanding of how LED professionals as a social group define the situation. However, it is recognised that this interpretative style of research does not cover a large enough range of situations to allow the scope or generality of its theories to be tested (Marsh 1984). Hence, more descriptive information was first collected in a survey to establish the generality and the breath of the situation before the intensive interviews took place.

A postal survey with a structured questionnaire was sent out to the lead person (named in the regional directories compiled by English Partnerships) of 103 organisations in the North West and 80 in the Eastern Region in Autumn 1995. These organisations were chosen on the ground that they had the prime responsibility for direct involvement in a wide range of LED initiatives, and it was not the remit of this survey to include individual companies or organisations which were only engaged in some form of LED activities on an ad hoc basis. Since the number of eligible organisations was less than 200, it was decided that a survey of *the full population* was highly desirable to eliminate potential sampling errors. Table 4.1 shows the distribution of organisations in the survey and their response rates. On the whole, the survey in both regions achieved a remarkable high response rate and the range of organisations was well represented in the final sample. Although some groups had lower response rates than others, this did not constitute a major threat of introducing any significant bias to the findings. Even those with the lowest response rates such as the Chambers of Commerce in the North West still reached a 50 per cent level, and the 'other private sector organisation' (which includes science parks and business partnerships) in the Eastern Region only consisted of a handful of organisations to start with. Of course, caution should still be made in the light of this context when interpreting the findings.

The survey was subsequently followed up by twenty-three (fourteen in the North West and nine in the Eastern Region) in-depth, semi-structured interviews with selective participants in Summer 1996. Due to the complex urban problems in the North West, most of the in-depth interviews within this region were strategically focused on the two main conurbations, and a good organisational spread in these two localities was achieved. The focus on the urban dimension in the North West provides a contrast to the experiences of the more rural Eastern Region. When choosing cases in the Eastern Region, there were fewer organisation types to be considered, which allowed more attention to be paid to the geographical spread of organisations to reflect the diverse socio-economic circumstances of the region.

Table 4.1 Distribution of organisations in the survey and their response rates

Organisations	*North West*		*Eastern Region*	
	target sample	response rate (%)	target sample	Response rate (%)
Central government	3	66.7	1	100.0
Local authorities	45	71.1	54	83.3
TECs	14	71.4	7	85.7
Chambers of Commerce/CBI	18	50.0	14	71.4
English Partnerships	3	66.7	1	100.0
Urban Development Corporations	3	100.0	-	-
Regeneration agencies	8	87.5	-	-
Public sector led partnerships	3	100.0	-	-
Other private sector organisations	6	66.7	3	33.3
Total	103	69.9	80	80.0

Compatibility of Objectives and Institutional Characteristics

Due to the pluralistic nature of LED activities which involve multiple agencies with multiple objectives, it is interesting to explore the compatibility of their objectives. LED has increasingly been interpreted by academics in a broader notion which extends beyond the purely economic dimension. For example, Beauregard (1993) views LED as what happens when individuals and organisations engage in the process of production, distribution and consumption. Turok and Richardson (1991, p.72) identify economic growth, social equity and local capacity building as the three basic objectives of LED. However, the message contained in the competitiveness White Paper of the European Commission (1994) and the UK Government (DTI 1994) is quite different. Both documents emphasise the importance of wealth creation and economic competition rather than the creation and retention of employment. Ward (1996), therefore, proposes that the desire for growth provides a linchpin of different actors' activities in urban partnerships.

The overall consensus (about 90 per cent) among the respondents over the narrowly defined objective of *economic growth* in the questionnaire survey clearly confirms Ward's proposition. *Employment growth*, the traditional concern of many local authorities, fell into second place. However, the research findings in Table 4.2 highlight a concomitant subordination of social objectives to the more economic oriented priorities. The more social equity related objectives, concerning the *improvement of access to socio-economic opportunities* and the *development of local resources*, were found at the bottom end of the hierarchy. Interestingly, the response patterns, on the whole, were found to be very similar between local authorities, TECs and other regeneration agencies as they all tended to have multiple objectives: it is clear that less emphasis were placed on the social aspect of LED by all these organisations. In a study of turf wars in LED, Haughton *et al.* (1997, p.89) argue that quasi-public agencies, such as urban development corporations and TECs, put a strong emphasis on wealth creation and relegate job creation and social distribution to a secondary role. They also comment on the changing attitude of local authorities who have become more willing to embrace the wealth creation approach without losing their traditional concerns of job creation and social distribution. The survey findings presented in Table 4.2 lend support to their arguments on the convergence between local authorities and other quasi-public agencies over the objective of local economic growth. However, it is difficult to detect any organisational differences (with the exception of the private sector) over job creation and other social oriented objectives. Further clarifications were thus made during the in-depth inquiry.

As Keating (1991) argues, the stated LED objectives very much reflect the prevailing political culture, value systems and institutional arrangements, as well as the specific socio-economic circumstances of a local area. During the interviews, policy-makers were thus specifically asked about their perceived linkages between the pure economic objectives and the more socially oriented ones. The interviews with practitioners from local authorities and quasi-public agencies revealed that they consistently viewed wealth creation and employment growth as going hand-in-hand together. It is clear that quasi-public agencies like TECs and regeneration partnerships did not draw a strong dividing line between economic growth and job creation as Haughton *et al.* argued. Employment growth, in many ways, was very much seen by the participants as a linchpin between the economic objective of wealth creation and other social oriented objectives.

However, it was true to say that local authorities tended to pay more emphasis on their responsibility to look after the multi-faceted welfare of the electorates who paid Council Tax. They were more likely to emphasise the Council's objectives to strike a balance between economic, employment and other social objectives. This strong sense of political accountability (see Hart *et al.* 1996) was particularly pointed out by a number of officers, as against the 'non-elected' status of TECs (Peck and Tickell 1995) who were tightly bounded by performance targets (managerial accountability) set by central government. The constraint imposed on their objectives and institutional remit was admitted by participants from quasi-public agencies. For instance, TECs had their performance indicators rigorously scrutinised and regeneration agencies and development corporations only had a very limited life span to achieve their targets. In order to meet the efficiency measures set out for each initiative, actors might have to make compromises between different types of projects to make up the numbers required. However, they did realise the political reality of the importance of training and social distribution to local residents.

It can, therefore, be argued that the differentiation of political and managerial accountability does not bear a strong relationship with the priority accorded to LED objectives, though it helps in explaining the subtle differences between local authorities and the non-elected agencies' views over social objectives. Although institutional remit and guidance from central government provide a framework within which quasi-public bodies have to work, they did have some leverage to react and adjust their activities to meet with political pressures from local communities and other actors. The findings in Table 4.2 clearly put this political complexity into view. It is also important to recognise that local authorities themselves are mixed entities which exhibit different approaches to LED. Job creation had been a dominant concern in declining areas like the North West where traditional, restrictive town planning control over development had been subsumed to the more market-oriented approach of development. The emphasis had also been shifted from physical and infrastructural development to a more social needs based approach, and recently with an accent on wealth creation. However, this was not necessarily the case in some affluent areas of the Eastern Region where coping with development

Table 4.2 Organisations' objectives of LED

North West							
Objectives	*Government offices* %	*Local authorities* %	*TECs* %	*Regeneration agencies* %	*Business sector* %	*All* %	*Difference between business sector and others (Chi-Square test)*
economic growth	100	100	100	87	92	96	0.00
employment growth	100	97	100	87	69	90	5.35*
skills development	100	84	100	73	62	81	3.66R
improve quality of living	100	91	60	80	23	72	16.23**
improve access to opportunities	100	75	60	73	23	64	9.40**
develop local resources	100	59	50	67	54	60	0.23

Eastern Region							
Objectives		*Local authorities* %	*TECs* %		*Business sector* %	*All* %	*Difference between business sector and others (Chi-Square test)*
economic growth		87	83		91	88	0.00
employment growth		89	67		64	83	2.00
skills development		64	100		55	66	0.72R
improve quality of living		78	50		36	69	4.79*
improve access to opportunities		56	50		45	55	0.46
develop local resources		49	50		45	48	0.05

Source: Author's survey

Notes: R: Chi-square = 3.88, $p < 0.05$, $df = 1$ to test regional difference.
$*p < 0.05$, $df=1$, $**p < 0.01$, $df=1$
since there was only one government office and one regeneration partnership in the Eastern Region survey, their responses cannot be released for confidentiality reasons.

pressure was their major concern. Land use planning functions were more widely used as strategic and regulatory instruments to control market forces in order to shape the development profile and regulate settlement patterns. These contrasting situations were plainly narrated by two local government officers:

> ... in the past, LED was not linked to social needs and we tended to focus on the development of hard infrastructure ... now we adopt a more balanced approach and try to look at both economic growth as well as the more socially related objectives. (a local authority in Greater Manchester)
>
> This is one of the wealthiest districts in the region ... our key role is to allocate employment area for B1 (office) development in the local plan ... we don't want any more big inward investors who do not have direct link with the area to increase the pressure of housing demand ... the hi-tech development profile is shaped by implementing development control. (a district council in Cambridgeshire)

The survey findings in Table 4.2 also single out business organisations from other institutions, especially in the deprived North West, because of their very narrow interest in wealth creation.

Private sector participants very much liked to demarcate themselves from the public sector. They regarded economic growth as their sphere of activity, and would like to see the public sector restricted to providing more social functions such as training and education. The majority of business organisations did not perceive themselves as playing a central role at all in LED. In spite of the government's effort to encourage local embeddedness of business organisations, many Chambers still regarded themselves as part of a wider national organisation. A Chamber manager described their minimal approach towards LED:

> The Chamber is the voice of the business community in this area and we pass their views to the HQ to lobby the government ... the business community has been responsible for the prosperity of this country, however, it would be scary if the private sector ran the country. (a Chamber in Greater Manchester)

Regional differences over the objectives of LED were also found in the survey response patterns. The attitude towards skills development was significantly different between the two regions, with more attention being paid by those in the North West (81 per cent, in comparison with 66 per cent in the Eastern Region). During the in-depth interviews, policy-makers in the North West consistently expressed their specific concerns over the low level of workforce skills.

Many industrial towns in the North West still suffered from the problems of an obsolete industrial structure left by the past legacy of coal mining, textiles and heavy engineering industries. The workforce in these declining areas needed re-training to develop appropriate skills, such as information technology and keyboard skills, to meet with the requirements of the new industries. Although some rural areas in the Eastern Region had the need to diversify the skills of their local workforce, the skills mismatch problem on the whole was less pressing. Instead, the pivotal attention of most practitioners in the Eastern Region was on the roads and infrastructure (see Wong 1998).

The findings of this study demonstrate that a consensus over wealth creation did exist across different organisation sectors in both the North West and the Eastern Region. Under the government's quasi-market philosophy and partnership ethos, the key issue is therefore to ascertain the extent to which this consensus on wealth creation overrides the deeply embedded values and norms of individual agencies and leads to collaborative relationships.

The evidence given above shows that there was a big gulf between the business sector and the public and quasi-public organisations. However, the differences between local authorities and other non-elected agencies were subtler. These diverse views over LED objectives may potentially shift the balance of interests between different organisation sectors in the partnership model. This issue will be further examined in the next section.

Resource Mobilisation and Partnership Building

The capacity of local actors to mobilise local resources has been the central concern of those who are engaged in LED research (e.g. Bennett and Krebs 1991; Blakely 1994; Syrett 1995). Resource assembly is also regarded by regime theorists as the power base upon which local coalitions are built upon. Walter Stöhr strongly advocates that a local initiative should be 'using mainly local resources under local control for predominantly local benefit' (1990, 33) . This strong sense of local identity was reflected in the survey data in that a large majority of respondents (over 80 per cent) either agreed or strongly agreed with Stöhr's statement. However when asked whether the chance of success was higher for locally based initiatives, the response was very mixed and uncertain. Table 4.3 shows that nearly a quarter of the organisations from both regions was very dismissive of the statement, and some of them simply could not make a judgement. The obvious discrepancy between the perceived ideal situation and the practical reality was due to the fact that nearly all LED initiatives in Britain had some sort of input from either central government or the European Union (EU). Although there were public-private partnerships, the limited resources provided by businesses were not sufficient to carry out large scale development programmes on their own. The crux to them, therefore, lay in the ownership and control of initiatives rather than the sources of funding. It was, however, worrying to note that the objective of developing local resources were not high on either public or private sector's agenda (see Table 4.2). This does not inspire confidence that LED professionals grasp the crux of developing a more sustainable local economy to achieve the ideal situation described by Stöhr.

Business resources and strong private sector participation forms the backbone of regime theory. However, the survey findings in Table 4.4 show that there was a lack of business inclination to take on any key roles in LED. The take-for-granted relationship between business participation and partnership development was thus further explored in the in-depth study. Observations made in the US and various European countries (e.g. Bennett and Krebs 1994; Marin 1987; Stoker and Mossberger 1994) suggest that stronger partnerships and business involvement tended to be found in more successful economies. However, the participation of the business sector in the Eastern Region was dismissed by one TEC manager

Table 4.3 Response to Stöhr's statement: 'locally-based initiatives tend to be more successful'

Response	*North West (per cent)*	*Eastern Region (per cent)*
strongly agree	18.1	15.6
agree	40.3	43.8
disagree	22.2	21.9
strongly disagree	2.8	1.6
can't say	15.3	17.2

No significant inter-regional or inter-organisational differences by Mann -Whitney U tests.

as 'putting their heads in the sand'. This criticism was echoed by six of the nine interviewees in this economically buoyant region. The lack of business interest in LED was also evident from the fact that businesses in Norfolk actually described themselves as 'comfortably undisturbed by national economic events' in a local survey. There were, nevertheless, early signs of changes in their attitude due to the hardship brought by the recent recession. There was only one interviewee from a more deprived seaside location who found that strong public-private partnerships were up and running in the area. These, therefore, produce significant counter-evidence to the 'strong economy, strong partnership' argument. It was the very economic success of the region which led to the complacent and apathetic attitude of businesses to be involved in the wider development of their local areas.

Although there was a higher level of business participation in the North West, the involvement of large companies still tended to be restricted to symbolic moral support such as turning up to meetings of funding bids, thrashing out new ideas and explaining the views of businesses. There were a few occasions when the private sector were more actively involved in an initiative but their ultimate motivation seemed to be their own commercial benefits. This was seriously criticised by a manager of a regeneration agency:

> ... they are supportive but with scepticism ... companies like NORWEB, AMEC and Kellogg's see that it makes good business sense to regenerate the area ... they provide moral support and top up extra need without a major input of resources. (a regeneration agency in Greater Manchester)

The lack of enthusiasm towards local development was also found to be true among small indigenous businesses. Their involvement was less driven by financial motives but more related to their immediate self-interest. They tended to support initiatives such as anti-crime campaigns and the holding of seminars on topics such as how to obtain business insurance. The lukewarm attitude of the private sector was thought to be mostly related to their reluctance to commit resources or time to LED. Their unwillingness to participate was further compounded by their worry about the high level of bureaucracy or risk involved in partnership programmes such as City Challenge and the Private Finance Initiative.

A few interviewees pointed out that some businesses genuinely did not know what their role was, and what they were expected to do. These reasons were found to be true in both regions. The reluctance to participate went beyond individual companies to some large business organisations like Chambers of Commerce and the CBI. Interviewees from a number of these organisations explained that their main roles were to provide business services to their members and to lobby on their behalf. Furthermore, they did not believe that the public sector understood the operation of the economy and business needs. Here are some explanations of their lack of faith in any intervention in market forces:

> ... businesses feel that the government should not be too involved in matters like investment in manufacturing plants and technological development ... a lot of the socio-economic policies are unhealthy. (an assistant regional director of CBI)

> ... the public sector should make less interference ... individual businesses should be as self-sufficient as possible rather than relying on grants. (a Chamber manager in the North West)

Table 4.4 Organisations' roles in local economic development

North West							
Role	*Government offices*	*Local authorities*	*TECs*	*Regeneration agencies*	*Business sector*	*All*	*Difference between business sector and others (Chi-Square test)*
	%	%	%	%	%	%	
Implementation	50	81	90	73	23	69	13.52**
coordination	100	91	90	73	23	75	19.56**
facilitator	50	91	70	80	38	75	11.30**

Eastern Region					
Role	*Local authorities*	*TECs*	*Business sector*	*All*	*Difference between business sector and others (Chi-Square test)*
	%	%	%	%	
Implementation	76	83	36	70	5.50*
coordination	84	100	18	75	19.36**
facilitator	89	67	27	77	14.82**

Source: Survey

Notes: * $p < 0.05, df = 1$
** $p < 0.01, df = 1$
# since there was only one government office and one regeneration partnership in the Eastern Region survey, their responses cannot be released for confidentiality reasons.

Similar to Strange's (1997) findings in Sheffield, this study shows that the involvement of both large companies and small indigenous firms in the two regions was driven by very pragmatic and instrumental motives, and there was a general lack of strategic vision for local development. Although a new tripartite partnership between the local authority, TEC and Chamber of Commerce was suggested as the legitimated vehicle to LED (see Haughton *et al.* 1997), the business sector largely failed to meet up with expectations to play a dominant role. The despair of their narrow business interest and failure to commit resources was not only expressed by local authority officers, but also shared by those from quasi-public agencies. There was a consensus that it would be very important for the public sector to continue to carry the torch of urban regeneration after the demise of various agencies. The explicit conflict between public and private interests means that the dominant roles within the partnership inevitably leans towards two legs (local authorities and TECs) of the tripartite stool. This was widely acknowledged by the participants in both regions.

With a weak business sector, partnerships were, thus found to be pre-dominantly led by local authorities and TECs. Since the 1980s, local authorities have had a well-established role in providing business advice and developing local economic strategies. The original remit of TECs was, however, focused on providing a more tailored implementation of government training schemes in local areas as well as providing small business support. With the gradual expansion of TECs' remit to education and enterprise support, the tension between TECs and local authorities eventually built up (Haughton *et al.* 1997). As shown in Table 4.4, it is very difficult to differentiate the unique roles of local authorities from those of TECs. Both of them perceived themselves as performing facilitating and coordinating roles in the LED process. Furthermore, many of their roles have been juxtaposed following a series of guidelines issued by central government to steer them towards partnership building. The widespread confusion and tension evident between the two partners is thus a consequence of a continuous process of role adjustment and changing inter-organisation relationships.

Despite the fact that TECs are funded by public money, they have been crowned with the status of 'private sector-led' in the 1994 strategic guidance 'TECs: Towards 2000' (Employment Department 1994). As admitted by the practitioners, the relationship between local authorities and TECs in the early years was not easy. However, it was further complicated by the 1994 guidance which was described by a TEC director in the Eastern Region as 'a gun pointing to a TEC's head to get them involved in partnerships with local authorities and be the key driver of the private sector'. Although some TECs thought it was more sensible for them to develop a strategy for local development because their spatial coverage was wider than a single local authority district, they did find this a very sensitive issue. Hence, TEC participants cautiously emphasised the importance of sharing the tasks between different parties, and emphasised that TECs could never replace local authorities to do the land and premises tasks. Local authority officers also played down the extent of duplication and highlighted the advantage brought by the division of labour between different parties. In some cases, a more harmonious working relationship was established between the two partners.

Another major top-down initiative from central government was the Single Regeneration Budget (SRB) which was thought to be a clever disposition that offers 'the carrot and the stick' to forge partnerships. Some practitioners were very cynical towards such funding sources because they were mainly the outcome of central government re-juggling the existing pool of public resources. This means each organisation did not only suffer from an immediate cut in their own budget, but also a loss of institutional autonomy and control over their activities. They were pushed very hard to work in partnership with other organisations in order to win the discretionary resources back. However, some policy-makers viewed SRB as a return of power to local authorities because they were increasingly expected to play a strategic role in coordinating different initiatives.

Business Link (BL) is another major partnership initiative (Oatley 1996) which aims to pull all agencies together to provide a one stop shop access to business services. Although BL was thought to be a good idea by most practitioners, they had strong doubts about its actual implementation. One stop shop could be interpreted as physical co-location of all partners in one site, but they could just be connected up in hyper-space. Of the twenty-three interviews, there was only one case where all the key partners were co-located under a single roof. The response made by practitioners in the two regions was somewhat different. Those in the North West tended to play down the problem of duplication and over-emphasise the minor differences between their services to justify their continuation. Despite their dismay over the take-over by BL and the subsequent closure of some of their operations, duplication was more readily admitted by practitioners in the Eastern Region.

According to the participants, the main incentives for a full merger of all partners under BL was to share staff resources in order to deal with the pressure of reduced budgets. It is, however, most surprising when they mentioned that a weaker Chamber actually fostered a successful organisational merger. From their own experience and knowledge, many strong Chambers were reluctant to subsume their power to BL and thus became a stumbling block to partnership development. This, once again, contradicts the theoretical expectation that strong partnerships are built upon the presence of a strong business community. In the own words of two TEC directors and a Chamber manager:

> The model of BL very much depends on local circumstances, for example, Oldham has a very weak Chamber, so it makes sense for a merger ... this Chamber is one of the strongest in the country and the TEC is only four years old, it is more sensible not to merge them ... the reality is BL becomes a referral agent, it is really a two-stop shop. (a TEC in Greater Manchester)

> ... TECs and the Chamber in Hertfordshire, Northamptonshire and Milton Keynes are all co-located with local authorities because their local Chamber is basically a one-man band. The whole idea of a TEC and Chamber merger in this area is very much up in the air ... (a TEC in the Eastern Region)

> ... this is a very strong Chamber ... the Chamber determines to remain independent, even it merges with BL in the future, the Policy Department will ring-fence itself to retain its lobbying power.(a Chamber manager in the North West)

Besides public and private resources, the capacity of LED can be enhanced by access to non-local power and resources especially when under difficult socio-economic circumstances (Bennett and Krebs 1991; Stoker and Mossberger 1994). Table 4.5 shows that there were significantly more respondents in the North West who regarded the EU as a key driving force in LED. Although they might not regard Europe as their local partner, the eligibility and success in securing a large amount of European assistance was the main factor underlying their opinion. However, the actual trade with Europe was not seen as important in both regions. Their positive and bitter attitude towards Europe were expressed:

> ... Europe is very important because it provides match funding for City Challenge and SRB bids, the Council has very little resources to do that. (a local authority in Greater Manchester)

> ... Europe is not 'on a level playing field' in that some areas are given large amounts of assistance which are not justifiable ... (a local authority in Suffolk)

Inward investment is another source of external resources that practitioners can draw on to enhance local development. Slightly less than half of the practitioners in both region found inward investors influential in LED (see Table 4.5). However, public and quasi-public organisations (63 per cent) in the North West tended to pay more emphasis on these external catalysts than their private sector counterparts (15 per cent). Due to the tremendous pressure of securing jobs for local residents in many deprived areas in the North West, local authorities and regeneration agencies had to work very hard to secure mobile investment. The circumstances in the Eastern Region were very different because the performance of many of their indigenous firms far out-ranked that of inward investors. There was a mixed view towards the actual benefits to be gained from inward investment in both regions. Some interviewees thought that inward investment was a zero-sum game to the nation, though it was far more glamorous and high profile. However inward investors, in some cases, could be a breath of fresh air to implant new skills and business culture to areas which were regarded as traditional backwaters.

The research findings presented here clearly debunk the application of the American model of public-private partnership in the British context. However, they lend strong support to Keating's (1991) argument that local partnerships in Britain are heavily reliant upon central state intervention. The business sector's lack of aptitude to care for the

Table 4.5 Perceived key driving forces of LED

Key driving forces of LED	*North West %*	*Eastern Region %*	*Chi-square test of regional differences*
Central Government	56.9	35.9	6.42*
European Union	52.8	18.8	17.45**
Inward investors #	48.6	42.2	0.68

* $p < 0.05$, $df = 1$
** $p < 0.01$, $df = 1$
# Difference between business sector and others: $\chi^2=16.9, p<0.01, df=6$

wider development of local areas and their reluctance to provide resources made it difficult to overcome the inherent conflict between the public and private sector. The overarching consensus over wealth creation did not satisfy the expectation of both public and quasi-public organisations over the local needs of regeneration and employment growth. Above all, the assumption of the presence of strong business partners in a successful economy does not stand, as counter-factual circumstances prevail: a strong Chamber was regarded as an obstacle to partnership building, and a buoyant local economy implied business apathy to LED. One can thus argue that the British partnership model is really public sector-led by local authorities and TECs (despite their rhetoric private sector-led status). The involvement of the business sector in local initiatives and the promotion of inward investment, in many ways, have been a ritual dance within LED activities rather than the substance. It is also clear that resource curtailment, top-down policy guidance from central government and its financial control over initiatives like SRB and BL, rather than private resource mobilisation, constitute the major mechanisms which motivate actors to form tentative, reluctant alliances. Because of its heavy dependence on public resources, the influence of central government and the EU was thus more strongly felt in the North West than in the Eastern Region (see Table 4.5).

The Interplay of Multi-spatial Policy Networks

Since the spatial policy and funding framework of central government and the EU was found influential to partnership development and LED activities, it is interesting to examine the relationship between actors operating at different spatial levels. The explosive relationship between local actors and central government was not concealed in the interviews. The over-centralised regime of the Whitehall was criticised as failing to maintain close relations with local actors. Due to the lack of consultation and local autonomy, a lot of initiatives and policies coming from the centre were not thought to be tailored to reflect specific local circumstances and the needs of businesses. The centralised structure also failed to deliver a clear strategic framework for LED which was reflected from the fetish of initiatives and the continual change in policy priorities. Local actors, therefore, frequently launched critical attack of central government, for example:

> ... central government has no framework, no strategy and no guidelines! ... They are currently in the process of introducing Challenge Funds to a wider arena. They just throw the core funding out of the window, it's a nightmare to secure long term changes. (a TEC manager in the Eastern Region)

The introduction of the Integrated Regional Offices (IRO) could be seen as a way to harmonise the relationship between central government and local actors. However, those who worked for the Regional Office were not too sure about the extent of regional autonomy given to local actors. One senior civil servant openly admitted that 'the IRO tries to integrate the Government Office and the region, but not the region and the centre'. On the whole, the attitude towards the IRO was more positive in the North West and a few interviewees found it provided a better support framework. The good relationships between local actors and the IRO very much depended on the contact and communication made between officers. The more favourable attitude in the North West was also due to the setting up of a new Government Office for Merseyside (GOM). The interviewees found that GOM provided a more coherent focus for social and economic renewal in Merseyside, and it was easier for them to gain access and have face-to-face interaction with civil servants. Turning to the down side of the IRO set-up, internal politics between different departments were frequently mentioned by the interviewees. The fact that different departments in the IRO worked to one Senior Regional Director as well as being responsible to their own Secretary of State in the Whitehall was considered as a formula for conflicts and tension.

The IRO was less well received in the Eastern Region not only because of the inter-departmental conflicts in the Office, but also due to its unusual physical set-up which is currently split into two locations: two departments in Cambridge, and the other two in Bedford. The interviewees also felt that the IRO failed to cope with the diverse socio-economic circumstances of six counties. Essex, Hertfordshire and Bedfordshire and southern Cambridgeshire, in many ways, shared more common characteristics with the South East, whereas the circumstances in the rural heartland of East Anglia was quite a different story. The development of historic towns and rural shire areas required a lot of dealings with the Department of National Heritage and the Ministry of Agriculture, Fisheries and Farming, but these two departments were not integrated with the so called 'Integrated Regional Office'. This, no doubt, made some interviewees feel that their problems were not attended to. One interviewee thus described this paradoxical situation as:

> ... it is really an *unintegrated* IRO. It may be slightly better elsewhere but probably not very much. We have to deal with four different bits of the Office ... this is one of the weakest regions with no assisted area status and has offices in separate locations. We get the 'lame and the sick' in this regional office. (a TEC director in the Eastern Region)

The contentious relationship between central government and local actors has increasingly encouraged local government to by-pass central government and be well-equipped to exploit European funding opportunities. The institutional structures and funding initiatives of EU are operated on a regional basis and stress the importance of partnership as an implementation mechanism. The policy framework of the EU was found to be influential especially in the peripheral areas such as Merseyside and the remote areas of East Anglia. Gaining the Objective One status no doubt gave Merseyside access to extra resources. However, the guidance from Europe played an important part in filling the policy vacuum left by central government. European assistance also provided stimulus to local actors to form partnerships at the regional level. According to several interviewees, the impetus behind forming the North West Regional Association in 1992 and its subsequent production of a regional economic strategy with the North West Business Leadership Team was a response to European pressure. This resource seeking motive is indeed openly admitted in the summary document of the Strategy that it: 'is to make the case for European Community structural funds for regional development ... At present these funds amount to over 100 million each year.' (NWRA and NWBLT 1993, p.1). Although these moves were positive signs of collaborative relationship, there was scepticism that it was just a forum to please Brussels.

The complex policy and funding frameworks of Whitehall and the EU made it very important for local actors to interact with those at the higher spatial levels to shape their local agenda. However, tension and conflict existed at all levels. The hostile relationship between local actors and the government was the most explicit and explosive one. Europe, in many ways, appeared to be a new light which offers both financial assistance as well as policy guidance. However, the function of Europe was largely a utilitarian one which impinged on the provision of match funding to unlock other resources from Whitehall. The building up of tentative partnerships was still very much a response to the state's funding initiatives.

The Role of LED Professionals

Most partnership literature adopts an organisation-agency approach to examine the process and networks of partnership development. There is, however, a lack of research on the role played by LED professionals in establishing the links and connections between different organisations. The focus of this study is to strip down the layers of network to elicit individual practitioners' opinion on the inter-relationship between LED organisations.

From their account, it is not difficult to identify the vital contribution made by some key individuals in the process of partnership development. Due to the rapid proliferation of local development activities and regeneration agencies, LED in the last twenty years has become a professional activity. With expert knowledge of the local area and a handle on the funding game, many economic development professionals have moved around to work for different organisations throughout their career paths. The mobility of these professionals inevitably helps to exchange the values and culture of different organisations across different sectors (Bryson and Daniels 1998). In some cases, they are the key catalysts in starting new relationships; in other occasions, they are the determinants of securing a long-term, successful alliance. This was definitely evident from the interviews in both regions:

> ... historically the TEC did not speak to us and vice versa. This has slightly changed because our new Chief Executive came from a TEC. In the last three years, a good relationship has been established for a lot of initiatives. (a local authority in Cambridgeshire)

> It was a threat when the TEC was first established because it covers a wider area. Now we find a key contact in their Chief Executive section, he used to work here ... (a local authority in Greater Manchester)

As commented by a Chamber manager, the success of partnerships is largely down to the individual personalities involved. In a way, individual professionals of LED organisations are the key engine behind the implementation of central government guidelines on partnership development. One can take Hart *et al.*'s (1996) discussion on administrative accountability further by unfolding its organisation and individual perspective. The obligation of regeneration agencies and local authorities to meet government guidelines and performance targets is not just a pure concern of local development, but also a direct challenge to their self-interest of survival. The threat of resource curtailment to any organisation will inevitably translate into a threat of individual job survival. More importantly, many posts in the LED field are offered on a fixed term contractual basis; officers may have to move around to work for different organisation sectors in the same locality. One can, therefore, put forward an argument that it is the very self-interest of the LED professionals which dissolves the organisational boundaries to make compromise in order to survive a very harsh funding regime imposed by central government. There were several occasions during the interviews, such individual feeling and concerns were freely expressed:

> There is still a lot of tension that we have to try to overcome ... I'm not sure about myself ... it doesn't really matter provided that I am paid by the Council, I'm a Council employee. (a senior local authority officer in Greater Manchester)

> ... the Council found itself sitting on the margins with a reduced budget, it has now co-located with TEC/Chamber to keep its staff employed. (an economic development officer in Greater Manchester)

> TEC now seconds staff to BL, but it is very confusing to staff because they don't know who they are responsible to ... there is a temptation to go for shorter term projects to cover your own back. (a TEC director in Cheshire)

Conclusion

The study here presents the views of LED professionals on the inter-relationship between different organisation sectors in two English regions. One of the key findings confirms a scepticism concerning strong business participation in local governance. Local partnerships in both the North West and the Eastern Region were characterised by the half-hearted involvement of businesses. The conservative outlook of the British business sector was evident in both large and small firms. Many of them are reluctant to take risks (Eisenschitz and Gough 1993) and are very much embedded in their traditional ways of thinking. They are very territorial and do not want their activities to be interfered with by the public sector. Meanwhile, many of them also fail to see their potential roles in LED and the wider benefits this could entail. The minimal involvement of businesses in local activities is very much related to their immediate self-interests. The evidence presented in this study casts doubt over the assumptions inherent in regime theory that business participation is a vital ingredient to partnership building.

In spite of the common objective of wealth creation, there is a gulf between private and public sector organisations over job creation and other social objectives. In the absence of a key resource input from the private sector, local partnerships in Britain are very much led by the public sector under a semi-coercive framework from central government. The result is that Whitehall has been pulling strings to orchestrate economic development activities at the local level. Thus, it is public resource mobilisation, rather than private resources as assumed by regime theorists, that forms the primary motive upon which collaborative partnerships are made. The continuous process of delegation of power to local actors to implement economic initiatives is ironically undermined by the ever strengthening process of centralisation of funding and performance control. Unlike the organic nature hypothesised by regime theory, partnership development in the two regions is very much a mechanistic arrangement to meet the requirements of an external funding framework. Local actors have also increasingly looked to Europe as a major funder, in some cases to provide a policy framework or innovative ideas to fill the policy vacuum left by central government.

The vivid interplay between the process of LED and the socio-economic conditions in the two regions is clearly evident in this study. Actors in the North West, at least those in the two urban conurbations, have become more experienced and sophisticated players. They have learnt how to manipulate the game rules set out by London and Brussels to seek resources. In spite of all the hidden hostility and distrust which no doubt still exists between different organisations, they have recognised the need to establish partnerships and work with each other in order to compete for resources from the highly regulated funding regime. The players are very capable of carving their own niche out of the proliferated web of LED organisations in the region, without forgetting to acknowledge others' role in order to avoid trespassing on each other's territory. This may signify a growing maturity in work practice among different stakeholders in the process of LED. The career move of LED professionals across different organisation sectors may also contribute to the more positive atmosphere of collaboration. Of course, one can take a cynical view towards such tentative partnerships and argue that it is purely a reflection of the depressing socio-economic circumstances in the region and that they are desperate to get any available financial aid. There is also tremendous internal pressure on the LED professionals to justify their own contribution in order to keep staff in employment.

The economic success of the Eastern Region means that local development has been largely left to private companies' own devices. Local authorities and TECs tend to offer assistance to overcome the supply side constraints and provide training and business services. In the very affluent areas of the region, LED is equivalent to planning control of the spatial distribution of activities. The lack of enthusiasm in partnership development in an economically successful area provides counter-factual evidence to Marin's (1987) argument that partnership building is a result of self-reproduction from a successful business community. Indeed, it is the changing economic climate in the recent recession which appears to be changing their complacent attitude. Local authorities have been stimulated to take a more active role in LED and to start thinking about potential funding opportunities. There are signs of closer collaboration between different organisations and talks are going on about the setting up of a regional association to raise the profile of the region. However, most organisations are as yet only in the early stages of getting a grip of the long learning curve of the funding game.

Finally, the methodology employed in this study has proved to be sufficiently robust to compare LED professionals' view across different organisation sectors in two contrasting regions on a systematic basis. The survey findings helped to establish the generality of the response patterns and highlighted key issues for more intensive inquiry during the in-depth interviews. Although the results could be regarded in part as proving the obvious, as Peter Worsley (1964, foreword) argues, 'Investigation of this kind are very necessary, since the obvious is very often denied or neglected ... The obvious, however, is often assiduously proved'. The political complexity and subtlety behind the survey response patterns on LED objectives is a fascinating example. The use of an interpretative approach to understand practitioners' views was found useful as they tended to express their own feelings and concerns and unfold issues beneath the official, bureaucratic organisational level. However, it is important for the researcher to be able to interact and comprehend the practitioners' own culture and maintain good rapport during the interviews. The background of the author as a local planning officer was, therefore, a beneficial factor when carrying out the field work and interpreting the field data.

To conclude, it is very important to interpret the dynamics of collaboration between different organisations against the wider spatial context, which is especially important in Britain because of the strong central control of local action and the narrow statutory basis for local development initiatives. The socio-economic context of local areas, the institutional characteristics of different organisations across different sectors, and the personal influence of the economic development professionals themselves have all played an important part in shaping the forms and nature of the partnership relationship. The resulting counter evidence to the assumption of strong business participation and the organic mechanism of partnership development hopefully provides some pointers for more refined theoretical development in partnership literature.

Acknowledgements

The research presented in this chapter forms part of a larger research project funded by the Economic and Social Research Council Research Fellowship Scheme (Grant number H52427003094). Supplementary funding was also provided by the University of Manchester Faculty of Arts Recurrent Grant to carry out the field work in the Eastern Region. I would like to thank both institutions for their support and Juliet McCormack for carrying out some of the field work.

References

Amin, A. and Thrift, N. (1994) 'Living in the global'. In A. Amin and N. Thrift (eds) *Globalization, Institutions, and Regional Development in Europe*. Oxford: Oxford University Press, 1-22.

Audit Commission (1989) *Urban Regeneration and Economic Development: the Local Government Dimension*. London: HMSO.

Beauregard, R.A. (1993) 'Constituting economic development: a theoretical perspective.' In R.D. Bingham and R. Mier (eds) *Theories of Local Economic Development*. California: Sage, 267-283.

Bennett, R.J. and Krebs, G. (1991) *Local Economic Development: Public-Private*

Partnership Initiative in Britain and Germany. London: Belhaven Press.

Bennett, R.J. and Krebs, G. (1994) 'Local economic development partnerships: an analysis of policy networks in EC-LEDA local employment development strategy.' *Regional Studies 28*, 2, 119-140.

Bennett, R., Wicks, P. and McCoshan, A. (1994) *Local Empowerment and Business Services: Britain's Experiment with Training and Enterprise Councils*. London: UCL Press.

Blakely, E.J. (1994) *Planning Local Economic Development: Theory and Practice*. California: Sage.

Bryson, J.R. and Daniels, P.W. (1998) 'Business Link, strong ties, and the walls of silence: small and medium-sized enterprises and external business-service expertise.' *Environment and Planning C: Government and Policy 16*, 265-280.

Bulmer, M. (1979) 'Concepts in the analysis of qualitative data.' *The Sociological Review 27*, 4, 653-677.

Coopers and Lybrand Deloitte, Bic and CBI (1991) *Local Support for Enterprise*. Coopers Lybrand, London.

Dicken, P. (1992) *Global Shift: The Internationalisation of Economic Activity*. (2nd edition) London: Paul Chapman.

DoE (1995) *Partners in Regeneration: The Challenge Fund Bidding Guidance* information pack. London: Department of the Environment.

DTI (1994) *Competitiveness: Helping Business to Win*. London: HMSO.

Eisenschitz, A. and Gough, J. (1993) *The Politics of Local Economic Policy: The Problems and Possibilities of Local Initiative*. Basingstoke: Macmillan.

Elkin, S. (1987) *City and Regime in the American Republic*. Chicago: University of Chicago Press.

Employment Department (1994) *TECs: Towards 2000. The Government's Strategic Guidance to TECs*. Crown Copyright, May.

European Commission (1994) *Growth, Competitiveness and Growth: The Challenge and Ways Forward into the 21st Century*. Brussels: European Commission.

Harding, A. (1990) 'Local autonomy and urban economic development policies: the recent UK experience in perspective.' in D. King and J. Pierre (eds) *Challenges to Local Government*. London: Sage, 79-100.

Harding, A. (1994) 'Urban regimes and growth machines: towards a cross-national research agenda.' *Urban Affairs Quarterly 29*, 356-82.

Hart, M., Haughton, G. and Peck, J. (1996) 'Accountability and the non-elected local state: calling Training and Enterprise Councils to local account.' *Regional Studies 30*, 4, 429-441.

Haughton, G. and Williams, C. (1996) *Corporate City? Partnership, Participation and Partition in urban development in Leeds*. Aldershot: Avebury.

Haughton, G., Peck, J. and Strange, I. (1997) 'Turf wars: the battle for control over English local economic development.' *Local Government Studies 23*, 1, 88-106.

Keating, M. (1991) *Comparative Urban Politics*. Aldershot: Edward Elgar.

Kearns, G. and Philo, C. (eds) (1993) *Selling Places: The City as Cultural Capital, Past and Present*. Oxford: Pergamon Press.

Levy, J.M. (1990) 'What local economic developers actually do?' *Journal of the American Planning Association 56*, 153-160.

Mair, A. (1993) 'New growth poles? Just-in-time manufacturing and local economic development strategy.' *Regional Studies 27*, 3, 207-221.

Marin, B. (1987) 'Contrasting without contracts: economic policy concentration by autopoietic regimes beyond law?' Working Paper 87/278, European University Institute, Florence.

Marsh, C. (1984) 'Problems with surveys: method or epistemology?' In M. Bulmer (ed) *Sociological Research Methods.* London: Macmillan, 82-104.

Martin, S. and Oztel, H. (1996) 'The business of partnership.' *Local Economy 11,* 2, 131-142.

NWRA and NWBLT (1993) *Regional Economic Strategy for North West England.* Summary Report, the North West Regional Association and the North West Business Leadership Team, Wigan.

Oatley, N. (1996) 'Business link.' *Local Economy 11*, 1, 70.

Peck, J. and Tickell, A. (1995) 'Jungle law breaks out: neoliberalism and global-local disorder.' *Area 26,* 4, 317-326.

Roberts, P., Collis, C. and Noon, D. (1990) 'Local economic development in England and Wales: successful adaptation of old industrial areas in Sedgefield, Nottingham and Swansea.' In W.B. Stöhr (ed) *Global Challenge and Local Response.* London: Mansell Publishing, 135-162.

Robson, B.T., Bradford, M.G., Deas, I., Hall, E., Harrison, E., Parkinson, M., Evans, R., Garside, P. and Harding, A. (1994) *Assessing the Impact of Urban Policy.* London: HMSO.

Sellgren, J. (1990) 'Local economic development partnerships in an assessment of local authority development initiatives.' *Local Government Studies 16*, 4, 57-78.

Stöhr, W.B. (ed) (1990) *Global Challenge and Local Response.* London: Mansell Publishing.

Stoker, G. and Mossberger, K. (1994) 'Urban regime theory in comparative perspective.' *Environment and Planning C: Government and Policy 12*, 195-212.

Stoker, G. (1995) 'Regime theory and urban politics.' In D. Judge, G. Stoker and H. Wolman (eds) *Theories of Urban Politics.* Newbury: Sage, 54-71.

Stone, C.N. (1989) *Regime Politics: The Governing of Atlanta 1946-1988.*, Lawrence, KA: University Press of Kansas.

Stone, C.N. and Sanders, H.T. (1987) *The Politics of Urban Development*, Lawrence, KA: University Press of Kansas.

Stone, C.N., Marion, E. and Orr, D.I. (1991) 'The reshaping of urban leadership in U.S. cities: a regime analysis.' In M. Gottdiener and C.G. Pickvance (eds) *Urban Life in Transition.* London: Sage, 222-39.

Strange, I. (1997) 'Directing the show? Business leaders, local partnership, and economic regeneration in Sheffield.' *Environment and Planning C: Government and Policy 15,* 1-17.

Syrett, S. (1995) *Local Development.* Aldershot: Avebury.

Turok, I. and Richardson, P. (1991) 'New firms and local economic development: evidence from West Lothian.' *Regional Studies 25,* 1, 71-83.

Ward, K. (1996) 'Rereading urban regime theory: a sympathetic critique.' *Geoforum 27,* 4, 427-38.

Weber, M. (1964) *Basic Concepts in Sociology.* New York: The Citadel Press.

Wong, C. (1998) 'Determining factors for local economic development: the perceptions of practitioners in the North West and Eastern Regions.' *Regional Studies 32*, 8, 707-720.

PART III

NETWORKING AND REGIONAL GOVERNANCE

Across the EU, if not the developed world, over the past two decades there has been an expansion in the reliance on joint actions between institutions and between different levels of government to address many of the issues facing contemporary society. Looser than many formal partnerships, and often based on perceived mutuality of problems and policies, local and regional organisations increasingly have been coming together to address issues which face them individually and collectively. The association of traditional industrial regions (RETI) was an early example of this in the EU, with joint intelligence and lobbying efforts funded through the member councils and authorities. Sector specific bodies have been created with similar remits, one of the best examples being MILAN - the network of European regions involved in the vehicle industry.

In a national context, such associations have been long established - for instance, COSLA, the Convention of Scottish Local Authorities has provided a platform for debate and the defining of common agenda and best practices, while in Germany the Federal Ministry for Spatial Planning, Building and Urban Development prompted the construction of eleven city networks under the ExWoSt programme over the period 1994-97 (Eser 1997). However, although these organisations and initiatives are fairly formal structures, the reality for many networks is that they are often ad hoc ways of addressing the problems of policy co-ordination, destructive competition between agencies, or a lack of institutional capacity at the local or the regional level. Improving accountability, albeit often indirectly, and adopting an integrated approach to policy administration and delivery are two of the main areas where networks have been embraced.

In this section, four contributions discuss the practises and experiences across a range of very different environments. In Chapter 5, using an institutionalist framework Henrik Halkier and Charlotte Damborg explore the attempts in North Jutland to enhance the patterns of business development support by the matrix of agencies in the region. Considering the developments there, they suggest how this networking approach could be applied to the study of regional governance in other parts of Europe.

Grigoris Kafkalas and Elisavet Thoidou (in Chapter 6), based on the case of Central Macedonia, assess the importance of European structural funds for the emergence of specific regional development agencies (RDAs). They then analyse the significance of the competitiveness of small and medium enterprises and of the gradual establishment of RDAs in the promotion of regional intelligence, and so place institutional thickness and capacity at the heart of the economic development process.

In the following Chapter 7, Peter Garside critically examines the present plans for new forms of regional governance in the constituent parts of Britain, contrasting the proposals for Scotland and Wales with those for the English regions. Basing much of his discussion around the importance of democracy and inclusion, he points out the key role played by networks in the relative success of the Celtic nations, in comparison with the limited devolution existing and promised for the sub-national parts of England.

Finally in this section, Christian Jensen and Svante Leijon (Chapter 8) adopt a very different approach to the study of developments in regional governance structures. Drawing from the experiences in West Sweden, they apply rhetorical analytical forms to describe the social construction of this particular region, explaining how some of the actors used imagery and 'persuasive storytelling' to create a region. Their examination of regional networks and institutional landscapes, the creation of artificial regions and the inevitable consequent inconsistencies with perceived realities provides a stimulating way of considering the importance of regional structures in the development process.

Reference

Eser, T. (1997) 'How do city networks contribute to regional development?' In M. Danson, S. Hill and G. Lloyd (eds) *Regional Governance and Economic Development*. London: Pion, 85-108.

5 Development Bodies, Networking and Business Promotion: The Case of North Jutland, Denmark

HENRIK HALKIER AND CHARLOTTE DAMBORG

Introduction

During the last decade, local and regional initiatives in economic development have mushroomed in Denmark, and today a multitude of separate public or semi-public bodies are active in the field of regional development and business support. All levels of government - national, regional and local - are involved, and the implementing agencies are typically small in size and offer different types of general or specialised advisory services. North Jutland, the northernmost Danish county, is a particular case in point: over 40 organisations are involved in business promotion in a region with less than half a million inhabitants.

While 'institutional thickness' in the academic literature is often claimed to be a prerequisite to regional development and learning (Amin and Thrift 1994), the explosive growth of bottom-up initiatives in Denmark has frequently been seen as a weakness (Industri- og Samordningsministereit 1994; Erhvervsministeriet 1995). The co-existence of a multitude of organisations allegedly impedes policy coordination, spawns competition between the organisations - and, ultimately, creates confusion among private sector clients. The presence of a host of specialised bodies does, however, not necessarily mean that these organisations cannot constitute an integrated approach to regional development. The nature of the system as a whole depends on how well efforts are coordinated, either by hierarchical means - one single agency to which all other actors are accountable - or through network types of coordination where overall integration is ensured on the basis of mutual resource dependencies between formally independent organisations.

The objective of this text is to explore the interaction of publicly financed actors involved in business promotion within the North Jutland region in order to establish patterns of formal and informal coordination, and to discuss the potential consequences of this for provision and development of business-related services within the region. The text is based on an analytical approach developed within an institutionalist framework for the study of organisations and policy-making, and a subsidiary aim of the text can therefore be said to explore the merits or otherwise of an approach that could be applied in the study of the governance of regional development in other European regions.

The paper proceeds in the following steps. The next section introduces the conceptual framework, and this is followed by an overview of the organisations involved in business promotion in North Jutland and the wider policy context in which they operate. Then a more detailed analysis of the policies, positioning and resource dependencies of these organisations is undertaken, and on the basis of this the patterns of cooperation between the organisations are discussed. Finally the conclusion will be accompanied by some more general reflections on the possible consequences of the existing institutional pattern for the capacity of the region to respond to new challenges.

Analytical Approach

The analytical framework which has formed the basis for the research design is inspired mainly by the so-called 'new institutionalism' and network theory,[1] and the concepts considered to be central in the analysis of interaction between development bodies are listed in Table 5.1. The 'regional development industry' in North Jutland will thus be investigated on three inter-related levels of analysis: the individual organisation, the way in which agencies interact with one another in bilateral relations, and the way in which the whole system of business promotion is coordinated in more or less formalised and hierarchical ways.

1 For an elaborate discussion, see Halkier and Damborg (1997).

Table 5.1 Organisations and policy-making - an analytical framework

Level of analysis	*Dimensions*	*Sub-dimensions*
Organisational	Domain	Territory Function
	Strategies	Policies Positioning
	Resources	Authority Finance Information Organisation
Inter-organisational	Institutionalisation	
	Resource dependencies	
Multi-organisational	Integration	

Source: Adapted from Halkier and Damborg (1997)

Domain is central to most organisations because their *raison d'etre* is to perform certain functions in a particular geographical setting. *Resources* are the means by which an organisation maintains itself and influences its surroundings, and therefore the question of resources and their exchange is essential, not least in the context of networks that are seen as driven by mutual dependencies with regard to four basic resources: authority, information, finance and organisation.[2] Closely associated with this is, however, also what the development bodies are trying to achieve for the regional economy - the question of *policies* - and the way agencies attempt to *position* themselves *vis-à-vis* other organisations in order to maintain their domain, resources etc. At the inter-organisational level of analysis, the mutual *resource dependencies* and the degree of *institutionalisation* of the relations between organisations will be examined. Finally, this should allow us to establish patterns of formal and informal coordination in the structure of the system of business promotion

[2] For a discussion of resources and relations of power, see Halkier (1996, pp.47-62).

as a whole, i.e. assess patterns of *integration* on the multi-organisational level.

In the light of the large number of organisations involved in business promotion in North Jutland to examine each and every bilateral relation in detail would have been prohibitively time-consuming. Instead a postal enquiry was undertaken in Autumn 1997 seeking copies of the latest annual report and other relevant materials from economic development bodies in North Jutland,[3] and this was supplemented by interviews were carried out in 17 organisations in order to investigate in more detail the nature of the interaction between the organisations.[4]

Development Organisations in North Jutland - An Overview

Since the late 1980s economic development bodies in North Jutland have operated within a system of multi-level governance where national and European levels of government not only regulate sub-national activities, but also to a certain extent have a direct presence within the region.

In terms of providing a regulatory framework, the national level clearly plays the most important role in Denmark. After all central government regional incentive schemes were terminated in 1991, its main role has been to regulate the economic development activities of local and regional authorities, and to co-fund European Structural Funds programmes. Most importantly, sub-national actors have not been allowed to subsidise individual firms but have instead been confined to employ so-called framework measures, i.e. collective forms of support that are not directed exclusively towards one particular firm such as advisory services, technological support facilities or joint marketing and promotion. At the

[3] The survey included providers of manufacturing and general business services, but excluded specific sectoral types of services for tourism and agriculture, workforce training initiatives, and organisations operating on a commercial basis without ongoing public subsidies. A list of the organisations included in the survey is provided in the Appendix.

[4] Interviews took place from November 1997 till January 1998. As can be seen from the list included in the bibliography, the interviewees represented organisations both at regional, sub-regional and local levels and were practitioners and civil servants rather than politicians.

same time the Danish approach to Structural Funds management has become a fairly decentral one in which central government maintain a role with regard to process management, legality and basic policy principles, but where substantive issues - i.e. programme development and evaluation of individual projects - have effectively been left for the regional partnerships to decide (See Halkier 1998, cf. Halkier 1997 and Damborg 1998). In both cases national policies would seem to reinforce European ones: not just limiting but ruling out national and sub-national financial subsidies as policy instrument, and taking the Commission's emphasis on regional involvement in the administration of Structural Funds programmes further than most EU member states.

A first overview of the large number of public development bodies in North Jutland can be obtained by grouping them according to two criteria, namely: 1) the spatial level on which they operate and 2) the nature of their main activities, i.e. political sponsorship or policy implementation. The result can be seen in Table 5.2, and in the following the key players and their roles will be introduced.[5]

At the regional level all Danish counties are involved in regional development, although resources, policies and implementation structures vary significantly (see Damborg and Halkier 1998a). In North Jutland the elected County Council is centrally placed as a political sponsor of economic development initiatives with its own programmes and a key role in the administration of Structural Funds programmes.[6] In order to involve social partners within the region, political responsibility for these activities has, however, been devolved to the *North Jutland Development Fund* (NJDF), established in 1992 and incorporating local authorities and business interests. The Fund recommends decisions on Structural Funds applications to central government and controls the regional development budget of the County, and thus it controls the two major single sources of funding for development activities within the region - and by chairing and

5 Unless otherwise indicated the basic information on the various organisations in the rest of this text is based on a database constructed from the annual reports and other materials of the organisations participating in the study, and personal interviews.

6 25 of 27 districts in North Jutland are covered by either Objective 2 or Objective 5b programmes and North Jutland is the main recipient of European Regional Development Fund monies in Denmark.

Table 5.2 Main regional actors in economic development in North Jutland

Spatial tier	*Political sponsorship*	*Implementing bodies*
Regional	North Jutland County Council Structural Funds Partnerships North Jutland Development Fund	Regional Policy Dept., North Jutland County North Jutland Business Service Technological Information Centres Business and Innovation Centre North
Sub-regional	Councils for sub-regional networks	Secretariat for sub-regional network Local Business Development Offices
Local	Local Authorities Local Business Development Councils	Local Business Development Offices

Source: Survey

financing the Fund as well as providing administrative support, the County in effect retains a dominant influence. Despite working in formalised partnership with other regional and local actors, regional government acting through the NJDF is in other words the most important political sponsor of economic development activities on the regional level, including the Structural Funds programmes (see Damborg and Halkier 1998b cf. Halkier 1997).

The implementing organizations with responsibility for the whole of North Jutland can be separated according to their main activities. The County's *Regional Policy Department* is in a unique position in that it acts as secretariat for both the NJDF and the Structural Funds programmes. This not only makes it the sole provider of financial subsidies to individual firms within the region, but also gives it a key role in assigning block grants to other development bodies and (co)financing so-called regional framework programmes. In contrast to this all other implementing bodies on the regional level are mainly providers of advisory services to individual firms, although they are backed by different political sponsors.

The first of the two *Technological Information Centres* (TICs) in North Jutland was established already in 1975 as part of a national network of self-governing institutions sponsored primarily by central government (c.75 per cent) with minor contributions from regional and local government (Erhvervsfremme Styrelsen 1998a and 1998b). The TICs provide information and advice to firms, and while services are free of charge, they are also limited in time, and therefore an important function of these organisations is to refer firms on to more specialised bodies. The *North Jutland Business Service* was established in 1994 with the explicit purpose of creating an organisation which could offer advisory services on a highly professional level to firms in North Jutland. The organisation is primarily sponsored by NJDF and has its own board of directors consisting primarily of members of the business community. Its core activities are different types of mainly free-of-charge-but-limited-in-time types of advisory services (financing, export and business development), but in addition to this the organisation also manages so-called framework programmes for NJDF and/or the Structural Funds partnerships like The Internationalisation Programme and The Enterprise Development Programme, special efforts running for a period of three or four years. The most recent development body to be established in North Jutland is the *Business and Innovation Centre North*, a European concept adopted towards the end of 1997 at the initiative of the NJDF, the adjacent Viborg county, the NOVI science park and sub-regional actors, and supported by major EU co-financing for the first two years. The centre covers both North Jutland and Viborg counties and is expected to act as a strategic partner for SMEs in industrial development projects by providing long-term advice and project support. Areas of expertise are to include technological, financial, organisational and market matters, and activities will be partly financed by charges paid by successfully assisted firms (Freddy Rano, personal interview).

On the local level political sponsorship rests with local government, either directly or via financial support for local business development councils. In North Jutland nearly all districts have a local business development office, but the structure, tasks and resources of the offices vary considerably. According to our data local business development offices exist in 25 of the 27 districts in North Jutland (of these three districts have a joint office). Nearly all of them are very small operations, mostly run by a local business council consisting of representatives of local business, social partners and local government, but in some districts they have been incorporated as part of local government administration. The tasks performed by the local business development office vary from district to district, but they often include promoting the area in order to attract new firms, initiating and/or participating in the preparation of large development projects in the district, assisting entrepreneurs and SMEs by providing different types of advice, being the link to the local administration, and arranging meetings, courses and participation in international activities for local firms.[7] An important exception to these general characteristics is *Aalborg Commercial Council*, the local business development office for the only major town in North Jutland and location of over a third of the total number of jobs in the entire region. Being a larger organisation with more resources, this organisation is able to supply more specialised types of advice, undertake larger development projects and devote more resources into place marketing.

During the 1990s a new type of actor has emerged on the scene, namely sub-regional networks established by adjacent districts in order to overcome the limited size of their local business development offices by pooling resources, increase their ability to engage in larger projects, and enhance their influence within the region. Some local authorities have embraced this approach more whole-heartedly than others, and by far the largest is the *Aalborg Region* network, based on the regional capital and administered by Aalborg Commercial Council. This network comprises more than 60 per cent of the region's population and has attempted to engage in far more specialised activities, including attempts to draw down funds for major projects from the regional level. The other strong network is the *Vendsyssel Development Council* which consists of five north-western districts representing c.18 per cent of the total population of North Jutland. Contrary to the Aalborg Region, this network has its own small secretariat and does not have a dominant partner acting as prime mover, and its activities are centred around various projects which relates to a development programme for the area covered by the network. At the north-eastern and southern peripheries of North Jutland the enthusiasm for sub-regional development networks is much more guarded, and what limited

[7] Some offices are also tourism offices.

initiatives there are seem to be driven mainly by the need to counter the perceived threat of dominance by the Aalborg Region.

All in all the economic development scene in North Jutland is clearly characterised by 1) the direct or indirect involvement of many levels of government as political sponsors or co-sponsors, and 2) a large number of implementing bodies operating on different territorial levels. This could either be seen as a recipe for duplication and inter-organisational strife, or as a situation prompting network cooperation between the major actors, and in order to illuminate the extent to which coordination is achieved, the organisations and their mutual relationships are analysed in the following sections.

Domains, Policies and Positioning

Having mapped out the basic features of the 'development industry' in the region of North Jutland, we can now proceed to the analysis of the organisational characteristics and inter-organisational relations involved. This section concentrates on three organisational features - domain, policies, and positioning - while the fourth, resources, will be discussed in greater detail in the following section in connection with the question of inter-organisational resource dependencies.

The local business development offices have two things in common, namely that they promote the economic development of their local community, and that they are relatively small organisations with one or two employees and annual budgets between 0.05 and 0.2 MECU (the exception is Aalborg Commercial Council with seven staff and a budget around 1 MECU). This group of development organisations is in other words characterised by operating in the same functional domain but inhabiting separate, yet neighbouring, territories, and as such they are mainly in direct competition with one another in connection with new incoming firms. The concrete policies through which the local offices pursue their parallel objectives vary between the localities, but as most of the local offices have to deal with a wide range of issues, the individual officer is typically a generalist and catalyst who provides practical help and develop ideas rather than more specialised types of advice (the larger Aalborg Commercial Council is again the exception). This was a profile stressed by most of the local business development officers interviewed.

Despite having a limited range of policies at their disposal, most officers insist that it is essential that they be the first point of contact and form the link between local firms and other business services.[8] Although the extent of this cautious positioning varies among the interviewees, local business development officers are generally on guard when it comes to the possibility of being circumvented by other publicly financed organisations, fearing to lose touch with local firms through competition from similar services offered at the regional level.

According to the members of the sub-regional networks interviewed, the purpose of cooperation is *not* to set up new business service organisations *nor* to merge the offices of the members, but to become able to undertake projects which reflect shared problems and ambitions through pooling of resources. Although the extent to which this will be realised remains to be seen at this early stage, both the Aalborg Region and the Vendsyssel Development Council can point to a reasonable number of projects which have been carried out or are under preparation. Some of these are relevant to North Jutland as a whole - districts outside the network areas have joined particular projects like the Aalborg Region Medico programme - and this would seem to reflect a positioning strategy that could ultimately see the sub-regional networks take over activities that are currently undertaken by actors situated on the regional level.

Turning to the role of the organisations operating at regional level, the county's Regional Policy Department is the largest player both in terms of staff (15) and, not least, budget: annual expenditure in the 1997-99 Objective 2 programme amounts to nearly 38 MECU in average and NJDF programmes to 4 MECU. Moreover, the organisation occupies a distinct domain as the only administrator of direct (Structural Fund) grants to firms and as financial supporter of other development bodies and their activities on the basis of European and/or NJDF funding. This of course makes the positioning strategies of the Regional Policy Department and its NJDF sponsors particularly important, not least because preference has been given to hiving off particular forms of business promotion to separate development bodies instead of keeping these activities in-house.

8 Virtually all local business development officers stressed this role.

The other organisations operating on the regional level are also larger than the typical local bodies in terms of staffing and budgets,[9] and among them the two TICs have a distinct profile as part of a national network and more than 20 years of presence in North Jutland. Although defined rather broadly, dealing primarily with 'technology-related issues' still provides the organisations with an identifiable functional domain that supplements rather than competes with those of the local business development offices. Increased involvement in the broader field of enterprise development may, however, place the TICs in a situation where they, at least in some respects, are competing with other providers of business services. In comparison the North Jutland Business Service is a much younger organisation, set up to assist firms with regard to sources of finance, internationalisation and enterprise development. Incorporating both general and more specialised services, at least some of its activities would certainly seem to be situated in the same domain as those of local and subregional actors. The recently established Business and Innovation Centre North has been set up to fill a perceived gap in the existing business promotion system with regard to support for innovative projects that are not very high-tech but could benefit from a long-term partnership possibly involving financial participation (Claus Midtgaard, personal interview). Although the new body has been purposely designed to operate in a hitherto neglected domain, it also has overlapping interests with the TICs, and Business and Innovation Centre North has therefore placed an employee in these centres in order to benefit from synergetic effects.

If we take an overall look at the various actors described above, they are, with one important exception, characterised by being relatively small and independent organisations operating advisory services alongside other suppliers in the broad domain of business services, ranging from general support to more specialised forms of advice on technology and internationalisation. This has two main consequences. On the one hand, the organisations have an obvious need to promote themselves: *vis-a-vis* the firms in order to be noticed and distinguished from other services, and *vis-a-vis* their political sponsors in order to justify their existence, something

9 The two TICs each have five staff and 0.4 MECU annual budgets, North Jutland Business Service 13 staff on a 0.9 MECU budget, and Business and Innovation Centre North seven staff and a 0.7 MECU budget.

that was certainly evident in the positioning strategies of some of the development bodies. On the other hand on their own each of the organisations is unlikely to be able to provide the range of advice and services which firms may need, and it would therefore seem natural that cooperation in the form of, for example, exchange of information and clients would take place between the public bodies. The only organisation that stands out from this general picture is of course the Regional Policy Department and its sponsors in NJDF because of its massive resource base and a distinct operational domain that not only sets it apart from the great multitude of advisory bodies and positions it as a key distributor of resources for other actors in economic development in North Jutland.

Resource Dependencies

The resources on which the organisations depend have been grouped according to four general types: authority, finance, information and organisation. In the following we will for each organisation attempt to identify the most important external resource dependencies, starting with the local actors and then moving on to the sub-regional and regional levels.

Basic funding for the local business development offices is supplied primarily by the local authorities, but it does usually not allow them to finance larger initiatives and development projects, and these therefore have to be developed in cooperation with their sponsoring local authorities and/or by seeking assistance outside the district. The ambition of local business development officers to operate as a first stop for firms carries with it new resource requirements, because local actors now more than ever have to have an overview of the options available so that relevant information can be unearthed and/or the firm referred on to more specialised providers of advice. The forming of sub-regional networks can be seen as an attempt to tackle such dependencies at the local level through pooling of existing resources - manpower, finance or projects - from participating organisations or using the combined strength of the network to attract external resources from regional, national or European programmes.

At the regional level NJDF and the Regional Policy Department are partly financed by their immediate political sponsor, the County Council, but the vast majority of the resources they allocate comes as co-funding from other, primarily European and national, tiers of government. Maintaining the role as the largest actor in economic development in North Jutland in other words depends on the continued designation of the region for Structural Funds support, i.e. on high politics in the run-up to enlargement of the EU towards the East. The TICs are in a position where they are financed by three Danish levels of government, but unlike in for example neighbouring Viborg County they are *not* used by the County to implement business development policies. Instead NJDF has set up a separate implementation body, North Jutland Business Service, which runs the majority of the regional framework programmes and has become the largest provider of business service in the region in terms of personnel. Business and Innovation Centre North depends more than any other regional body on the cooperation of the various suppliers of business service in order to be able to identify a sufficient number of viable industrial development projects (Claus Midtgaard, Svend Valentin, personal interviews). As a new organisation the Centre is hardly likely to be able to trace down enough development projects, and this is of course especially important because it will be charging for some of its services and thereby contribute to its continued existence.

Summing up the patterns of resource dependencies, three things are conspicuous with regard to relations of authority. Firstly, the activities of sub-national actors are subject to national and European regulation and thus have to operate within certain more or less clearly defined limits. Secondly, and not very surprising, the implementation bodies draw their authority from their political sponsors. And thirdly, no single actor within the region has the authority to direct the actions of all other actors, not even if we discount the organisations that are part of nation-wide networks. In terms of authority, the picture of the economic development bodies in North Jutland is in other words one of fragmentation.

With regard to financial resources, the origins of the *basic* budgets of the development organisations generally reflect the fragmented pattern of political sponsorship and authority, but it is also important to stress that the regional level via its influence on the largest single source of external funding available for economic development purposes in North Jutland, the European Structural Funds programmes, would seem to have considerable influence on any *additional* activities sub-regional and local actors may wish to pursue.

Turning to informational and organisational types of resources, a much more complex pattern of exchange and dependency is in evidence. The resources on which the local business development offices draw depend on the type of activities they prioritise, and as there will often be a range of options at their disposal, they need not necessarily rely on one particular source of, for example, information or refer their clients on to one particular advisory body. The regional organisations to some extent depend on the cooperation of other suppliers of business service - locally, regionally and nationally - but there is no clear-cut pattern of dependency: individual organisations will often have different partners to chose between when accessing additional information or pointing clients on to other service providers, but at the same time they also to a certain extent depend on having SME clients referred to them from especially local development bodies. In terms of information and organisation a quasi-market situation exist where the presence of a number of competing providers operating in broadly similar domains offering overlapping business services would appear to give individual organisations, especially those on the local level, a considerable degree of freedom with regard to what partners they chose as suppliers of additional organisational or informational resources. In these circumstances the scope of individual organisations for pursuing different strategies of collaboration would seem to be considerable, and hence it will be important to investigate concrete patterns of cooperation between development bodies in North Jutland.

Patterns of Cooperation

The analysis of actual patterns of cooperation first deals with horizontal cooperation between organisations operating at the same spatial level, and then considers vertical cooperation between organisations operating on different spatial levels.

Formalised *horizontal cooperation* between local districts has achieved a high profile recently through the emergence of sub-regional networks. It is, however, interesting to note that districts faced with similar problems due to similarities in economic structure often fail to cooperate because they see each other primarily as competitors, for example the districts of Skagen and Hirtshals which have traditionally had competing fishing industries. Further, activities entailing a physical location and a very visible choice between job creation in different districts - like infrastructure projects or attraction of investments from outside - will often be avoided because they collide with the fundamental objective of the participating local offices, namely to create growth in *their* local community.

The extensive institutional engineering on the regional level could be expected to affect patterns of cooperation adversely. At the time of its establishment North Jutland Business Service actually took over some of its functions from the TICs (Preben Mousten, personal interview), but as most of their services are not overlapping and the TICs are co-sponsored by the ultimate sponsor of North Jutland Business Service, the County, reasonable working relations are not an unlikely outcome (Preben Mousten, personal interview). Similarly Business and Innovation Centre North, despite scepticism in some quarters about the relevance of the new organisation, generally seemed satisfied with the level of cooperation it had met (Freddy Ranø, personal interview). All in all reasonably cordial and constructive working relations would seem to prevail between the regionally-based development bodies.

With regard to *vertical cooperation*, the relations vary greatly depending on which regional body we look at. By setting up NJDF the County of North Jutland has formally included local and sub-regional interests in the policy-making process surrounding the largest development programme in the region, and although inter-district and inter-tier conflicts still exist, establishing a forum in which these issues can be discussed must be seen as a constructive attempt to create inter-tier consensus on the political level. But when we turn to implementing bodies, the relationship between regional and local/sub-regional actors is very uneven indeed. While Business and Innovation Centre North at the time of the study was too new to have made any great impact, cooperation between the local business development offices and the TICs seemed to be reasonably smooth,[10] albeit in many cases without involving much interaction, probably because the distinct functional domain occupied by the two Centres was seen as complementing rather than competing with local efforts. Cooperation is, however, not what has characterised the relationship between the majority of the local business development

Preben Mousten, personal interview, cf. almost all local business officers interviewed.

offices and the North Jutland Business Service. Despite the fact that almost all local business development officers stress the importance of the availability of more specialised sources of advice at the regional level with regard to finance and export, many of them have until recently refrained from using these advisory services, allegedly because North Jutland Business Service originally promoted itself very aggressively at the expense of the local business development offices. The local business development officers did not want to be reduced to a local vehicle for promotion of regional services, and many saw it as trespassing when North Jutland Business Service began to offer services which were already provided locally in some, but not all, districts. In practice this meant that fewer firms were referred from local business development offices to North Jutland Business Service, and that the latter could not rely on the cooperation of the local offices in generating interest for particular projects or initiatives. Most offices only used North Jutland Business Service in connection with 'monopoly services', i.e. the regional framework programmes which for example co-funds the use of private consultancy services in firms while oher suppliers were preferred for non-unique advisory services. The new regional body appears to have underestimated the extent to which it depends on the assistance of the local business development offices, and the ensuing poor relationship may well have increased the incentives for local business development offices to cooperate horizontally in e.g sub-regional networks (Andy Jensen, Jorgen M. Jorgensen, Preben Mousten, and Claus A Nielsen, personal interviews).

The most conspicuous vertical conflict has, however, been between North Jutland Business Service and Aalborg Commercial Council. The basic conflict is that between on the regional capital of Aalborg which is able to supply a wide range of services for business and on the other side North Jutland County Council which has set up the North Jutland Business Service to cover parts of the same functional domain for the whole county. The conflict has been reinforced by the formation of sub-regional networks which allow the Aalborg Region to become an even more important actor. Strong sub-regional networks are able to undertake services, projects and

Only two of the districts in which interviews were carried out had pursued a policy of cooperation.

programmes supplied by regional organisations such as the framework programmes currently implemented by North Jutland Business Service on behalf of NJDF, something which the County has been more than reluctant to endorse. This conflict about the ownership of business services between the regional and sub-regional levels of government would seem to suggest that while sub-regional networks can improve horizontal coordination between actors in economic development, they may at the same time challenge the system vertically.

In this situation it is hardly surprising that the question of coordination has surfaced on the political agenda in North Jutland, and several attempts have been undertaken to improve day-to-day and strategic cooperation between the many actors by means of instruments such as allocation of financial resources, development of common strategy, and organisational changes. Although NJDF has no direct authority over the other actors, an instrument which could be used to influence other organisations is the allocation of annual grants and the decision as to who should implement framework programmes on the regional level. Influencing the activities of the sub-regional networks and the local business development offices is, however, more difficult as NJDF do not allocate annual grants to these actors (Henning Christensen, personal interview), and the long-term strategic potentials of ad-hoc funding for local projects are more limited. Coordination at the regional level could also be furthered through formulation of a regional development strategy, and currently the Objective 2 programme is what comes closest to such a strategy (Nordjyllands Amt 1997). This programme resulted from an extensive process of consultation among partners at all levels in the region, something which has undoubtedly contributed to a feeling of joint ownership of the programme. The programme is, however, very broad in its strategic focus and does not attempt to define which tasks are to be undertaken at what level and thus leaves important organisational and spatial issues unresolved. Recent reports prepared for the NJDF have attempted to fill in the gap and clarify the division of labour between the organisations, and this may herald new and better times in terms of cooperation, although especially the way in which the sub-regional networks will fit into the system in practice remains to be seen. So far the County has blocked the formal recognition of the sub-regional networks as Business Centres supported by central government, and it is therefore likely that new moves to bolster the position of the sub-regional networks may also be resisted from the regional level. Perhaps the introduction of many new actors over the past decade cannot be expected to take place without some degree of conflict, but a key challenge for the future is whether the actors will be able to align themselves with each other through voluntary cooperation and networking, or whether some sort of hierarchical relations will eventually be introduced coordination in order to improve the functional efficiency of the overall system. Until now attempts to improve coordination of economic development activities have clearly not been able to square the circle of territorial politics within the region.

Conclusions and Perspectives

The North Jutland system for business service has been found to have the following general characteristics. All levels of government have chosen to be active within the field of business promotion in North Jutland, not only as sponsors but by setting up their own implementing bodies, and there is thus a range of business services available to North Jutland firms. The vast majority of organisations are characterised by being small and operating in broadly the same functional domain, especially with regard to provision of general forms of advisory services, and even though various forms of formal and informal cooperation take place, business promotion has gradually become a somewhat crowded and competitive field in the 1990s. While this may enable private firms to chose between different public providers of advice, it certainly also has a series of drawbacks, some of which are recognised by the development bodies themselves. Firstly, the splitting up of activities into too many different organisations may not be appropriate from the perspective of an enterprise which may have to involve different organisations in what the firm sees as an integrated complex of problems. Secondly, the plethora of small organisations does not allow the most effective use of the total resources allocated because competition as well as cooperation with other organisations take up a significant part of the resources available. Thirdly, the constant search for additional external funding would appear to tempt small organisations to branch out into new functions and thereby add to problems of coordination. And finally from the perspective of long-term development of competences and strategies the preponderance of organisations that are primarily project or programme-driven increases the risk that specialist knowledge and competences will disappear if organisations are shut down or the personnel cut down or replaced.

No formal structure of authority exists which can remedy these problems: neither the County nor the NJDF can order the organisations to cooperate by exercising authority over them. One may of course expect the regional level to have some degree of leverage through the resources allocated via the NJDF and the Structural Funds programmes, but this influence manifests itself primarily at the regional level, whereas the sub-regional and local level find their main sources of finance elsewhere. Similarly, the presence of a number of regional and national providers of more specialised types of advisory services ensures that sub-regional actors do not depend on one particular provider and thus regional actors cannot use informational or organisational resources to compel local and sub-regional actors to cooperate, simply because these resources are not irreplaceable. Essentially, the system therefore consists of formally independent actors with different political sponsors and the degree of coordination and cooperation therefore to a large extent depend on the willingness of the actors to cooperate, something which may reflect not only functional but also for example territorial interests.

A similar picture may be found in other regions in Europe where several tiers of sub-national government vie for position in the domain of economic development, but in North Jutland the interaction of the internal territorial politics of the region with European and national policies would seem to have combined to produce an even more intricate situation. Large sums have been available from the European Structural Funds and have, among other things, been used to set up a range of separate institutions. This line of action would partly seem to have been prompted by the general preference of Danish governments for framework measures: European funding should be used for institution building rather than direct subsidies to individual firms. The extensive institutional engineering would, however, also appear to be propelled by territorial politics with the County setting up its own organisation in order to control policy implementation and thereby colliding with the ambitions of other organisations and levels of government intent on operating in the same policy domain.

Underlying these ongoing attempts to reshape the division of labour within the 'development industry' in North Jutland we find the uneven economic structure of the county. The dominant city of Aalborg has built up its own fields of competence and enhanced them by instigating a sub-regional network comprising other relatively prosperous districts within the region, and this again seems to have triggered, or at least sped up, the formation of other sub-regional networks. These institutional developments point towards a central strategic dilemma facing actors in economic development within the region: should resources be directed towards strengthening growth industries or target peripheral areas? In this context sub-regional networks could have a function in drawing attention to the peripheral areas *if*, in terms of resources and size, they are able to form an adequate counterweight to networks in more prosperous areas. The positive interpretation of the ongoing institutional transformation could in other words be that the introduction of new sub-regional actors in economic development will highlight the diversity of North Jutland and thereby make choices made on the regional level more explicit and transparent. But still an obvious risk would seem to be that adding a new tier to the already complex system of economic governance will increase the importance of territorial politics in the decision-making process at the expense of functional considerations.

On a more general note the case of North Jutland would seem to suggest that 'institutional thickness' is not unambiguously a blessing, but something which may well imply significant drawbacks if the balance between cooperation and competition amongst public development bodies is skewed too far towards the latter. Compared to other European regions which have sometimes been labelled 'intelligent' due to their successful adaption to economic challenges from their national and international environment, perhaps a very real problem for North Jutland is what the region is *not*. It is neither a relatively homogenous industrial district like for example Emilia-Romagna in Italy, nor a nation like Wales or Catalonia, and hence it lacks the trust or sense of national purpose that may generate a social environment conducive to constructive interaction between public and private partners in regional development. Instead what we have is something that is undoubtedly more common from a European perspective, namely a comparatively new and essentially artificial administrative region with a heterogenous economic structure in which the system of business promotion has been established even more recently and thereafter constantly transformed and adapted. From this perspective, the methods employed in making sense of bottom-up regional policy in North Jutland may prove to be useful in other settings in a period where integration and enlargement on the European level put new pressure on the institutional set-up for economic development at the regional level.

Acknowledgements

This text is based on work undertaken as part of the LEONARDO-sponsored project *The Intelligent Region*. Thanks are due to the regional and local development organisations in North Jutland for participating in the study, and the Ministry of Business and Industry in Denmark for supplying information. The financial and other support of DGXVI of the European Commission and Aalborg Univesity's Department of Languages and International Culture Studies is also gratefully acknowledged, as is the inspiration provided by the project coordinators at the Welsh Development Agency and the other project partners. Full responsibility for the text in its present form does of course remain with the authors.

References

Amin, A. and Thrift, N. (1994) 'Living in the Global.' In A. Amin and N. Thrift (eds) *Globalization, Institutions, and Regional Development in Europe*. Oxford: OUP, 1-22.

Damborg, C. (1998) 'The North Jutland Objective 2 Programme: Coordination and Evaluation.' *IQ-NET Occasional Paper 2*, Aalborg University.

Damborg, C. and Halkier, H. (1998a) 'Regional development agencies in Denmark - towards a Danish approach to bottom-up regional policy.' In H. Halkier, M. Danson and C. Damborg (eds) *Regional Development Agencies in Europe*. London: Jessica Kingsley, 80-99.

Damborg, C. and Halkier, H. (1998b) 'Development bodies, networking and business promotion in North Jutland.' *European Studies Series of Occasional Papers 28*, European Research Unit, Aalborg University.

Erhvervsministeriet (1995) *Regionalpolitisk Redegørelse 1995*. København: Erhvervsministeriet.

Erhvervsfremme Styrelsen (1998a) *Evaluering af Teknologiske Informationscentre (TIC)*. Kobenhavn: Erhvervsfremme Styrelsen.

Erhvervsfremme Styrelsen (1998b) *Evaluering af Teknologiske Informationscentre (TIC) - Casestudier*. Kobenhavn: Erhvervsfremme Styrelsen.

Halkier, H. (1996) 'Institutions, power and regional policy.' *European Studies Series of Occasional Papers 16*, European Research Unit, Aalborg University.

Halkier, H. (1997) 'The North Jutland Objective 2 Programme: institutions and implementation.' *IQ-NET Occasional Paper 1*, Aalborg University.

Halkier, H. (1998) 'Danish regions and the Europeanization of regional policy.' *European Studies Series of Occasional Papers 27*, European Research Unit, Aalborg University.

Halkier, H. and Damborg , C. (1997) 'Networks, development agencies and intelligent regions - towards a framework for empirical analysis.' *European Studies Series of Occasional Papers 22*, European Research Unit, Aalborg University.

Industri- og Samordningsministeriet (1994) *Koordinering af regional erhvervsfremme.* Betænkning afgivet af et udvalg nedsat af industriministeren. København: Industri- og Samordningsministeriet.
Nordjyllands Amt (1997) *Globalisering. Et Program til Styrkelse af Nordjyske Virksomheders Konkurrenceevne.* Aalborg: Nordjyllands Amt.

Interviews

All interviews undertaken in the period 12 November 1997 - 27 January 1998 by Charlotte Damborg. Taped and summarised, not 1:1 audiotyped.

Ole Albæk, Programme Coordinator for the Vendsyssel Development Council, Hjørring.
Poul Erik Andersen, Local Business Development Officer, Hobro.
Henning Christensen, Head of the Regional Policy Department, North Jutland County.
Ole Christensen, Consultant, the Aalborg Commercial Council, Aalborg.
Andy Jensen, Local Business Development Officer, Aabybro.
Lene Jensen and Anette Petersen, Business librarians, The Library's Business Service, Aalborg.
Kurt Jepsen, Local Business Development Officer, Dronninglund.
Jørgen M. Jørgensen, Consultant, the Himmerland Development Council, Aars.
Claus Midtgaard, Consultant, the North Jutland Business Service, Aalborg.
Preben Mousten, Manager of the Technological Information Centre South, Aars.
Claus A. Nielsen, Local Business Development Officer, Skagen.
Per Husted Nielsen, Local Business Development Officer, Hadsund.
Jørn Munk Nielsen, Local Business Development Officer, Hirtshals.
Freddy Ranø, Chief Consultant, the Business and Innovation Centre North, Aalborg.
Svend Valentin, Managing Director of NOVI A/S, Aalborg.
Helge Wittrup, Local Business Development Officer, Sæby.
Hans Peter Wolsing, Local Business Development Officer, Lokken-Vra.

Appendix

Organisations included in the survey

Regional

Erhvervssekretariat, Nordjyllands Amt (The Regional Policy Department, North Jutland County Council)
Arbejdsmarkedsrådet Nordjylland (The North Jutland Labour Market Council)
Bibliotekernes Erhvervsservice (The Libraries' Business Service)
BIC Nord (The Business and Innovation Centre North)
dk-TEKNIK
Lindholm 21

Netværkscenteret, Aalborg Universitet (The Network Centre, Aalborg University)
Nordjyllands Erhvervsservice (The North Jutland Business Service)
Nordjyllands Udviklingsfond (The North Jutland Development Fund)
Nordjysk Eksportklub (The North Jutland Export Club)
Nordjysk Informatik og Virksomhedsudvikling (The North Jutland Information Technology and Enterprise Development)
NOVI A/S (The North Jutland Science Park)
TIC Nordjylland Nord (The Technological Information Centre North)
TIC Nordjylland Syd (The Technological Information Centre South)
Videnskabsbutikken, Aalborg Universitet (The Science Shop, Aalborg University)

Sub-regional

Region Aalborg (The Aalborg Region)
Vendsyssel Udviklingsrad (The Vendsyssel Development Council)

Local business development offices

Brovst Turist- og Erhvervsrad
Dronninglund Erhvervskontor
Frederikshavn Erhvervsrad
Hadsund Erhvervsrad
Himmerlands Udviklingsrad (covering Farso, Norager, Aars)
Hirtshals Kommunes Erhvervsrad
Hjorring Erhvervsrad
Hobro Erhvervsrad
Lokken-Vra Erhvervsråd
Sejlflod Erhvervs- og Udviklingsråd
Skagen Kommunes Erhvervssekretariat
Sæby Erhvervskontor
Aabybro Kommune, Erhvervskontoret
Aalborg Erhvervsråd

6 Cohesion Policy and the Role of RDAs in the Making of an Intelligent Region: Lessons from the Southern European Periphery

GRIGORIS KAFKALAS AND ELISAVET THOIDOU

Regional Learning and the Making of Intelligent Regions: From Theory to Policy Making

The idea of regional learning and the intelligence of regions as the key mechanism for the understanding of regional development is in itself an innovative conceptual breakthrough of regional development theory. The genealogy of the concept goes back to the notions of industrial districts, clustering and system areas and it is also associated with the themes of innovation strategies, institutional thickness and the embededness of development. The existing literature makes a strong case for the potential of intelligent regions to compete effectively in markets, to adapt quickly to crises, to exploit new opportunities and to achieve convergence with the most successful areas.

For the purposes of the present article regional learning is considered to be the process through which a regional system acquires the necessary knowledge and the practical expertise in order to deal efficiently with structural change. In this respect learning itself becomes a factor enabling change because it changes our perceptions and our practices in dealing with structure. On the other hand, different definitions of the notion of 'region' sometimes contrast sharply with each other. For example geographical definitions could not always coexist with historical or political ones (Kafkalas 1995). And in any case the criteria used to define a region vary extensively in terms of size, socio-economic factors, time horizons, etc. Is Europe a region in relation to Southeast Asia? Is a metropolitan area a region within a national territory? Are regions complementary in a puzzle-like horizontal structure or can they contain each other in a more hierarchical way? These are questions to which no general answer can be provided and it seems that a region is a 'region' only in relation to a specific question or purpose.

The article adopts a definition compatible with our concern with public development plans and innovation strategies. Thus, a region is considered to be a geographically delimited area for which there exists a locally based public agency or network of agencies (not necessarily representative or directly elected) with administrative capacities (not necessarily exclusive) to formulate and/or implement comprehensive regional development plans in the sense that it has both the political legitimisation and the command over the necessary resources. Thus regions are defined here as basically programme regions at the level of public policy making.

A number of tentative efforts have been made to utilise these insights on learning and innovation in urban and regional development theory. Morgan and Cooke (1991) and Morgan (1992) should be credited with the use of the term 'intelligent region' in their effort to capture the importance of the complex web of relations, roles and functions of the different regional actors.

Another sophisticated attempt, according to Morgan (1995), is to be found in Storper (1994) who seeks to explain what he considers to be the principal trend of contemporary spatial economies: the rise of the local at the time when the forces of globalisation appear to reduce the world to a 'placeless' mass. A key part of the explanation is the association between innovation, technological learning, and the agglomeration.

This association has two roots: the first concerns localised input-output relations in the agglomeration, which are essential to information exchange and the user-producer co-ordination. The second concerns the role of untraded interdependencies (like labour markets, local conventions, norms, values, public or semi-public institutions) which co-ordinate the process of organisational and interactive learning. Both localised input-output and untraded interdependencies make interactive learning to be place specific, and the respective agglomeration a par excellence site for innovation. The birth of the intelligent region concept thus comes together with an extension of interest from private sector inter-firm networking to civil society, societal institutions, public policy making and innovation support strategies.

The idea of an innovation strategy as an aim of regional development policy focuses more upon the regional innovation system in its totality rather than on the more restricted notion of the innovative cluster. We can associate this idea with a new theoretical contribution that was added to the discussion on regional innovation based upon the pioneering work of Lundvall (1992) on national systems of innovation. This widened the debate on districts, flexible specialisation, new industrial spaces, and technopoles.

Lundvall gives no strict definition for the concept of systems of innovation, but introduces two basic propositions: (1) that innovation is an interactive learning process between firms and the basic science and technology infrastructure, and (2) interactive learning between firms is supported by a wide range of institutional mechanisms, such as habits, routines of everyday life and social conventions which are rather 'intangible' and 'invisible', embodying knowledge which is tacit and skill-like. This view opens a much wider debate and provides a direct theoretical link for the formulation and implementation of innovation strategies as a means to promote regional learning capacities and thus to contribute in the making of an intelligent region.

We are particularly concerned with the generalisation of the policy implications of the 'Technopole' and innovation support debate (Kafkalas and Komninos 1993; Komninos 1993; Kafkalas 1995). This is a step that needs still to be taken further by theoretical research and current practice.

So far the debate seems to focus too much on high tech and the cutting edge of technology and science at the expense of the more routine and close-to-everyday experience aspects of innovation; this means the study of innovation within the context of specific regional productive systems.

It seems that there is a disproportionate focus upon the discontinuity triggered by major innovations while insufficient importance is attached to the continuity of minor innovations occurring through engineering and other supposedly 'lower' applications of knowledge (Morgan 1997, forthcoming). But it is exactly this form of piecemeal innovation, which happens in the less developed regions at all times and even in the developed regions most of the time, that enables both normal functioning and gradual upgrading of a regional productive system.

The underlying rationale for the support of a regional innovation system lies in its attempt to bring to the surface the main factors behind the region's innovation deficit: the archaic character of its small and medium-sized businesses, the inadequacies of its mechanisms for the diffusion of innovation and, first and foremost, the inadequate integration of technology supply and demand.

The basic concern of an innovative region strategy is the promotion of a more decentralised regional innovation system, which stands on the existing industrial and research capability of the region, and insists on institutional mechanisms for adaptability, interactive learning and networking.

The intelligent region concept refers to the ability of an area to control effectively the process of its structural economic transformation. Two factors are particularly crucial in relation to this ability:

1. planned state intervention dealing with the issues of development and structural adjustment of the regional productive system, and
2. the way in which the various regional agents, especially local firms, deal with increasing market competition.

Moreover, the intelligent region concept is closely related to the attempts to implement strategies for innovation and technology transfer, especially in the productive systems of lagging regions. These strategies stress the importance of inter-firm networking and the establishment of the appropriate common services for small and medium-sized enterprises (SMEs).

Concerning regional policy, the promotion of regional institutions as well as the creation of the structure and infrastructure capable of responding to the needs of regional productive systems in general, and of providing support to SMEs in particular, are two basic parameters in the above context (Komninos 1997). Regional development planning and its implementation could be considered to reflect the above mentioned intelligent region's characteristic: the ability of regional bodies to act and co-operate in order to achieve the development and structural adjustment of the regional economy in the context of the intelligent region strategy.

European Structural Policies: An Overview of the Greek Experience in Relation to the Regional Competitiveness of SMEs

European Union structural policy, as the main redistributive mechanism aimed at the narrowing of regional inequalities and the maintenance of the socio-economic cohesion of the EU, can support substantially the implementation of intelligent region strategies through the co-financing of regional development programmes. By supporting regional adjustment and increasing regional competitiveness, EU structural policy plays a twofold role: on the one hand it directly finances the creation of the necessary infrastructure and, on the other hand, it helps to establish and support local agents in their efforts to plan and implement the necessary actions. Moreover, EU structural policy is aimed at strengthening the local and regional level, regarding the procedures of development planning, administration and implementation, by both financial and institutional means (Andrikopoulou 1995; Andrikopoulou and Kafkalas 1995; CEC 1992).

As far as SMEs are concerned, EU structural policy offers to the European regions a series of policy instruments in support of their productive system. This is due to the substantial role that is attributed to SMEs for the improvement of regional competitiveness. Service provision as well as co-operation and networking support constitute the main elements of the innovative measures/actions directed at SMEs. In other words, EU structural policy measures addressed to SMEs are providing to the regions, especially to the lagging ones, potentialities and specific tools in support of their regional innovation systems. The intelligent region strategy constitutes a key concept for the incorporation and utilisation of these tools within the development strategy selected for each specific region.

On the other hand, as already argued, the region's reaction to the potentialities created in the context of the EU structural policy could be supposed to constitute a measure of what the intelligent region concept refers to, that is the region's ability to control the process of its structural economic transformation effectively. The contribution of regional development agencies (RDAs) is substantial in this direction. Their emergence to a large extent represents an area's reaction to the rising challenges within the context of the intelligent region strategy. Therefore, the composition and characteristics of the EU co-financed programmes, as well as the role of RDAs, are crucial points in our consideration.

In the context of EU regional policy, Greece is considered as an Objective 1 region. Objective 1 is concerned with 'promoting the development and structural adjustment of the regions whose development is lagging behind'. The successive Community Support Framework (CSF) for Greece are nationwide programmes with regional sections that account for about 40.4 per cent (in CSFI) and 28.2 per cent (in CSFII) implemented through regional multifunded operational plans. During the 1980s and 1990s, regional policy in Greece became spatially organised, aiming at structural interventions related to all the sectors of the Greek economy. To a large extent this is due to its connection to the EU structural policy, especially after the reform of the Structural Funds in 1989. Both the doubling of Structural Fund resources and the impact of structural policies on the system, methods and contents of regional planning in Greece led to the introduction of some very useful ideas and instruments (such as networking, innovation and technology transfer). National, regional and local authorities, which now have at their disposal new strong tools capable of enriching and specifying regional policy measures, are facing the challenge of the intelligent region strategy.

The co-financed programmes of national and community interest exercised considerable influence over this direction. Their contribution must not be considered only by the volume of available funding (e.g. to enterprises, supporting agents or other kinds of investment and actions that in the long term support the regional productive system).

Equally and perhaps even more important is the fact that, within this context, problems are being recognised and defined, different ways of resolving them are being proposed and adopted, several supporting agencies are being created or reactivated, forms of enterprise co-operation and networking are being introduced, the corresponding legal framework is being renewed and the experience of the other EU member states is being utilised in a number of cases (EP 1991; EC 1996).

The strong relationship between EU structural policy and the establishment of regional institutions, RDAs in particular, is clearly shown in the case of the CSF. The establishment of the regional public administration authorities (General Secretariat in each region) in 1987, to a large extent corresponded to the new emerging needs for regional planning in Greece, particularly in the context of the EU co-financed programmes.

During this initial phase, regional public administration authorities in each region were functioning the most in support of these programmes, and of the regional multifund operational programmes (MOPs) in particular. This task has been proved to be of great importance for their transformation and the redefinition of their new role, through a new institutional framework, in 1997.

The emergence and the role of RDAs also reflect this course. Since 1978, the Greek Government had made provision for the establishment of RDAs in areas characterised either by specific developmental problems or by significant developmental resources. The emphasis given to endogenous local development during the 1980s, to a large extent favoured the RDAs' creation and function. However, despite these measures, only a few agencies had been created during the 1970s and the 1980s, most on the state's initiative.

The majority of RDAs that are functioning nowadays at a local or regional level have been created during the second half of the 1980s, mostly after 1990. This is due to their close and systematic connection to the European structural policy, which is creating significant opportunities and yet poses particular preconditions and regulations regarding the role of the RDAs.

It has to be mentioned that this course is generally meeting the prevailing developmental trends and patterns during the same period. The emphasis given to the locality as well as the revision of the role of the state is of great importance in this regard. RDAs are usually acting in support of regional productive systems and local/regional authorities, while in some cases they are expanding their activities in preferential state's fields of action.

As far as SMEs are concerned, development priorities and specific measures have been selected for funding through the CSF and Community initiatives, both at national and regional levels. These are expected to affect particular factors which are considered as influencing the competitiveness of the less developed areas (i.e. those supported as Objective 1 regions by Community regional policy). Given the wide range of factors behind their competitiveness, interventions for SMEs have included many so called 'soft', innovative actions, in contrast to the traditional hard infrastructure provision. Development problems and potentialities concerning the country's productive system are identified and stressed in both the CSF I and CSF II for Greece. 'Improvement of the competitiveness of firms' is one of the five priorities selected for the national section of CSF I (1989-93). The aim is to 'support development of the productive sector by providing finance towards measures to improve the technical and economic environment for industrial and service firms (industrial estates and advisory services), towards the training of managers and workers, and towards an effective aid scheme.' (CEC 1990, p. 12). Aid to industrial firms, promotion of Greek products to markets abroad and creation of infrastructure are the specific aims for this sector. 'Development and competitiveness of the economy' is also one of the five priorities selected for the national section of the ongoing CSF II (1994-99). This priority comprises the Multifund Operational Programme for industry and services[2] which is aimed to 'encourage investment from abroad and to assist firms which can meet the challenge of technological change and market globalisation' (EC 1994: 46). CSF II acknowledges the fact that, concerning industry, the aid scheme selected by the CSF I did not have the expected impact on business competitiveness. The overall estimated cost for the priorities addressed at SMEs is about 1,197 (at 1989 prices) and 3,318 MECU (at 1994 prices) for CSF I and II (Objective 1) respectively, which accounts for almost 9.9 per cent and 12.6 per cent of their total cost.

It follows from the priorities set out by the successive CSFs for Greece concerning SMEs that the improvement of business competitiveness is becoming an increasingly important priority. The increased share of this priority in the budget, as well as the adoption of significant innovative measures (along with traditional ones), indicates the efforts undertaken in support of regional productive systems during the last period. This fact also indicates the extent to which the Structural Funds, by providing the proper reorientation of priorities, can actually promote the intelligent region strategies.

1 The level of infrastructure (in particular telecommunications, transportation, energy and environmental infrastructure), the qualification of employees, along with the level of R&D, and the attraction of direct foreign investments are considered as factors underlining regional competitiveness (EC 1994b).

2 It also comprises the MOPs for Research and Technology, Tourism and Culture, Agriculture and Fisheries.

Regional Planning and RDAs in the Making of an Intelligent Region: the Case of Central Macedonia

The region of Central Macedonia constitutes one of the thirteen programme regions of Greece and has three independent tiers of administration. The regional tier is part of the decentralised central state structure, while both the prefectural and the municipal tiers are directly elected local authorities. There are three administrative tiers below the National Government level: the Regions and the two Tiers of Local Authorities - the Prefectures and the Municipalities (or Communes in certain cases). The Regional Tier consists of 13 administrative units. Central Macedonia is one such Region. Each Region is headed by the General Secretary of the Region appointed by central government, with nominal responsibility over the co-ordination of all public agencies decentralised at the peripheral level. The most important function of the Regional Secretariat concerns its direct involvement in the formulation, monitoring and implementation of the Multifund Operational Programme (MOP) for regional development as an integral part of the European Community Support Framework. The Prefectural Tier consists of 50 administrative units. The Region of Central Macedonia is subdivided into seven Prefectures. The Prefectural Tier constitutes the Second Tier of Local Authorities and corresponds to a directly elected self-government. Its organisational structure resembles that of the central state with various directorates and departments with concrete administrative capacities. However, this tier lacks substantial economic and political power as the controversies over the devolution of administrative functions continues since its transformation from a decentralised state machine to a directly elected body in 1994. The Municipal (or Communal) Tier is composed of 900 Municipalities and 133 Communes. There are 134 Municipalities in the Region of Central Macedonia. They constitute the First Tier of Local Authorities, which has a long history of self-government in Greece. They possess, however, little economic power and their administrative capacities remain restricted to specifically defined local issues, including items such as the collection of garbage and the running of pre-school and primary education establishments.

The role of Central Macedonia is substantial in the development of the entire country due to the region's specific characteristics, such as its geographical position along with the presence of the city of Thessaloniki as well as the characteristics of its productive system. Central Macedonia is a large and dynamic region in Northern Greece that maintains a prominent role in the Greek regional system, especially as a pole of international significance in the wider Balkan area and a European Union gateway-region in its south-east borders. The region, and Thessaloniki in particular, is a meeting point for the main axes of the transport networks at both a national and international level. The geographical position of the Region of Central Macedonia is shown in Figure 6.1.

To a large extent its development is based on manufacturing activity. Thessaloniki, which is the second largest Greek town, is also the second pole of attraction of industrial activity in the country, constituting a zone of important manufacturing activity together with the surrounding areas. At the beginning of the 1990s, Central Macedonia had a per capita GDP (in PPS) of 46.8 (with Europe-12=100), ranking fifth among the thirteen Greek regions but occupying one of the lowest (17th from the poorest) positions among the European regions.

Enterprises of Central Macedonia, especially those in manufacturing, make a significant contribution to the overall development of the region as well as to the development of the secondary sector of the Greek economy. The region's long-lasting specialisation in traditional manufacturing branches and its notable exporting activity, coupled with its main characteristics (level of infrastructure, services and human capital, geographical position with regard to the transportation network and the wider Balkan peninsula), define its development perspectives.

Considering the characteristics of the regional productive system as well as the developments in the neighbouring regions and in the wider area (the Balkans, Europe and at the international level), new challenges have arisen for Central Macedonia. The need for restructuring, which was obvious since 1980, became urgent during the 1990s and the efforts to meet it should be intensive.

The prevailing development strategy, which has been selected in the context of the CSF 1994-99 for Greece, is aimed at the promotion of the metropolitan role of the region as well as at the strengthening of the region's role in the wider Balkan area. The strengthening of the potential of the regional economy (industry, SMEs and human resources, in particular) is among the main objectives adopted by the selected development strategy. Within this context, a wide range of the regional and national section measures/actions of the CSF concerns the improvement of the economic, technical and social infrastructure of Central Macedonia (transportation, communication, environment and services). Besides, there was a major effort to support the activity of SMEs, both by 'hard' and 'soft' types of action. The structure of the implemented development programmes represents the prevailing aspects about the region's main development priorities as well as the selected main axes of action.

Within this context, the regional MOP 1989-93 for Central Macedonia included the 'improvement of the competitiveness of firms' among the seven objectives of its first priority. This objective was specified through a sub-programme that comprised six measures. The measures entitled 'establishment of agencies supporting SMEs' and 'services to SMEs' can be considered as the most innovative.

According to the relevant text: 'The combination of these two measures is the core of the sub-programme. Specialised, viable agencies with high standards and good knowledge of the region's structural problems are expected to be founded, in order to support enterprises at the whole spectrum of their activities' (Region of Central Macedonia 1990, p.89). Indeed, the first measure financed the creation of a new RDA, namely the 'Business and Cultural Development Centre' (KEPA), which is developing a significant activity, while the second included some small-scale actions, such as studies and databases.

According to the objectives and the preliminary choices described in the regional MOP 1994-99 for Central Macedonia: 'The secondary sector which is capable of: converting idled private resources into long-term productive investment, securing the production of added value and constructing a, more or less, integrated productive system, is posed by the development strategy for Central Macedonia in the centre of the overall development effort' (Region of Central Macedonia 1990, p.3).

'Improvement of SMEs competitiveness' is one of the eight sub-programmes of the regional MOP 1994-99. The measures and actions in it cover quite a large range. Specifically, the measure 'improvement of SMEs competitiveness' has a financing role (aid to enterprises, either under the Greek Incentive's Law or under the unified guidelines set out by the Ministry of Development for all the country's regions). The measures 'industrial and business infrastructure' and 'development of inter Balkan co-operation' mainly comprise the creation of infrastructure for organisations providing services. Last but not least, the measures 'training' and 'research and production linking' have an innovative character due to their specific actions such as the 'industrial informatics' that are included in the latter.

It is clear that the approach for SMEs has been gradually enriched, both in financing terms (see Table 6.1) and in terms of their innovative character, at least at the initial planning stage.

However, comparing the initial estimated budget to the final payments shows, as far as the regional MOP 1989-93 is concerned, that there is a remarkable reduction of the share of the relevant sub-programme as a percentage of the total programme's cost. The same has happened at a national level (CSF 1989-93): 'Even though the initially selected priorities were right and despite the efforts made by both Greek authorities and the Committee, other reasons caused a change in the emphasis given to the selected priorities, during the first CSF period' (EC 1994a, p.18).

In the current regional MOP, an improved perception of the needs of the enterprises seems to have been included. However, to a large extent, the so-called 'soft' and/or innovative actions of the sub-programme are facing difficulties regarding their implementation.

Table 6.1 Financing the competitiveness of SMEs 1989-1999 (estimated figures)

Regional MOP for Central Macedonia	*Total Programme Budget (MECU)*	*Improvement of Competitiveness of SMEs (MECU)*	*Sub-programme Per Cent of the Programme*
1989-93	366 (1990 prices)	14	3.8
1994-99	817 (1994 prices)	73	8.9

Source: Annual reports

Concerning the region's RDAs, many of them are functioning in Central Macedonia in several fields of activities. They can be distinguished into two categories: state organisations on the one hand and non-state organisations on the other. The majority of the region's non-state RDAs have been created in the context of EU co-financed programmes and/or they are implementing such programmes. Therefore, their establishment and operation is directly or indirectly connected to EU structural policy.

This connection is clearly shown in the following most common cases of RDAs setting out in the region of Central Macedonia.[3]

(i) Creation of an agency in order to meet specific EU regulations concerning a specific EU co-financed programme. This is the case of the Local Action Groups that have been established in each one of the region's prefectures in order to implement the LEADER initiative. It is remarkable that only one out of seven LEADER RDAs was created before LEADER was established in 1989. Four out of the seven region's Local Action Groups were established in the period 1992-93 in order to implement LEADER I, while two of them started only in 1995, within the context of LEADER II.

(ii) Creation of an agency in order to overcome the problems and restraints that characterise the traditionally responsible state organisations or to expand in a new field of action. Problems and opportunities of this kind usually concern the planning, management and implementation of EU co-financed programmes at a regional or a national level. These are the cases of the 'Business and Cultural Development Centre' (KEPA) and the 'Development Agency for Private Utilities in Northern Greece' (EAIYBE). As mentioned above, the first is an intermediary agency for quite a lot of sub-programmes, measures and actions from both the CSF and the Community Initiatives. The second is responsible for the action 'Private Utilities in Northern Greece' which is in the Operational Programme for Industry of the national section of CSF II.

(iii) Support of an agency that has been created in order to form and implement a strategy on specific themes of interest, through the possibility of being financed for the implementation of particular EU programmes and initiatives. This is the case of the 'Inter Balkan and Black Sea Business Centre' (DIPEK) and the 'Thessaloniki Technology Park' (TTP). The main goal of the former is to support and co-ordinate the activities of the Greek enterprises in the Balkan and the Black Sea countries, while the latter is generally aimed at supporting regional development, technology transfer, commissioned research, and training provision.

[3] The case of Euro Info Centre, which functions in the context of the Association of Industries of Northern Greece, is not mentioned here, given that it is not included in the EU structural policy.

(iv) Implementation of a specific action of CSF. This is the case of the 'Industrial Change Offices' that have been created in four out of seven region prefectures, within the context of the Operational Programme for Industry and Services (measure 'recovery of the country's declining areas'). The Offices, which co-ordinate several actions aimed at the recovery of declining areas, function in the context of each Prefecture.

Concerning their specific activities, RDAs in Central Macedonia have developed a variety of activities in support of the region's productive system. These can be broadly summarised as follows:

- dissemination of information
- development studies/plans on either a spatial or a sectoral basis
- financial and business services
- databases/geographical information systems
- consulting
- vocational training, education
- management, administration and/or implementation of EU co-financed programmes/measures/actions
- co-operation and networking at a regional, national or EU level
- assistance in participating in EU and national programmes.

The composition of their activities indicates the specific characteristics of each RDA. In the region of Central Macedonia two main categories can be distinguished: services provider on the one hand and intermediary financing agencies on the other. In our consideration it is very important to say that, to a great extent this differentiation is in accordance with their geographical range.

The existing status, concerning the agencies' structure and control, is also in accordance with their spatial range. Their shareholders usually come from both the private and public sectors.

- Local agencies' main shareholders are local authorities of the first and second degree as well as the representatives of the important corporate interests or collective activities of the prefecture, as the case may be.
- Non-local agencies have a quite different range of shareholders, namely a specific region's prefecture, Northern Greece as a whole (i.e. the regions of Western Macedonia, Central Macedonia and

Eastern Macedonia and Thrace), or the entire country. The Federation of Industries of Northern Greece and the Association of Exporters of Northern Greece have the leading role in most of the cases. Specifically, they are shareholders in KEPA, EAIYBE, DIPEK, TTP, while the Euro Info Centre functions in the context of the Federation of Industries. Chambers of various prefectures as well as the regional branches of state organisations established in the city of Thessaloniki are also shareholders in some of the development agencies of the region.

Direct activity of the state in supporting the regional productive system, especially SMEs, is carried out by the relevant state organisations which have branches in Thessaloniki (the region's capital), while their headquarters are established in Athens. Many of the measures/actions of the national and regional section of CSF and the Community Initiatives that are implemented at regional level are administered by them locally. However, mostly, this is due to decisions made centrally by their headquarters in Athens and does not exclusively reflect their own dynamism at a regional level.

However, the presence of the state RDAs could be considered to be of great importance in the context of the intelligent region strategy.[4] The reason is that they usually decentralise some of the central state's activities, while also facilitating the function of the relevant non-state organisations (RDAs) at the regional level, e.g. by being their shareholders

The recent political choice for the restriction of the role of the state regarding many traditional areas of its action is expected to have considerable impacts on their perspectives at the regional level. Coupled with the overall legislative and organisational restraints and shortages, as well as the existing insufficiencies and rigidities of the public sector in general, these trends demonstrate the significance of the role of the non-state RDAs.

[4] Many state organisations that support SMEs have branches in Thessaloniki. The most important among them are: EOMMEX: Hellenic Organisation for Small and Medium Size Enterprises and Handicrafts; ELKEPA: Greek Centre for Productivity; OPE: Organisation for the Promotion of Exports; ETBA: Hellenic Industrial Development Bank S.A.; HELEXPO: Thessaloniki International Fair, an important nationwide organisation with its headquarters established in the city of Thessaloniki.

Conclusions on the Impact of the Plans and the Role of Development Agencies

The conclusions concerning the combined impact of regional development plans and regional development agencies is presented below in three interlinked themes: the spatial level of action, the structure and content of the programmes, and the character of the agencies.

(i) The spatial level of action for the programmes and agencies supporting SMEs: the degree of integration on a regional or a local basis.

It is clear, in the case of Central Macedonia, that there is a strong relationship between development programmes on the one hand and institutions (RDAs in particular) that support the regional productive system on the other, with regard to the spatial level of their activities and the degree of their spatial integration.

Concerning the spatial level of CSF and Community initiatives, two cases could be distinguished:

- the regional section of CSF and the LEADER initiative - which are planned, implemented and administered on a regional or local basis, respectively.
- the national section of CSF and the other initiatives - which have a horizontal character for the whole country, with the exception of some particular sub-programmes, measures and projects that are locally implemented, such as the RETEX initiative and the Operational Programme for Industry, which comprise particular actions in the region of Central Macedonia.

It is remarkable that the successive CSFs for Greece make provision for the spatial integration of regional MOPs through the spatial integration of the corresponding administrative and financial management procedures.

CSF 1989-93 points out that for the projects 'for which technical monitoring and financial management are at present centralised ... the Greek authorities have committed themselves to taking the measures necessary ... to complete gradually the desired decentralisation process by the end of 1991' (CEC 1990, p.21). Further, CSF 1994-99 reminds that the regional programmes should comprise only of projects for which the legally, financially and technically responsible organisations are based in each region (EC 1994a, p.70).[5]

In the case of the national section of CSF and the Community Initiatives, the need for the decentralised administration and management of those projects, measures or sub-programmes that are spatially allocated in many cases has led to the establishment of RDAs. Besides, some RDAs which already existed have been supported in order to undertake this role.

With the exception of regional MOPs and LEADERs, regional development programmes that are totally or partly implemented within Central Macedonia are not correspondingly planned and administered on a regional or a local basis. When this happens, it is almost certain that new RDAs will be created or existing ones supported.

Concerning the geographical range of the region's RDAs, they can be broadly grouped into two categories: those acting at a local level and those acting on a non-local level (such as a group of prefectures, the whole region, a group of regions, or the whole country).

The Local Action Groups that have been set up in order to manage and implement the LEADER initiative in each one of the region's prefectures, particularly in their disadvantageous areas, are the most important RDAs in the first group; some other local agencies with specialised objectives act beside or in parallel with them. This is the case with the Industrial Change Offices, which have a rather official character, since they function in the context of the Prefectural Self-Administration of second degree. In some cases (e.g. the BIC of Serres) the agency covers areas that not only belong to the region of Central Macedonia but also to a neighbouring region.

The second group (non-local RDAs) comprises agencies with a regional, multi-regional or a national range, such as KEPA, DIPEK, Thessaloniki Technology Park, etc. It is characteristic that, at least in the case of Central Macedonia, there is a remarkable lack of RDAs with a regional character and orientation only.

The case of KEPA is typical: even though it was established in the context of the first regional MOP (1989-93), it has since developed various activities on a regional, a multi-regional (i.e. groups of regions, usually the

[5] The recently established organisation called 'Regional Fund' (1998) which functions in the context of the region's General Secretariat aims to support the procedure of decentralisation.

regions of Northern Greece) or a nationwide basis. This corresponds to the spatial range of several programmes/measures or actions that KEPA is managing as an intermediary agency.

(ii) The structure and the content of the programmes: innovative or traditional / 'hard' or 'soft' types of actions - the case of MOPs for the region of Central Macedonia.

Regional MOPs in general are locally prepared and administered within the context of 'democratic planning' from below, according to the principle of partnership. For this reason regional MOPs are considered as reflecting an important characteristic of the intelligent region: the ability of both regional authorities and social partners to co-operate in order to plan and implement interventions aimed at the structural adjustment and the development of the regional economy.

In the case of Central Macedonia, their composition indicates that both the state and the regional authorities of SMEs at the regional level have a clear picture about the needs of the productive system, and of SMEs in particular. They also seem to be capable of describing and formulating the necessary measures to achieve the objectives of the programme.

It is remarkable that the first regional MOP, relatively early, recognised the need and the importance of supportive mechanisms and procedures, in order to improve the overall competitiveness of SMEs at a regional level. As a result, as mentioned above, it supported the establishment of an important RDA.

Further, the current regional MOP comprises a variety of actions, both 'soft' and infrastructural, which involve the public and private sectors as well as public and private agencies in order to be implemented.

In general terms, the design of the regional MOPs suggests that the planning authorities, to a large extent, adopt approaches which correlate regional inequalities in Europe with the lack of institutions for the encouragement of inter-firm co-operation and networking, with the lack of institutions for specialised support, as well as with the lack of links between research institutions and enterprises.

The presence of measures and actions, in both the examined programmes, which try to resolve these kind of problems, implies the existence of a wider political consensus between the main 'social partners' (e.g. governmental regional authorities, employees and employers).

However, the experience of the implemented first regional MOP as well as the existing indications from the ongoing second one, shows that there are serious difficulties when implementing actions of this kind. Besides, the traditional methods of resolving regional problems (e.g. by the provision of infrastructure and direct financial aid to SMEs) always retain their advantage of the fast absorption of funds. The result of this might be the incremental reallocation of resources from innovative to traditional actions.

The differences between the design and the implementation of the programmes, in the final analysis, mean that the observed political consensus is weakening when it comes to the implementation phase. However, it must be noted that, year by year, things seem to be moving towards the recognition of the importance of a better balance between innovative measures and the traditional priorities favouring hard technical and economic infrastructure.

(iii) The character of the agencies: an intermediary financing or a service providing role?

Despite the fact that the most of the RDAs of the region have been created to implement or administer particular EU programmes, there are significant differences in their character and functions.

The charter of each RDA usually makes provision for a broad possible range of activities to be undertaken. However, from the character of their main activities, two basic groups can be distinguished: RDAs that provide services, mainly to SMEs, and RDAs with an intermediary financing role.

Notably, this specialisation of RDAs is related to their geographical range. On the one hand, local agencies have already expanded their activities to many fields of action, covering a wide range of business supporting services, in addition to the administration or the implementation of EU programmes or initiatives. On the other hand, a lot of non-local RDAs have developed an intermediary role in order to facilitate the implementation of various programmes in a most effective and flexible way and to overcome the existing restraints that the corresponding public sector organisations are facing.

As argued above, this can be additionally attributed to the revision of the role of the state, at least at the local and regional level, as well as to the changing relationship between the public and private sectors.

The comprehensive analysis of the role and the activities of the RDAs of the region pointed out different trends in their perspectives. Local RDAs usually try to widen the range of their activities as well as to deepen the contents of each activity, in order to undertake a more substantial role in the procedure of local development. On the other hand, non-local RDAs usually concentrate their efforts on specific activities concerning the implementation, administration, intermediary financing, etc. of EU co-financed programmes, measures and actions. Thus, they seem to undertake a managerial and administrative role in regional planning.[6]

As already argued, the above-mentioned characteristic concerning the spatial range of regional development programmes and agencies as well as their role (innovative or traditional concerning the programmes, service providers or intermediary financing concerning RDAs) generally can be correlated with the progress of the regional development planning procedure, particularly in terms of the state of the regional institutions.

Table 6.2 RDAs in Central Macedonia: role and geographical range

	Local	*Non-local*
Intermediary		2
Service provision	5	2
Both, mainly service provision	7	

Source: Authors' survey

Concerning the regional level, it could be argued that the institutions operating in support of the regional productive system, and the regional development planning procedure especially, are still under formation. It is characteristic that the institutional framework for the establishment of the regions as administrative and development entities, which has remained in constant flux until recently, has been completed only in 1997. On the other hand, the long lasting regional specialisation in manufacturing and exporting activities, which are represented by well organised and powerful associations, is related to the leading role that the latter have undertaken in support of the regional productive system,

6 It has to be stressed that this is a broad classification mostly showing the existing trends. For example, there are non-local RDAs, such as DIPEK and TTP, which have a service providing role, while RDAs usually can have both an intermediary and a service providing role.

specifically the programmes and the agencies supporting SMEs (Komninos 1997; Foutakis and Kafkalas 1998).

It can be argued that the local level presents an interesting dynamism, which can be attributed to the long-lasting constitution of the local state at the level of the prefecture. Public administration mechanisms are strong enough at this level, since they have a long tradition of action, while the establishment of the Prefectural Self-Administration (Local Authorities of the second degree) in 1994 proves the potential of the existing trends. Further, many institutions which address both the private and public sectors have developed a significant role for the development of the prefecture. It is apparent from the case of Central Macedonia that to a great extent EU cohesion policy contributes to the formation of regional systems that provide support to the regional SMEs. This support is basically channelled through the synergy created between regional development planning and the operation of regional development agencies. However, it should be stressed that this synergy is not a self-realised goal of the regional system but should be both carefully planned and politically promoted in order to achieve the desired multiplier effects for the promotion of regional intelligence and the creation of a flexible, adaptable and competitive regional economy.

Acknowledgements

This paper is based upon the research project on 'The Making of an Intelligent Region: the Role of Structural Funds and the Profile of Regional Firms in Central Macedonia', undertaken by the Aristotle University of Thessaloniki team led by Grigoris Kafkalas within the framework of a broader LEONARDO DA VINCI project - 'Intelligent Region' - coordinated by the WDA. Its theoretical anchorage relies also upon the article by Kafkalas and Komninos (1999), 'The innovative region strategy: lessons from the Central Macedonia Technology Plan'.

References

Andrikopoulou, E. and Kafkalas, G. (1995) 'Peripherality and integration in the new European territory.' Paper presented at the RSA Conference Regional Futures: Past and Present, East and West, May 1995, Gothenburg, Sweden.

Andrikopoulou, E. (1995) 'The regions in the European Union: the evolution of regional policy from the Treaty of Rome to Maastricht.' Themelio, Athens. (in Greek)

CEC (1990) *Greece, Community Support Framework 1989-93*. Office for Official Publications of the European Communities, Luxembourg.

CEC (1992) *The Structural Policies of the Community. Evaluation and Prospects*. COM (92) 84 final, Brussels.

EC (1994a) *Greece, Community Support Framework 1994-99*. Office for Official Publications of the European Communities, Luxembourg. (in Greek)

EC (1994b) *Competitiveness and Cohesion: Trends in the Regions*. Fifth periodic report on the social and economic situation and development of the regions in the Community, Office for Official Publications of the European Communities, Luxembourg. (in Greek)

EC (1996) *First Report on Economic and Social Cohesion 1996*. Preliminary Edition, Office for Official Publications of the European Communities.

EP (1991) *The Regional Impact of Community Policies* (by F.Frazmeyer, P.Hrubesch, B.Seidel and C.Weise of DIW-Berlin), Research and Documentation Series of the European Parliament on 'Regional policy and transport' No. 17, Office for Official Publications of the European Communities, Luxembourg.

Foutakis, D. and Kafkalas, G. (1998) 'Innovation and technology transfer in regional productive systems'. In E. Sefertzi (ed) *Technology Transfer, System-Areas and Innovative Development in Greece*. Athens: Gutenberg, 41-82. (in Greek)

Kafkalas, G. (1995), 'Innovative Growth and Peripherality in the New European Territory' In H. Cocossis and P. Nijkamp (eds) *Overcoming Isolation*. The Netherlands: Springer, 41-52.

Kafkalas, G. and Komninos, N. (1993) 'Strategies of local development and the new role of social policies'. In P. Getimis and D. Gravaris (eds) *Welfare State and Social Policy*. Athens: Themelio, 203-221. (in Greek)

Kafkalas, G. and Komninos, N. (forthcoming), 'The Innovative region strategy: lessons from the Central Macedonia Technology Plan'. In K. Morgan and C. Nauwelaers (eds) *Regional Innovation Strategies and Peripheral Regions*. London: Jessica Kingsley Publishers.

Komninos, N. (1993) *Technopolises and Development Strategies in Europe*. Athens: Gutenberg. (in Greek)

Komninos, N. (1997) *Innovation in Central Macedonia: The Regional Technology Plan*. Athens: Gutenberg.

Lundvall, B. A. (ed) (1992) *National Systems of Innovation. Towards a Theory of Innovation and Interactive Learning*. London: Pinter.

Morgan, K. (1992) 'Innovating by networking: new models of corporate and regional development.' In M. Dunford and G. Kafkalas (eds) *Cities and Regions in the New Europe*. London: Belhaven Press, 150-169.

Morgan K. (1995) 'Institutions, innovation and regional renewal. The development agency as animateur'. Conference on Regional Futures: Past and Present, East and West, Gothenburg, Sweden, 6-9 May.

Morgan K. (1997) 'The learning region: institutions, innovation and regional renewal.' *Regional Studies 31*, 5, 491-503.

Morgan K. (forthcoming) 'A regional perspective on innovation: from theory to strategy.' In K. Morgan and C. Nauwelaers (eds) *Regional Innovation Strategies: The Challenge for Less Favoured Regions*. London: Jessica Kingsley Publishers.

Morgan, K. and Cooke, P. (1991) *The Intelligent Region - Industrial and Institutional Innovation in Emiglia-Romagna*. Regional Industrial Research Report No 7. Cardiff: Welsh Development Agency.

Region of Central Macedonia (1990) *Regional Operational Programme 1990 – 93, Region of CM.* Thessaloniki. (in Greek)

Region of Central Macedonia (1994) *Regional Operational Programme 1994 – 99, Region of CM.* Thessaloniki. (in Greek)

Storper M. (1994) 'The resurgence of regional economies. Ten years later: the region as nexus of untraded interdependencies'. Paper at the conference 'Cities, Enterprises and Society at the Eve of the XXIst Century', Lille, 16-18 May 1994.

7 Regional Government in the United Kingdom: Democratic Representation or Economic Success?

PETER GARSIDE

Introduction

There are many contentious issues surrounding the development of regions, ranging from what actually constitutes a region to what is regional development (Rhodes 1995; Amin and Thrift 1995a; Morgan 1997; Asheim and Dunford 1997). This has produced abstract concepts such as 'decision space' to cope with the notion of region (Sharpe 1993) and long running arguments as to the purpose of regional development (Lovering 1996; Brand *et al.* 1997). The aim of this chapter is to confront some of these common debates relating to regional development and, utilising research conducted in the UK (Harding *et al.* 1996), to question the role of elected and non-elected forms of regional representation.

In the final analysis, this chapter goes beyond the typical product/process dichotomy usually associated with this type of study, whereby the end product of economic success subjugates the social process of development. This is achieved by questioning the role of democratic processes within regional futures and the purpose of regional development (Lovering 1998).

Socially embedded processes are important, not just because of their ability to increase economic competitiveness, but because of the manner in which they construct inclusive and exclusive networks within civil society. This is significant for several reasons. First, because it draws attention to one of the most enduring tensions associated with neo-liberal development, social justice versus economic growth. Second, because in Britain a central agenda for New Labour is to address the issue of local democracy and related processes of local empowerment (Labour Party 1995). Third, because the research into regional government, upon which this chapter is based, avoided detailed discussion of a democratic imperative. The intention is to increase the significance of social processes affecting change, so that they become as critically important as the end products they create.

This type of approach is becoming increasing important, because those engaged in the regional development debate are still wrestling with the fundamental question of what development should be expected to achieve (Lovering 1996, 1998; Morgan 1997; Amin 1998). Some commentators dismiss the supposed link between new regional innovation strategies, based upon supply architecture and social capital, and any attempt to alleviate social exclusion, including mass unemployment (Morgan 1997, p.501); whilst others highlight the manner in which these new forms of regional governance operate, effectively exacerbating the problems of social exclusion, even though their agenda is supposedly not designed to enhance social justice (Lovering 1998).

Examining this dichotomy between process and product is becoming a central theme within both contemporary British politics and new theories of regional development (Amin and Thrift 1995b). In both these contexts, the distinction is used to question whether democratic approaches, as opposed to non-elected approaches, have any intrinsic value to deliver more equitable and successful forms of development. This theme, of linking democracy and economic development, was encapsulated by the 'Yes' arguments, which supported the devolution referenda for the Welsh Assembly and the Scottish Parliament in the United Kingdom (UK) during 1997. These pro-devolution arguments directly linked the concept of democratic subsidiarity to enhanced national economic performance and increased equitable development.

The considerations underlying this belief in liberal democracy, to provide the most efficient type of framework for free market development, are assessed in this chapter. They offer a critical insight into different perceptions of democracy and its role within regional development. In addition, this discussion also brings into question many issues surrounding the politics of place, concerns about identity, economic competitiveness and the moral issues of democratic accountability (Murphy and Caborn 1995; Digiovanna 1996; Patchell 1996).

All these relevant issues inform this chapter, but particular attention is given to a developing division at the centre of the regional development debate. On one side are those supporting some form of community democracy, accused of taking the moral high ground to defend all attacks on their democratic ideology. On the other, there are those who demand localities should maintain whatever level of flexibility necessary to acquire competitive economic advantage, accused of prostituting their sense of identity and democratic principals to the forces of globalisation. Of course, this is an over simplification of the realities which exist, but the choices that people will make to decide the future of their political structures will be based upon this kind of subjective rhetoric. As such, it is important to understand how these forces affect the issues of regional development in the UK.[1]

Contemporary Debates and Issues

The following introductory sections have a dual purpose. First, it is necessary to unpack some of the common assumptions linked to the issue of regional government in the UK, and second, it is important to state why regions, regionalism and regionalisation have grown in importance during the 1990s. The sections offer clarification of a range of problematic terms and concepts, providing a benchmark for future discussion, and highlight the contemporary significance of the arguments. This is important because the significance of these issues has recently changed due to a shift in political context and because misunderstandings have occurred due to a lack of consensus on language.

The definitions of region and regionalism are vague and invariably replaced with the concepts of devolution and decentralisation. Confusion is especially problematic when discussions move from a single national structure to international comparisons of sub-national government structures. Therefore, in an attempt to overcome these problems the application of the terms used in this chapter, and in previous works, are addressed.

1 Due to limiting factors on the research Northern Ireland has been omitted from the study.

Contemporary political history informs us the UK is a nation state or unitary state. Even with the advent of the Welsh Assembly and the Scottish Parliament, allowing these nations secondary legislative powers, institutional sovereignty still resides with one parliament as the constitutional status of these sub-tiers of the union is limited. Alternatively, it would be equally wrong to assume all the administrative regional parts of the UK are the same. This would simply associate nations with English regions, and ignore the differences in their cultural identity, institutional structures and desires for constitutional change.

If these differences are ignored the concept of regionalism becomes confused with nationalism. Regionalism is a collective consciousness that can be used as an organising platform for political and administrative forms based upon cultural affinity. The motivations for regionalism are generally a combined result of political will and cultural identity, linked to a desire for greater local control of regional governance. This does not necessarily challenge the dominant national structure of the central state; it merely advocates enhanced regional power in an attempt to provide greater efficiency. In contrast, nationalism supports total independence and denounces the basic legitimacy of any external power structure attempting to control sovereignty of that nation.

The autonomy of a region is rooted in its power to control its assets without external interference. This autonomy relies upon the degree of control the region has over all the resources within its boundaries. Rhodes (1988) categorised these resources as anything from human capital to environmental and others have noted that controlling these resources does not have to be embodied in constitutional structures (Paterson 1994). In addition, some have clearly stated that without a defined financing mechanism, regions have very little autonomy, whether their autonomy is constitutionally based or not (Blow, Hall and Smith 1996).

Under the conditions of new regional governance, the issue of regional autonomy is not just restricted to the public sector. As regimes, in the 'true' sense (Stoker 1995), bridge the gap between the division of public and private labour, the issue of autonomy resides more within new regional networks than the public sector. As such, the private sector acts as a controlling force within these networks and exposes the region to two possible development paths.

Regional autonomy, set within this context, confronts the forces of globalisation and, for some, one path is the continued penetration of external capital with associated external control (Turok and Richardson 1991). Whilst others favour the concept of firm embeddedness, enhancing the power of regional regimes (Ohmae 1993). In reality the two forces combine and fluctuate between place and over time, producing a dynamic set of relationships upon which autonomy is based.

The decision making capacity of a region is synonymous with its autonomy. This is directly supported by the process of hollowing out of the nation state (Jessop 1997), whereby regional institutions gain power not only from above, but from the creation of new regional structures with new capacities. In addition, regionalisation is also expanded when strategic roles adopted by regional structures relieve lower levels of government of their functions.

It is now important to discuss how these trends manifested themselves in the UK during the 1990s. This acts as a brief introduction to questioning the role of democracy within the changing patterns of regional governance. All these trends and issues reveal not only the resurgence of the regional government debate in the UK, but the wide variety of inputs into the discussion surrounding the concept of regional democracy (Mawson 1997; Donnelly and McQuail 1996).

Prior to the devolution referenda in September 1997, there had been a trend of regionalisation based upon increased transference of administrative functions from central government to the Scottish and Welsh Offices (HMSO 1993; Parry 1993). The Scottish and Welsh national parties advocated increased regional autonomy as a lead into their demands for sovereign independence (SNP 1992). In England regionalisation of administrative functions has also taken place through the Government Offices for the Regions and related administrative arrangements established to deliver the Single Regeneration Budget (Hogwood 1995). This is in addition to the realignment of a variety of administrative and statutory organisations, conforming to the boundaries of the traditional English planning regions.

This development of a regional tier of governance in the UK is underpinned by a growing non-democratic, unaccountable and, supposedly, inefficient quangocracy (Stewart *et al.* 1995). The key debate surrounding this type of institutional trend is whether or not these organisations, which already create a *de facto* level of regional governance, should be democratised in some form (Salt 1994). This would supposedly promote efficiency and allow a directly accountable new government structure to act as a catalyst for regional economic competitiveness (Murphy and Caborn 1995).

Supporting these arguments is a diverse range of contemporary issues. There is a demand for regional organisations to offer a strategic overview considering the move towards unitary single-tier local authorities (Tomaney 1996). There is a shifting trend towards constitutional change, advocated by New Labour and its closest allies: the Liberal Democrats (Donnelly and McQuail 1996). However, devolution for the English regions is far from settled. The two-staged process, moving from indirectly elected regional chambers to elected regional authorities (Straw 1995), has stalled, and many see the new government's ambitions going little beyond the introduction of regional development agencies.

The watered down version of New Labour's original proposals (Straw 1995), effectively promotes economic development agencies for the English regions, charged with encouraging inward investment, supporting small businesses and co-ordinating regional economic development. Under this approach, the thorny question of finance for regional government is avoided, and the emerging agencies are more akin to what Blow, Hall and Smith (1996) refer to as an 'agency' model rather than 'choice' model: the former being a case for more efficient performance from regional bodies, set within national standards, and without the need to levy additional taxes on the area.

European development policies have also brought a distinct regional dimension to the discussion of administrative structures within the UK. This has been driven by the issue of a 'Europe of the Regions', the implementation of Structural Funds and the possibility of a more significance role for the Committee of the Regions. This influence links directly with the historical trend of strong European regional structures in comparison to the UK. Britain has constantly been described as being out of step with the rest of Europe, due to its centralisation tendencies, and held up as a nation lagging behind the innovative regional structural trends found in other leading member states (Crouch and Marquand 1989; Harvie 1994).

The conceptual significance of the 'region' has also been elevated during the 1990s. New regionalism (Morgan 1997) and globalisation, linked to intensified inter-regional economic competition and regional innovation systems, offer the region a new theoretical focus (Amin and Thrift 1995b; Gamble and Payne 1996). This conceptual realignment has been enhanced by two factors. First, the declining role of the nation state in western economies to manage macro economic demand side policies. Second, the expanded role of local institutions to deliver supply-side functions. This applies throughout the political economy of western Europe and the increasing opportunities for new forms of regional governance to control new factors of production (Harding *et al.* 1996).

Ultimately, and contemporary debates surrounding the Welsh and Scottish referendums support this, there are two ongoing central arguments, which sum up the polarised position concerning regional government. The proponents of regional government argue for a sensitised, strategic level of democracy, which will link into localised development priorities and deliver efficient services to support increased economic development (Coulson 1990; Murphy and Caborn 1995; Tomaney 1996). In opposition to this, there is a general feeling that regional government will duplicate functions between central and local government, confusing issues and obscuring the truly sensitised function of local authorities (Jones 1988).

However, in most of the demands for promoting regional development the need to develop an accountable structure is not always made explicit. The question of democracy is sometimes assumed or ignored and, within the regional literature, there are many misplaced assumptions on its role which need to be discussed before any empirical analysis is introduced (Donnelly and McQuail 1996).

The Role of Democracy in the Regions

Certain reports, supporting the role of regional government, present democratic arguments based upon issues of identity, representation and accountability (Donnelly and McQuail 1996). They do not presume that democracy equals economic success. Other authors have assumed that democratic mechanisms may in fact prohibit economic success, primarily based upon the idea of introducing bureaucratic inefficiencies (Harding *et al.* 1996). But there are very few who have considered the notion of democracy and the implications of what an accountable system for the English regions and UK nations would entail.

This next section introduces some arguments, which will open the door on a much wider debate than previous attempts. The first argument introduced rehearses the classic interpretation of democracy as a political method, the second considers the implications of democratic associationism and the third deals with some contemporary politicised issues of democracy.

Consider the basic ideas underlying democracy as a political method, and the manner in which it can be achieved, and there is no basis for assuming that it will bring any predetermined result other than a utilitarian natural perception of the 'peoples' will' (Schumpeter 1961; Birch 1993). On this basis, democracy, as a political method, cannot be used to achieve an end in itself and hence cannot be used to deliver any specific form of development, economic or otherwise. This understanding derides claims that associate a democratic imperative to economic development assuming a 'common good' and 'common will', which will produce economic dynamism promoting regional growth (Murphy and Caborn 1995). From this perspective, assuming an allegiance between the method and the end result could be construed as anti-democratic, for:

> To try to force the people to embrace something that is believed to be good and glorious but which they do not actually want - even though they may be expected to like it when they experience its results - is the very hall mark of anti-democratic belief. (Schumpeter 1961, p.237).

Alternatively, counter to this position, some espouse a link between regional government and economic success based upon a moral component. In this context, if 'the people' are fundamentally involved within the process of economic development through democratic channels, then not only is the process the 'will of the people', but the benefits of development will be accrued in an egalitarian manner. But, those supporting the narrow Schumpeterian definition of democracy would consider this to be flawed on two accounts: first, the inability to link the 'will of the people' to any directed end result of economic success, and second, the confusion of democracy with individual rights. In the case of the latter, there is no guarantee that just because a democratic process is utilised, the rights of individuals to access the benefits of economic growth will be enhanced.

The use of whatever form of democracy, such as 'bourgeois' or formal (Dahl 1971; Rueschemeyer *et al.* 1992), as distinguished from other forms of rule, will make a difference in the process of political decision-making. But, those supporting a limited definition of democracy see the need to democratise the decision-making processes within areas such as Wales as separate from the need to increase its economic competitiveness. This perspective determines that new spatial development strategies (Hudson 1997) and the development of learning economies and innovation systems (Gregersen and Johnson 1997), which can act as the corner stone for the resurgence of specialised and self-contained regional economies, are not dependent upon a democratically elected decision making process.

Essentially, the Schumpeterian concept of democracy is an ultimate value of the way in which society should operate, not the definitive means by which social justice can be achieved to mediate the uneven affects of capitalism. However, democracy cannot be ignored because of economic imperatives or reduced to the ballot box and should, for a range of reasons, all opposite to those above, be considered as fundamental for regional development.

Many have argued that a democratic framework is fundamental for maintaining a successful free market system. These include Neo-Marxists, such as Jessop (1997), neo-Liberals, such as Fukuyama (1991) and pluralists, such as Dahl (1971); this is considering the nature of the liberal democracies espoused by each is significantly different. But the critical link, which directly relates to contemporary theories of associative democracy (Hirst 1994; Cohen and Rogers 1993), is that democracy is not simply reducible to elections. This follows a much broader understanding of democracy, which can be used to contradict a basic understanding of democracy as simply a political method.

At this broad level democratic space offers opportunities for a multitude of overlapping associations to exist. The associationist position relies upon this understanding, as do pluralists, because it allows for decentralised groups and initiatives to develop, and for elected and non-elected representation to operate in an open learning environment. The learning and feedback mechanisms are more innovative than in any approach which is directly based on a hierarchy and privileged position of decision makers. For some (Lovering 1998), it is essential that this broader approach be adopted within regional development strategies, not just to create economic competitiveness but, to halt the social exclusion generated by existing regional networks.

The process of regional development is far more vital in these terms, than the end product, because of the manner in which learning capacity can be engendered throughout all areas of a regional network; thereby, equating more to the principles of the network paradigm (Morgan 1997). In addition, it is an essential contribution to the way accountability can be ensured in the decision-making process and provides 'ethical dignity' to the results of the process, however desirable.

This understanding closely mirrors the ideas surrounding the new regionalism (Hudson 1997). Regional innovation systems and social capital are determined to maximise their potential in an open learning environment, without any path dependent trajectories governed in a closed system. The clear manner in which this inclusive, open system can be created is by allowing all voices from civil society to contribute to the development system, and not to offer control to appointed decision makers, with similar backgrounds, functioning within a very restricted environment.

Finally, there are some contemporary politicised reasons for considering the role of democracy in the regions. Why is it not feasible or desirable to leave regional development to the new quangocracy or privately-led regimes? The 'quangos bad, elected organisations good' argument is not as clear cut as imagined (Clark 1995), and there are more persuasive reasons for its inclusion within regional development.

First, it is essential to promote democratically elected representatives within a local area, with a mandate from the community they try to serve.

> We believe that it is through the institution of democracy that political activity can take place most productively and in an orderly way. Politics is the essential activity of free people in the resolution of conflicts of interest, the disposition of power, and the

pursuit of solutions. (Commission for Local Democracy 1995, p.3)

Second, the case for subsidiarity is an argument as much in favour of efficiency as it is a requirement for direct accountability. In addition, this provides a counterweight to the levels of government above and below the region. Openness and access are an integral part of this theme and it is essential to generate a regional strategy, which is best placed to offer this form of transparent delivery.

Third, the 'accountability deficit' that has accrued in Britain over the past decade has focused attention on the need for reclaiming democratic power at a more local level (Morgan and Roberts 1993). The increasing administrative regionalism that has occurred in the UK has merely served to heighten the general awareness of the role of non-elected organisations. In addition, this growing trend has also been linked to highly competitive neo-liberal tendencies that are being reproduced in the regions. Therefore, there is a growing demand for an alternative framework, including all voices in the community, which will give back responsibility to the people, to decide if these competitive processes generating socially excluded groups are acceptable.

Research Questions and Regional Audit

Two central questions guided the original research upon which this chapter is based (Harding *et al.* 1996):

1. Has the regional dimension of governance in the UK increased during the 1990s enabling a democratic process of regional decision making?
2. Is there a relationship between regional institutional structures and economic competitiveness?

However, due to the nature of the research, there is a third implicit question, which links these two lines of inquiry together and provides the focus for this chapter. Will a democratically elected form of government enhance economic competitiveness within the UK regions, including the non-English nations? Considering the recent changes in the planned constitutional status of Scotland and Wales, and the (stalled) proposals for regional representation in the English regions, this third question is crucial for the future of the UK's regional economies (Mawson 1997).

In the original study two English regions and two nations were investigated: the North West; the North East; Scotland and Wales. Initially, however, to assess the regionalisation of policy set against devolved democratic regional autonomy, the changes in administration across the English regions were examined. This was because the English regions had witnessed the bulk of recent additional regional activity before the devolution referenda in Wales and Scotland. Moreover, whilst it was apparent quangos and non-departmental public bodies had come to dominate English regional administration, it was not apparent what role democracy or regional autonomy was expected to play.

The analysis of regional administrative change across different sectors in England revealed a wide diversity in the institutional nature of recent developments:[2]

- integrated regional offices where different central government regional departments have been consolidated into one organisation - Government Offices for the Regions;
- national government departments, quangos or agencies with regional offices - Housing Corporation, Office of Standards in Education (OFSTED), various Next Steps Agencies e.g. Highways Agency;
- national government departments or quangos whose head offices are internally structured on a regional basis - Funding Agency for Schools;
- freestanding regional organisations which operate within an overall framework collectively agreed with their national equivalents and substantially dependent upon central government grants - Regional Arts Boards, Regional Tourism Boards;
- regional utility companies - Regional Water Companies and Electricity Companies;

[2] The detailed status and autonomy of these institutions is fully explored in the original report produced for the Joseph Rowntree Foundation (Harding *et al.*, 1996).

- regional advisory committees of regulatory bodies – Office of Water Services (OFWAT), Office of Gas Supply (OFGAS), Office of Electricity Regulation (OFFER);
- joint regional authorities in metropolitan areas, created after the abolition of the Greater London Council and the metropolitan county councils, overseen by councillors appointed by district and borough authorities and responsible for fire and civil defence, police and waste disposal;
- umbrella organisations formed by local bodies in order to articulate regional interests of common concern - English Regional Associations of local authorities;
- bodies promoted by central government to provide a jointly agreed contextual statement to support regional actions - Regional Planning Conferences.

Based upon this audit, there are clear signs of regionalisation taking place. However, to answer the research questions it was necessary to discover if this had been accompanied by an increase in regional autonomy.

This increase in regional activity has predominantly been caused by a growth of administrative arms of central government, particularly quangos or agencies which have replaced administration by local authorities. The growth in the number of such organisations in the education sector, for example, could be recognised as a veiled form of centralisation rather than evolving regional autonomy. This is because such organisations are directly accountable for all their resources to central government and operate within a highly rigid, centrally determined, framework.

The same is true of the growing number of Next Steps Agencies, organised on a regional basis. Under most circumstances, these organisations were previously recognised as government departments with remote regional offices. For example, those questioned at the Highways Agency revealed the centralised nature of their resources and procurement policy; not unsurprisingly, considering their operations are heavily determined by several central government departments which issue their contracts and devise their operating policy.

There have been some counter measures to this centralised control, through moves to improve the decentralisation of higher levels of administrative. These developments have occurred due to the increased emphasis on quality control in service delivery, reflected in the citizen's charter and targeted performance rates for new forms of commodified services. This is the basis for the continued operation of Regional Health Authorities, the regional structures of Office of Standards in Education and the Social Services Inspectorate. Nevertheless, as with the other forms of regionalisation, those within these organisations acknowledged their limited ability to manoeuvre around centrally determined budgets.

Other sectors reflect this same trend, especially where tighter central control and tough fiscal constraints have offset gains in regional autonomy. Regional Tourist Boards and Regional Arts Boards have become independent from their national organisations and been permitted greater autonomy over expenditure patterns. Yet, as with other similar regional institutions, they are hampered by the constraints of reduced grant aid and the imposition of a stringent output and monitoring system.

The government has also made increased use of contractual and licensing arrangements, which have given quangos and agencies more managerial freedom in deciding internal priorities, in exchange for tighter financial regimes and stricter output targets. This is especially true of the Training and Enterprise Councils, who, as other research has also revealed, are locked into narrowly defined target outputs with limited entrepreneurial capacity (Evans and Garside 1995; Hart, Haughton and Peck 1996).

All these examples represent an institutional turn which does not equate with the ideal type of regional capacity required for engendering a learning economy or enhancing competitiveness (Hudson 1998). The developments described are predominantly designed to generate increased productivity and better value for (public) money. Whilst effectively, they increase efficiency in a path dependent trajectory and promote the type of 'lock-in', which, Morgan (1997) states, is counter productive for creating an innovative milieu.

In addition to central constraints upon regional institutions, there are other inbuilt restraining influences within their structures. This is particularly evident where institutions predominantly function as information providers for their superiors, or where their capacity relies upon, for whatever reason, the circumscribed commitment of members. In the case of the former, the remit of the institution determines functional capacity. For example, the regional offices of the utility regulators are charged with the responsibility of market research, whilst their centralised head offices wield regulatory power. In the case of the latter, the institution relies upon drawing a consensus from a wide range of members, each of whom have primary responsibilities elsewhere. This applies to both Regional Planning Councils and English Regional Associations, who are reliant upon a diverse range of local authority members with localised, and sometimes conflicting, agenda. This is notwithstanding the veto authority of the Secretary of State.

At the highest level of regional institutional authority sits the Senior Regional Director, with responsibility for the Government Office for the Regions. There are many who recognise this as a step forward whilst understanding the limited ability of these institutions (Mawson 1997). The directors have to report to the Secretaries of State for their four constituent departments, and central government controls the distribution of funds (Single Regeneration Budget). Considering directors command the highest level of regional authority, they are only responsible for approximately ten percent of public expenditure in each region.

All these examples reveal a reconstitution of central-regional relationships to achieve greater efficiency and the manner in which regional autonomy has been withheld from the English regions. Additionally, what little increase there has been in regional responsibility has compromised the power of local authorities, because of the upward transfer of power to the regional level rather than downwards from the centre. In effect, the regionalisation process that has taken place has not been associated with any increase in regional autonomy. As a result, it has not conformed to the institutional developments advocated by those supporting new forms of regional development (Morgan 1997; Amin 1998), primarily because these types of stunted administrative structures prohibit the development of a learning region (Hudson 1998).

UK Institutional Networks, Performance and Democracy

This final section examines empirical research carried out in four case study areas: Scotland, Wales, the North West and the North East. In the original study, the basis of the research was simply to link together economic indicators with institutional activity, to reveal the drivers behind economic performance, and to question those engaged in delivering development programmes on accountability issues (Harding *et al.* 1996). This section opens up the methodological flaws within the original research and reinterprets the evidence based upon insights drawn from debates surrounding new regional development theories (Lovering 1998; Amin 1998).

The information for this section was taken from secondary sources, relating to the institutional structures in the four areas and their economic performance, and primary sources, mainly based upon an investigation of perceptions held within non elected agencies (Harding *et al.* 1996; Appendix A). The presentation of the formal institutional structures operating within the areas is a relatively simple exercise; Table 7.1 taken from the original research summarises the principal organisations.

As this Table reveals, at present, the key institution in Scotland is still the Scottish Office, represented in cabinet by the Scottish Secretary of State; although this will be replaced by the new parliament at the turn of the century. As a nation, Scotland has particular legal, administrative and educational systems and the high levels of administrative devolution it has experienced have been driven by a strong nationalist influence (McCrone 1993). This influence has also surfaced in the form of distinctive nationalist politics, in the form of the Scottish National Party, based upon significant cultural heritage (Midwinter, Keating and Mitchell 1991).

The power of the Scottish Office to co-ordinate executive decision making at the national level far exceeds that of the English regions and there is a much broader range of statutory and non-statutory economic development bodies. The two development agencies, Scottish Enterprise (SE) and Highlands and Islands Enterprise (HIE), co-ordinate a network of independently-constituted Local Enterprise Companies whose boards comprise of key non-statutory and public sector leaders. This arrangement has clear advantages over the previous Scottish Development Agency, in that economic development and labour market programmes are integrated and it is a much more sensitive, decentralised operation within a strategic Scottish framework (Hayton 1992).

Table 7.1 Principal institutions operating at the level of the case study regions

Institution	*Scotland*	*Wales*	*North East*	*North West*
Governmental	Scottish Office, Scottish Secretary, Four Ministers, Select Committee, Grand Committee	Welsh Office, Welsh Secretary, Two Ministers, Select Committee, Grand Committee	Government Office for the NE, Minister for the NE	Two Government Offices (North West and Merseyside and Ministers)
Development Agencies	Scottish Enterprise, Highlands and Islands Enterprise	Welsh Development Agency, Development Board for Rural Wales	English Partnerships Regional Office	English Partnerships Regional Office
Inward Investment Agencies	Locate in Scotland, Scottish Trade International	(part of WDA)	Northern Development Company	INWARD
European Lobby	Scotland Europa	Wales European Centre	Local authority European Offices	Local authority European Offices
Local Authority	Council of Scottish Local Authorities	Council for Welsh Districts, Assembly of Welsh Counties	North of England Assembly	North West Regional Association
Business	CBI Scotland, Scottish Chamber of Commerce, Scottish Business in the Community	CBI Wales, Welsh Chamber of Commerce, Business in the Community Wales	Northern CBI, North East Chamber of Commerce	North West CBI, North West Chamber of Commerce
Public/Private Partnership	Scottish Council		Northern Info Applications Agency, Regional Technology Centre	North West Regional Partnership
Trade Unions	Scottish TUC	Welsh TUC	North East TUC	North West TUC
Private Groupings	Scottish Electronics Forum	Institute of Welsh Affairs, Wales Engineering Centre	Manufacturing Challenge	North West Business Leadership Team
Private Organisations	Scottish Financial Enterprise	Wales Quality Centre, World Trade Centre	Northern Offshore Federation	NIMTECH (technology transfer)

This level of autonomy and co-ordination extends to a variety of Scottish development agencies, including the inward investment agencies (Locate in Scotland and Scottish Trade International) and the local authority organisation. Even those organisations located in Scotland for simply organisational reasons, have become more embedded and autonomous within the national framework, such as CBI Scotland (CBI Scotland 1995).

Wales has also been granted similar national administrative status in the form of the Welsh Office. In principle, the Welsh Office is as powerful as its Scottish counterpart but, due to geographical proximity and relatively weaker institutional capacity, there has been a much closer association with central government than in the Scottish case. This reduced relative status exhibited by the Welsh Office and, generally, a weaker nationalist inclination were reflected in the comparatively subdued devolution campaign and movement towards a Welsh Assembly, rather than parliament. The latter offers no powers of legislation (only secondary legislation within a central government framework) and no control over revenue generation.

The Welsh Office, whilst it has 2,000 staff and is responsible for 70 per cent of public expenditure in Wales, has not typically adapted national legislation. Its more passive role reflects the cultural aspect of Welsh nationalism, rather than economic, and the absence of a significant Welsh corporate elite (Thomas 1995).

The North West and North East do not possess anything approximating these governmental structures, but do differ from each other in terms of a governmental regional presence. The North East is presided over by a single Government Office for the Region, whilst the North West, reflecting the more divided nature of the region, has two Government Offices for the Regions: Merseyside and the remainder.

The sense of regional identity in the North East is much more coherent and there has been a stronger tradition of corporatist relations between public and private institutions, particularly in economic development (Shaw 1993; Tomaney 1996). The rivalry between the three counurbations in the North East: Tyneside, Wearside and Teeside, is limited in comparison to the regional split in the North West between Manchester and Liverpool, and has allowed much greater cultural and institutional integration (Burch 1993).

The North East has one of the best track records for inward investment amongst the English regions, which is a result of the regional commitment to the Northern Development Company (NDC) from employers, trade unions and local authorities. Figures 7.1 and 7.2 reveal that whilst the North West has a greater propensity for developing projects, they are much smaller in terms of employment creation. This regional collaboration is also reflected in the North of England Assembly of local authorities (covering the North East), which offers a united local government voice on regional issues, and orchestrates development work with internal and external organisations, particularly Brussels.

By contrast the North West's development structure is still in its infancy and is constrained by the size of the area, physical diversity and the continued rivalry between the two main conurbations. This was epitomised by the independent expansion proposals by the airport authorities in Manchester and Liverpool. However, the recent development of the North West Regional Partnership (1994), linking business representation and local authorities, is a clear attempt to overcome these difficulties and promote a strong identity.

This diversity of co-ordination and co-operation is reflected in the regional development strategies of the four areas. The process of developing these strategies has differed greatly between the locations and reveals the strength of association across the institutions or what contemporary commentators have called the supply architecture (Morgan 1997) or institutional thickness (Amin and Thrift 1995b). However, it must also be remembered that these, so called, development strategies are economic development structures designed to enhance economic competitiveness. They are not social programmes, even though those developing the strategies believe they will offer a sustained or improved quality of life for those in the area.

The established development strategy in Scotland depends upon a chain of accountability that runs upwards from the Local Enterprise Companies to their parent bodies (SE and HIE) and through to the Scottish Office's Employment and Industry Department. Scottish Enterprise provides a crucial link in this chain and, through formal reviews, offers strategic guidance to other associated bodies. But the formal stage has also been supported by informal interaction between key corporate and public agency decision makers and Ministers (Moore and Booth 1989). This has proved successful by addressing crucial economic concerns about sectoral clusters, the role of manufacturing (CBI Scottish Manufacturing Group 1994), inward investment and indigenous growth (Turok 1993).

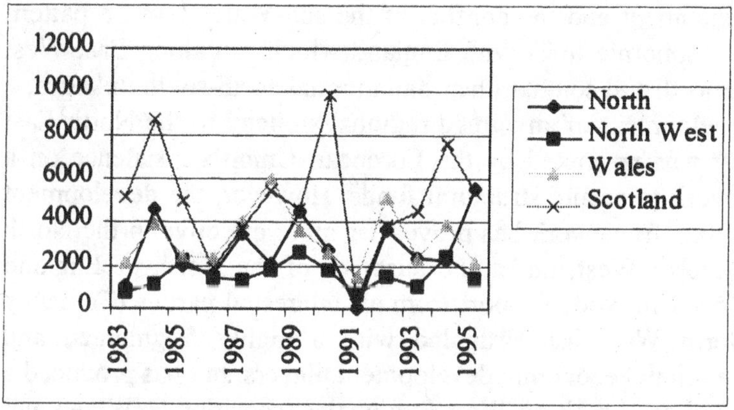

Source: Invest in Britain Bureau (1997)

Figure 7.1 Number of new jobs created by investment projects 1983-1995

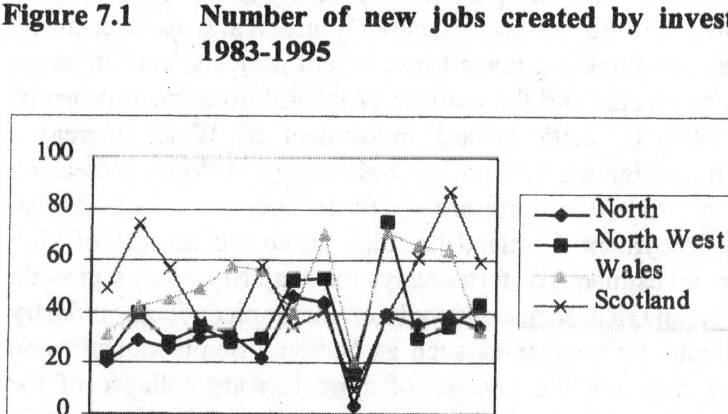

Source: Invest in Britain Bureau (1997)

Figure 7.2 Number of investment projects 1983-1995

In contrast, the Welsh Development Agency and the Development Board for Rural Wales have only recently started to co-ordinate their efforts. And, strategic visions, such as those provided by the Institute for Welsh Affairs, have generated little interest across government organisations, and little external input, unlike Scotland. This absence of a unified development strategy is symptomatic of the limited Welsh corporate establishment and the conflict at the sub-Wales level, a pattern reflected in the economic links with England which run along East-West corridors in the north and south, rather than internal north-south linkages.

The development of an agreed regional strategy in the North East and North West was prompted by the European Union's insistence on a regional framework to secure structural funds. However, the development and delivery of this framework has proved far more effective in the North East, than the North West, under the auspices of the North of England Assembly (NEA), with wide support from all interested parties (Tomaney 1996). The North West has struggled with a highly fragmented and complex set of regional economic development players, but has produced a strategy supported by the North West Regional Association (NWRA) and North West Business Leadership Team (NWBLT), covering skill, knowledge, environment and transport development (Pieda 1993).

As Figures 7.1 and 7.2 show, Scotland and Wales have been the key success areas for attracting inward investment projects, both in terms of numbers of jobs created and the number of inward investment projects. In the period 1986 to 1995 inward investment in Wales increased dramatically, with foreign manufacturing employment in Wales increasing from 44,000 to 73,000, representing thirty per cent of Welsh manufacturing employment. Scotland has also tasted the success of high levels of foreign investment. Unfortunately, the majority of this growth, particularly in Silicon Glen, focused heavily on the semiconductor industry and related products, by companies such as National Semiconductor and Viasystems, now suffering the ravages of a world-wide collapse of the semiconductor market. However, it was the ability of single purpose agencies, such as Locate in Scotland, to embed incoming firms into the local supply economy, which brought this medium term success (Turok 1993).

Agencies in the North East and especially the North West have found it much more difficult to approach regional development problems with such strategic purpose. Where in Wales and Scotland success has occurred, through network building and targeted resources orchestrated at the highest level, the same has not been true of the English regions. The North East and particularly the North West struggle against limited development resources and diverse interest groups, which negate rapid response rates and defined priorities. This comparatively limited ability is also reflected in the approach of their development agencies towards international associations, international networks and a European profile, which Wales and Scotland have adapted as part of their national development strategies for foreign relations.

All of these performances reveal the varying abilities of the different development agencies to meet the challenge of creating a facilitative milieu for regional/national development. However, judging the success of these agencies in improving the development of their area and whether or not they would have performed better based upon an elected system is something the original research failed to consider successfully. This is based upon certain key assumptions made and methodological approaches used without any critical interpretation of the data generated.

In the first instance, the perceptions of those interviewed in the non-elected agencies were not subjected to close scrutiny. This can be achieved in retrospect by applying some principles from public choice theory (Simon 1995) and concepts from the literature on regional innovation systems (Morgan 1997). Under these conditions the objective truth as represented by those operating in these agencies can be assessed against considerations on the nature of rationality, selfishness and altruism. In addition, the concept of a closed development system, which draws its impetus from a relatively small group of individuals with similar backgrounds, also needs investigation considering the claims for open innovative systems to be developed.

To support this reinterpretation, the economic data gathered for the original research can also be reassessed, as little attention was paid to matching anecdotal evidence with the statistical information or other related economic research (Lovering 1996; Brand *et al.* 1997). It is hoped this approach reveals that the assumed arguments the original work presented, against increased democratic devolution, are not as diaphanous as stated.

One conclusion from the research was that the institutional machinery in Scotland and Wales was better able to understand, articulate, engage with and act upon regional problems than their English counterparts. Considering the level of resources available to SE (£380m per year) as opposed to the NDC (£6m per year), this perceived difference is not surprising. However, it also emerged that institutions, whatever their formal powers, work better when their central focus and priorities are part of a wider social consensus. In that, they are functioning as a legitimate part of civil society, rather than an imposed administrative structure. This was the primary reason why the Scottish institutional arrangements, although not totally dissimilar to the other areas, were seen to perform more effectively.

This finding would appear to support the call for a more integrated and embedded institutional network, with increased empowerment and legitimacy. Therefore, what better way to move towards a fully developed institutional system, to function as a legitimate part of civil society, than to base it upon elected forms of representation? This does not mean that all functioning levels of regional development should be run through popularly elected agencies with multiple functions, as to dismiss the role of single purpose, semi-detached, agencies, run by experts and managed by business representatives, is to revert to the 'quangos bad, local authorities good' argument (Clark 1995). This, as the research revealed, is obviously not the case, considering the inward investment performance of the Scottish and Welsh institutions (Figures 7.1 and 7.2), and the mutual support they have been given from the private sector.

The key issue, as stated in the introduction to this chapter, is to examine the process by which development is managed and the representative base supporting it. Even if all the evidence points towards the success of these institutions in achieving specific tasks, it is quite clear that their cumulative affect on regional development is restricted. Figures 7.3, 7.4, and 7.5 display three principal economic indicators that reveal, on balance, the North West was one of the more successful of the four areas studied.

This is contrary to the institutional evidence already presented because, even though the Scottish, Welsh and, to a lesser degree, the North East institutions performed far better than their North West counterparts, this outcome evidence indicates the continued relative strength of the North West economy. Therefore, revealing that the lack of institutional thickness in the North West has not dramatically hindered its relative progress, whilst in other areas, particularly Wales, the institutional impact has been relatively limited. This suggests that, whilst structural change in these areas is the key driving force underpinning economic movement, the present organisation of institutional capacity for economic development is a minor factor.

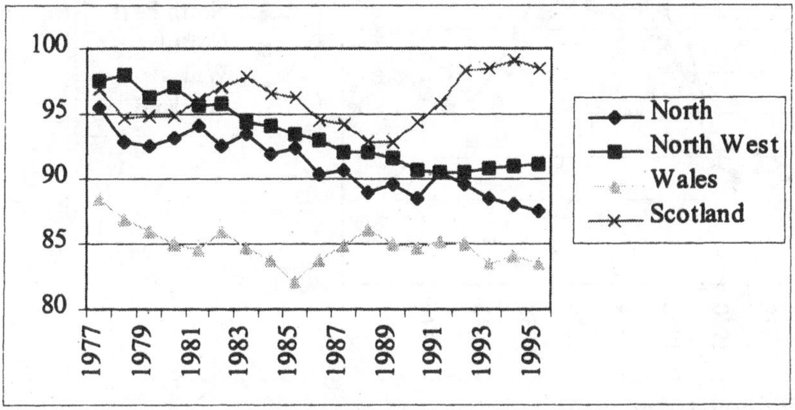

Source: Regional Trends (1997)

Figure 7.3 GDP per capita 1977-1994 (Index UK = 100)

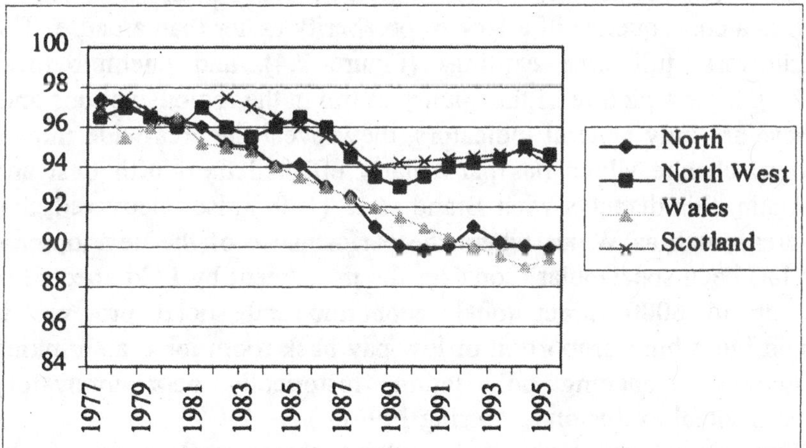

Source: NOMIS (1997)

Figure 7.4 Average gross weekly earnings (full-time) 1977-1995 (Index GB = 100)

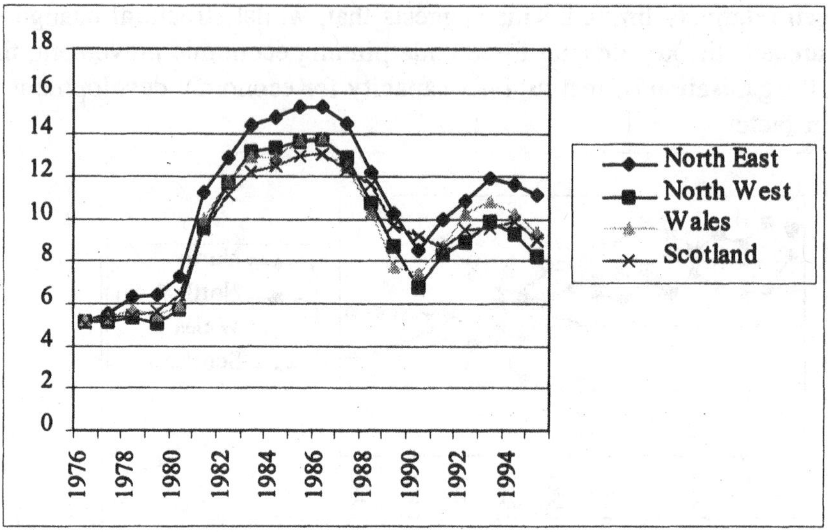

Source: Regional Trends (1997)

Figure 7.5 Seasonally adjusted unemployment 1976-1995

The main indicator, GDP per capita (Figure 7.3), reveals the relative low economic activity rates in Wales, which, as Brand *et al.* (1997) point out, is a consequence of a lack of prosperity rather than a cause. The other indicators, full time earnings (Figure 7.4), and unemployment (Figure 7.5), offer a picture of the quality of life in the regions/nations and, whilst these are only general indicators, they reveal the area-wide impact of structural change which has particularly effected the North East and Wales. Again, this displays what Brand *et al.* (1997) also uncovered, that even in areas such as Wales where the performance of the development agencies has been spectacular (consider the investment by LG expected to generate up to 6000 direct jobs), economic and social progress is constrained by: a high proportion of low-pay back room jobs; a shrinking labour market; deepening polarisation; historically poor innovatory capacity and social exclusion (Lovering 1996).

This does not mean that without the contributions of the development agencies the economic outcomes of the areas would have been the same. The counterfactual arguments may show that regional economies would have performed worse without the activities of development agencies. But, as also stated in the introductory sections, the end-result of a slightly improved economic performance cannot take precedence over the processes which exacerbate social exclusion, of which the development agencies are part, especially when research reveals these processes to be restricting wider economic development (Lovering 1998).

The original research, upon which this chapter is based, presented a case against the introduction of a more democratised institutional system (Harding *et al.* 1996). In fact, the main conclusion from the research was that economic performance would be hampered by proposed democratic change now under way in Scotland and Wales. This was based upon the views of those representing the institutions most likely at threat from these changes and the business community which, as the regime theorists show, are unlikely to favour a settlement based upon social criteria (Stoker 1995). In addition, it was also assumed that the people representing these development institutions, just because they are non-elected, have a greater closeness to and understanding of business needs.

There is obviously a problem with both these conclusions. First, those most at threat of losing their autonomy, or those whose economic principles do not equate with social development, are the key candidates to pursue a self serving, bureau building agenda, rather than representing the objective truth. This is quite ironic, considering the call from these non-elected representatives was for a system of linkages based upon greater openness, trust and transparency. The second incorrect conclusion was that the people on the management committees and boards of these institutions offer entrepreneurial wisdom, when the majority of them operate within a closed system, are mainly ex-civil servants or local government officers, with the principle function of disbursing state funds.

Therefore, based upon the empirical evidence, additional research (Brand *et al.* 1997; Lovering 1996), theoretical discourse (Lovering 1998, Amin 1998) and flaws in the methodology, the original finding against a more democratised development system appears weak. In addition, there are signs that for marginalised economies, the process of social exclusion, inhibiting economic development, cannot be addressed if the social capital geared towards development is not based upon accountable representation.

This does not necessarily go against Schumpeter's (1961) principled view that democracy is not a means to an end, merely that without it certain systems of development are less likely to exist. It also supports the arguments of the neo-marxists, neo-liberals and pluralists that a democratic settlement is the best framework for maintaining a successful free market system. And finally, it concurs with those promoting some form of associative democracy, which states democracy cannot be reduced to elections, and allows greater potential for feedback and learning than hierarchies of privileged decision makers.

Conclusion

Essentially the research set out to uncover the extent to which governance in the UK had undergone regionalisation in the past ten years and the links between regional institutional capacity and economic performance. However, as part of this, the focus of the work shifted towards examining the underlying assumption that elected regional structures bring enhanced economic competitiveness. All these propositions are used in one form or another to support arguments for constitutional change and regional government (Coulson 1990; Cheshire *et al.* 1992; SNP 1992; McCrone 1993; Murphy and Caborn 1995).

Because of this change in focus, this chapter includes a more theoretical critique of democracy, omitted from the original research, to link with the empirical analysis. This provides a range of understanding with regards to the purpose, effect and role of democracy. In addition, this chapter offers a clearer insight into the links between these different perspectives on democracy, new regionalism and the economic performance of regions. This reveals that the call for regional government can not be dismissed simply because business representation believes it will politicise and embed problems rather than provide the means to solve them. However, this does not mean that all levels of development administration need to be directly elected and the research shows there is a role for semi-detached single purpose agencies.

Further to this, the possibility of regional government based upon democratising non-elected regional governing capacity has its problems. The contradictory impulses that lie behind the recent growth in regional executive activity have produced a variety of barely related initiatives, across a range of inconsistent boundaries. This fragmented system primarily serves the government's convenience in streamlining administration, cutting costs, pushing the process of priority setting further down the governmental ladder, regulating regional utility markets, whilst retaining control over the direction of policy. This is something which does not appear out of place with New Labour, considering the wording of the white papers for Scottish and Welsh devolution.

> Scotland will remain an integral part of the United Kingdom, and The Queen will continue to be Head of State of the United Kingdom. The UK Parliament is and will remain sovereign....The financial framework for the Scottish Parliament will be closely based on existing financial arrangements for financing the Scottish Office. (The Scottish Office 1997).
>
> The Government proposes that a directly-elected Assembly will assume responsibility for policies and public services currently exercised by the Secretary of State for Wales.....The Assembly will also....make detailed rules and regulations, through secondary legislation, within the framework laid down in Acts of Parliament. (Welsh Office 1997).

Regional autonomy, during the recent period of regionalisation, has been marginally extended in a patchy, ad hoc way and selective decision making capacity at regional level has grown. Nevertheless, regional autonomy drawn from other levels of government has only really been enhanced by the movement of local authority functions upwards, in effect producing centralisation. Realistically, this increased autonomy is limited and in most cases central government determines the framework, sets performance targets, appoints key personnel and provides most of the financial resources. Therefore, any move to regional government, especially in the case of the English regions, would have to start from scratch, and the present system offers little to equate with the ideas for a learning regional environment (Hudson 1998).

The arguments in favour of withholding any movement towards a system of regional government are weakly based upon existing empirical evidence. The position of those engaged within the new regionalism debate clearly show that an inclusive approach to development can deal with both social and economic development (Lovering 1998). And, the role and function of development agencies, whilst not intentionally engaging with social processes, do serve to exacerbate the problems of a marginalised workforce. The need for innovative systems to be developed is not questioned, just the manner in which this goal is achieved; especially as the need for a form of associative democracy would improve the chances of their success.

Contrary to this, there are arguments in favour of regional government, which point to Britain being out of step with the rest of Europe, that do not stand up. Across Europe each country has virtually completely different arrangements for regional sub-national governmental structures (Sharpe 1993), these do not always make economic sense (Rhodes 1995), and in many cases they hold less autonomy than the structures presently operating in the UK (Harding and Le Gales 1997). But this is no reason why Britain should not have a more developed sub-national democratic regional system.

In conclusion, the case for regional government is not unfounded when based upon general economic indicators or the perceptions of those engaged in delivering development policies. Giving greater autonomy to a region, especially if democratic, would, at worst, guarantee the potential of that area to become more active within its own destiny or, at best, offer a more inclusive innovative system providing both economic and social progress. Obviously, as some have pointed out, democracy cannot guarantee an outcome (Schumpeter 1961).

There is no certainty as to how regions would use democratic power, or that it would bring economic competitiveness or reduced levels of social exclusion. Ultimately there is no guarantee regional government will be better at delivering economic success than any other form of regional institution. But, there are clear signs that the present system has not been able to achieve this and the democratic alternative could offer a more holistic learning environment with greater development potential.

Finally, none of this means that the case for regional government cannot be argued on other grounds, such as the grounds for democracy. This should also be at the heart of the argument, as it is a political decision about where democracy lies, about who should be represented in the decision making process, about accountability and, most of all, about responsibility. If people are prepared to accept responsibility for their own destinies, whatever they may be, then they should be in favour of a democratic process, which brings the responsibility closer to them.

Acknowledgements

I would like to thank the British Academy for their financial support, which covered part of the travel expenses to the RSA conference in Frankfurt Oder. I would also like to thank Allan Cochrane and Alan Harding for their comments on previous drafts.

References

Amin, A. (1998) 'An institutionalist perspective on regional economic development.' Paper presented at the Economic Geography Group Research Seminar Institutions and Governance, Department of Geography, UCL, London, July.

Amin, A. and Thrift, N. (eds) (1995a) *Globalization, Institutions and Regional Development in Europe.* Oxford: Oxford University Press.

Amin, A. and Thrift, N. (1995b) 'Institutional issues for the European regions: from markets and plans to socioeconomics and powers of association.' *Economy and Society 24*, 1, 42-66.

Asheim, B. and Dunford, M. (1997) 'Regional futures'. *Regional Studies 31*, 5, 445-455.

Birch, A.H. (1993) *The Concepts and Theories of Modern Democracy.* London: Routledge.

Blow, L., Hall, J. and Smith, S. (1996) 'Financing regional government in the UK: Some issues.' *Fiscal Studies 17*, 4, 99-120.

Brand, S. *et al.* (1997) 'Why isn't Wales richer? Economic change and GDP per capita'. *Local Economy*, November, 219-233.

Burch, M. (1993) 'The political dimension: the scope for a regional initiative?' In M. Burch and M. Rhodes (eds) *The North West Region and Europe: Development of a Regional Strategy.* EPRU Paper 3/93, Manchester: University of Manchester.

CBI Scotland (1995) *Scottish Business Agenda for a More Prosperous Scotland.* Glasgow: CBI Scotland.

CBI Scottish Manufacturing Group (1994) *Manufacturing Matters.* Glasgow: CBI.

Cheshire, P.E. *et al.*. (1992) 'Purpose built for failure? Local, regional and national government in Britain.' *Environment and Planning C: Government and Policy 10*, 355-69.

Clark, D. (1995) 'Call for democratic testing on quangos.' *Municipal Review and AMA News*, January, 220-221.

Cohen, J. and Rogers, J. (1993) 'Associations and Democracy.' *Social Philosophy and Policy 10*, 2, 282-312.

Commission for Local Democracy (1995) *Taking Charge: The Rebirth of Local Democracy.* Final Report of the Commission for Local Democracy, London: CLD.

Coulson, A. (1990) 'Devolving power: the case for regional government.' *Fabian Tract 537*, London: Fabian Society.

Crouch, C. and Marquand, D. (eds) (1989) *The New Centralism: Britain Out of Step in Europe?* Oxford: Blackwell.

Dahl, R.A. (1971) *Polyarchy: Participation and Opposition.* New Haven: Yale University Press.

Digiovanna, S. (1996) 'Industrial districts and regional economic development: a regulation approach.' *Regional Studies 30*, 4, 373-386.

Donnelly, K. and McQuail, P. (1996) *Regional Government in England.* London: The Constitution Unit.

Evans, R. and Garside, P. (1994) 'TEC local economic development policy and activity in Merseyside.' A report to the North West Regional Office of the Employment Department, mimeo.

Fukuyama, F. (1991) 'Liberal democracy as a global phenomenon.' *Political Science and Politics 24*, 4, 659-664.

Gamble, A. and Payne, A. (eds) (1996) *Regionalism and World Order.* London: Macmillan.

Gregersen, B. and Johnson, B. (1997) 'Learning economies, innovation systems and European integration.' *Regional Studies 31*, 5, 479-490.

Harding, A. *et al.* (1996) *Urbanisation and the Functions of Cities in the European Community.* Brussels: European Commission.

Harding, A. and Le Gales, P. (1997) 'Globalization, urban change and urban policies in Britain and France.' In Scott, A. (ed) *The Limits of Globalization.* London: Routledge, 181-201.

Hart, T., Haughton, G. and Peck, J. (1996) 'Accountability and the non-elected local state: calling training and enterprise councils to local account.' *Regional Studies 30*, 4, 429-441.

Harvie, C. (1994) *The Rise of Regional Europe.* London: Routledge.

Hayton, K. (1992) 'Scottish Enterprise: a challenge to local land-use planning?' *Town Planning Review 63*, 3, 265-78.

Hirst, P. (1994) 'Associative Democracy.' *Dissent 41*, 2, 241-247.

HMSO (1993) *Scotland in the Union: A Partnership for Good.* CM 2225, Edinburgh: HMSO.

Hogwood, B. (1995) 'The integrated regional offices and the Single Regeneration Budget.' *Commission for Local Democracy,* Report no. 13, London: CLD.

Hudson, R. (1997) 'Regional futures: industrial restructuring, new high volume production concepts and spatial development strategies in the new Europe.' *Regional Studies 31*, 5, 467-478.

Hudson, R (1998) 'The learning economy, the learning form and the learning region: A sympathetic critique of the limits to learning.' Paper presented to the Annual Conference of the Institution of British Geographers, Kingston University at Guildford.

Jessop, B. (1997) 'Capitalism and its future: remarks on regulation, government and governance.' *Review of International Political Economy 3*, 3, 561-581.

Jones, G. (1988) 'Against regional government.' *Local Government Studies,* Sept/Oct, 1-11.

Labour Party (1995) *A Choice for England: A Consultation Paper on Labour's Plans for English Regional Government.* London: Labour Party.

Lovering, J. (1996) 'New myths of the Welsh economy.' *Planet 116*, 6-16.

Lovering, J. (1998) 'Theory led by policy? The inadequacies of 'The New Regionalism' in Economic Geography, illustrated from the case of Wales.' Paper presented at the Economic Geography Group Research Seminar Institutions and Governance, July, Department of Geography, UCL, London.

Mawson, J. (1997) 'New labour and the English regions: A missed opportunity?' *Local Economy,* November, 194-203.

McCrone, D. (1993) 'Regionalism and constitutional change in Scotland.' *Regional Studies 27*, 6, 507-512.
Midwinter, A., Keating, M. and Mitchell, J. (1991) *Politics and Public Policy in Scotland.* London: Macmillan.
Moore, C. and Booth, S. (1989) *Managing Competition: Meso-Corporatism, Pluralism and the Negotiated Order in Scotland.* Oxford: Clarendon.
Morgan, K. (1997) 'The learning region: Institutions, innovation and regional renewal.' *Regional Studies 31*, 5, 491-503.
Morgan, K. and Roberts, E. (1993) 'The democratic deficit: a guide to quangoland.' *Papers in Planning Research 144*, Department of City and Regional Planning, University of Wales in Cardiff.
Murphy, P. and Caborn, R. (1995) *Regional Government for England: An Economic Imperative.* Sheffield, PAVIC, Sheffield Hallam University.
Ohmae, K. (1993) 'The rise of the region state.' *Foreign Affairs,* 78-87.
Parry, R. (1993) 'Towards a democratised Scottish Office?' *Scottish Affairs 5*, 41-57.
Patchell, J. (1996) 'Kaleidoscope economies - the processes of cooperation, competition, and control in regional economic development.' *Annals of the Association of American Geographers 86*, 3, 481-506.
Paterson, L. (1994) *The Autonomy of Modern Scotland.* Edinburgh: Edinburgh University Press.
Pieda (1993) *Regional Economic Strategy for the North West of England: Final Report.* Manchester: Pieda.
Rhodes, M. (ed) (1995) *The Regions and the New Europe: Patterns in Core and Periphery Development.* Manchester: Manchester University Press.
Rhodes, R.A.W. (1988) *Beyond Westminster and Whitehall: The Sub-Central Governments of Britain.* London: Unwin Hyman.
Rueschemeyer, D. *et al.* (1992), *Capitalist Development and Democracy.* Cambridge: Polity Press.
Salt, H. (1994) 'Taking control of regional government.' *Municipal Review and AMA News 753*, 198-99.
Schumpeter, J.A. (1961) *Capitalism, Socialism and Democracy.* London: George Allen and Unwin.
Scottish Office (1997) *Scottish Devolution: A Summary of the Proposals.* http://www.scottish-devolution.org.uk.
Sharpe, L.J. (ed) (1993) *The Rise of Meso Government in Europe.* London: Sage.
Shaw, K. (1993) 'The development of a new urban corporatism: the politics of urban regeneration in the North East of England.' *Regional Studies 27*, 3, 251-59.
Simon, H. (1995) 'Rationality in political behaviour.' *Political Psychology 16*, 1, 45-61.
SNP (1992) *Independence in Europe: Make it Happen Now!* Edinburgh: SNP.
Stewart, J. *et al.* (1995) *The Quango State: An Alternative Approach.* Commission for Local Democracy, Report 10, London: CLD.
Stoker, G. (1995) 'Regime Theory and Urban Politics.' In D. Judge *et al.* (eds), *Theories of Urban Politics*, London: Sage, 54-71.
Straw, J. (1995) 'Labour and the regions of England.' Regional Studies Association Annual Lecture, Labour Party press release, 28 September, 1995.

Thomas, A. (1995) 'The Welsh Assembly debate: 1979 revisited?' *Public Money and Management*, April-June, 6-8.

Tomaney, J. (1996) 'Regional government and economic development.' *Local Economy*, May, 27-38.

Turok, I. (1993) 'Inward investment and local linkages, how deeply embedded is 'Silicon Glen'?' *Regional Studies 27*, 5, 401-17.

Turok, I. and Richardson, R. (1991) 'External takeovers of Scottish companies in the 1980s.' *Area 23*, 1, 73-81.

Welsh Office (1997) *An Assembly for Wales: An Overview.* http://floor.ccta.gov.uk.

Interviews

Below is a list of representatives who gave valuable time to discuss development issues. This work was carried out by Alan Harding and Richard Evans, European Institute for Urban Affairs (Harding *et al.* 1996).

K. Aitken, Freelance journalist and former Industrial Editor, The Scotsman.

J. Armstrong, Industrial Advisor to the Government Office for the North East and Northern Development Company.

G. Baird, Executive Director, Scottish Financial Enterprise and former Chief Executive, Scotland Europa.

H. Bernstein, Deputy Chief Executive, Manchester City Council.

P. Bounds, Chief Executive, Liverpool City Council.

R. Craig Campbell, Chief Economist, Scottish Council (Development and Industry).

Sir A. Cockshaw, Chairman, AMEC plc and joint chairman, North West Business Leadership Team.

Prof P. Cooke, School for Advanced Studies in the Social Sciences, University of Wales Cardiff.

H. Conway, Chief Executive, Cardiff Chamber of Commerce and Industry.

K. Davies, Chief Executive, Plaid Cymru.

P. Denham, Regional Director, Government Office for the North East.

A.N.A. Dicken, Teeside Site Manger, ICI.

L. Ellmann, Leader, Lancaster County Council.

J. Elvidge, Under-Secretary, Scottish Office Industry Department.

Dr A. Foord, Director, North East CBI.

T. Gernon, Head of Corporate Affairs, Teeside Training and Enterprise Council.

C. Gibaud, Chief Executive, Merseyside Partnership.

L. Gold, Chief Executive, Scottish CBI.

J. Graham, Under-Secretary, Scottish Office Environment Department.

J. Hamilton, Economic Development Officer, Northumberland County Council.

J. Hansen, EC Commissioner for Wales.

D. Henshaw, Chief Executive, Knowsley Borough Council.

M. Hollingsworth, Chief Planner, Land Authority for Wales.

J. Harris and J. Jones, Convention of Scottish Local Authorities.

Prof N. Hood, Marketing Department, Strathclyde University (formerly of Locate in Scotland).
R. Howarth, Director, Wales Quality Centre.
Prof J. Hughes, Development Director, Development Board for Rural Wales.
E. Haywood, Director, CBI Wales.
R. Howard, Regional Secretary, TUC Northern Region.
D. Jenkins, Director, Wales TUC.
N. Jones, Assistant Secretary, Assembly of Welsh Counties.
S. Knighton, Director, Business in the Community, Wales.
R. Leonard, Assistant Secretary, Scottish TUC.
J. Lewis, Lecturer, Geography Department, University of Durham.
G. Lord, Kellogg UK Ltd.
J. Lord, Director of Strategy, Scottish Enterprise.
J. Madden, Chief Executive, The Engineering Centre for Wales.
D. McCrone, Sociology Department, University of Edinburgh.
A. McKenzie, Chief Planner, Scottish Office Environment Department.
N. Meachen, Deputy Secretary, North of England Assembly of Local Authorities.
P. Mitchell, Welsh Development Agency.
J. Moorhouse, Director, Scottish Business in the Community.
B. Morgan, Chief Economist, Welsh Development Agency.
Prof K. Morgan, Department of City and Regional Planning, University of Wales in Cardiff.
P. Nicholls, Manager, World Trade Centre.
G. Parker, Senior Business Advisor, Tyne and Wear Development Corporation.
G. Piper, Chief Executive, North West Business Leadership Team.
K. Richardson, North East Chamber of Commerce.
P. Price, Head of European Affairs Division, WDA.
G. Price-Jones, Secretary, Council of Welsh Districts.
Prof B. Robson, Geography Department, University of Manchester.
G. Robson, Under-Secretary, Scottish Office Industry Department.
P. Shakeshaft, Director of Corporate Affairs, Northern Development Company.
Sir J. C. Shaw, Deputy Governor, Bank of Scotland.
P. Sheldon, Chief Executive, South Glamorgan TEC.
M. Shukman, Head of Co-ordinating Division, WDA.
J. Snaith, Economic Development Officer, Chief Executives' Department, Sunderland City Council.
J. Tomaney, A. Pyke and D. Charles, Centre for Urban and regional Development Studies, University of Newcastle.
T. Thomas, Chief Executive, The Co-operative Bank.
I. Turok, Centre for Planning, Strathclyde University.
D. Walsh, Chair, Economic Development Committee, Cleveland County Council.
Prof J. Ward, IBM UK.
E. Weeple, Under-Secretary, Scottish Office Industry Department.
T. Wetherby, Chairman, INWARD.
J. Wright, Economic Development Officer, Development Department, Newcastle City Council.

8 Persuasive Storytelling about the Reform Process: The Case of the West Sweden Region

CHRISTIAN JENSEN AND SVANTE LEIJON

Regions, Reforms and Rhetoric: Introduction

Can a commissioner work to create a new institutional order? Can a commissioner break up identities and shape new ones, change organisational structure, bring about a law change, or serve as a weapon in a national struggle concerning depleted resources? These are some of the large-scale, direct, social and political effects which have been ascribed to certain reformatory activities. How seriously should they be taken?

A parliamentary system is based upon ideological differences and the conflicts this causes in society. Government official commissions are an arena for such conflicts where different interests can find and articulate their opinions. This commissionary work has a long tradition in Sweden. Its roots go back to the beginning of the 17th century. Its function then and then now is to generate knowledge, to prepare a decision and to exercise pressure in a given direction.

There are several advantages with these commissions. The first is that the commission is a constructive way of solving problems as an ongoing dialogue between different parties and interests. The next is that the submission of the proposal for comments has a democratic value through the possibility of critical examination of the proposals through an open debate. A final advantage is the way it functions: as a preparatory area for compromises and agreements - thus it is possible simultaneously to secure reform proposals and to test the reaction in a congregation of different opinions. The commissionary work thus facilitates the formulation and implementation of a long range policy, as well as solving current problems concerning multiple opinions. In this chapter we will describe and analyse different parts of a comissionary work regarding the creation of a new regional institution in West Sweden.

During the 1990s there has been a debate in Sweden - partly because of EU membership and partly because of the budget deficits arising from the creation of a new institutional structure - about regions playing a dominant role. The discussion is new, but only to a certain extent. Over the post-war period, at regular intervals and mainly pushed by the work of commissioners, there have been intensified discussions about the need for extended regional self-government which would help the inhabitants and decision-makers of a region to govern the development and future of their region themselves to a greater extent. However, other solutions to problems generated by multiple administrative borders as well as by a lack of political influence have been chosen: during the 1950s and the 1960s, by amalgamating many small municipalities (about 5000) into a much smaller number of municipalities (approximately 290), and during the 1970s and 1980s, by expanding responsibility for Goverment planning and co-ordination. The regional level has mainly been engaged in healt-care issues, which certainly have been expanded during the post-war period, too. But now, again, discussions are being conducted on extending regional self-government, where counties are to be amalgamated and responsibility and authorities are being decentralised from Govermental level to a newly established regional level.

In a previously published article (Jensen and Leijon 1996) we described and analysed the progress of the West Sweden region. One of our conclusions was that there were some uncertainties concerning the outcome of the process. The discussion has been ongoing since then, and today we can ascertain the general tendency of the process. In this paper, we will develop our discussion and give a clearer description of the reform process in terms of negotiation and persuasion.

After this brief introduction, in the next section we will present a constructivistic frame of reference, emphasising the importance of symbols and rhetoric if the process of reform work is to be understood. Then we will present our case, partly as a short historical background, following this introduction, partly as a section which is intended to catch a phase which is important for the process in creating a region. The second section will be interspersed with a rhetorical analysis. In our conclusion, by means of our case study we will conduct a more fundamental discussion on the need for a reform of ideologies and the need they, in their turn, have of good rhetoric.

A Constructivistic Perspective on Reformation

The conception of a reform is connected with a modernist enterprise (Baier, March and Sætren 1986; March and Olsen 1983). Through reforms the society and the institutions can develop in an almost linear way, they claim. However reform scholars have been proposing a wide variety of alternatives to the modernist concept. One of them is a social constructivistic perspective, which we will describe here.

A social constructivistic manifesto (Berger and Luckmann 1967) sees institutions and organisations as products of human beings. They are instruments used to deal with different tasks placed before man. There are no universal organisational forms which are able to resolve all the problems that may confront an organisation; rather organisations need to change when new challenges present themselves. Understanding change is to understand how we introduce different types of tangible structures – organisational forms, control models, executive systems, policies, etc. – from an abstract and general viewpoint, i.e. to express values at a level of abstraction at which agreement can result. The latter is without doubt the representation of a region as a device for creating a new institutional order.

To introduce another order is a construction activity in organised forms. The order referred to in situations of change is something that does not exist, but ought to be made visible and comprehensible. Although order does not exist, somebody has a vague idea, an aiming point, as to how things should look when order rules. Organisational theory tries to capture this through the concepts of the 'plan', 'strategy' and 'vision', which are perceived by all organisations as essential but volatile activities.

However, in order for an organisation to work, it is assumed, firstly, that there is an image of current reality as being disordered and full of problems but also, secondly, an image of the future reality as being orderly. The reality which the organisational activity intends to organise must thus, for it to be put in order, first be constructed through a mutual social negotiation, so that aiming points will be defined and given a content which seems meaningsful to the participant. How can this be done?

The image of some kind of order is, thus, an important prerequisite for the creation of reforms. Although the concept of a 'region' according to Oxford Advanced Learner's Dictionary of Current English is said to be an 'area or division *with or without* definite boundaries or characteristic' [our italics] the concept still symbolises a future possible order.

The concept of a region therefore in this article will be understood as a socially and culturally constructed category, a typically historically contingent discursive formation, which emerges from communications and social action. The use of words, argument and communication are in this respect part of the process of reforming and organising. Argument is an attempt to try to change something the majority understands as a problem to something that they will consider as being genuine, through the use of something that has already been approved.

To see organising as a rhetorical enterprise is also a way of highlighting the politics of reorganising. Edelman argues in his 'The Symbolic Uses of Politics' (1964) that political cognition is not a representation of reality, but a selective construction of non-referential symbols. Edelman claims that: 'For most men most of the time politics is a series of pictures in the mind, placed there by television news, newspaper, magazines and discussion. (p.5)'

Moreover, Edelman (1964, p.5) argues that because of the absence of personal contact with political events, people see politics '...as a passing parade of abstract symbols'. The gap between experience and perception causes the relationship between political symbolism and language, on the one hand, and political event, on the other, always to be problematic. In Edelman's world both language and symbolism help to constitute political reality. He views them as performances, that is, as political action in themselves.

Argument is often defined as the endeavour to convince. The argumentative dimension is essential to language in that any discourse tries to persuade the person it addresses – this very paper is no exception. Argument, however, is also characterised as nonformal reasoning (Perelman 1982; Shotter 1993). One only argues because it is not an absolute necessity that reasons should follow each other in a logical pattern thus leaving room for possible disagreement. Rhetoric and argument scholars attend to the ways symbolic action produces transformation – change, assent, or most generally, movement and development – in assumptions, beliefs, practices, and affiliations. The rhetorical nature of reforms and changes stems from the fact that alternatives are open, sometimes deliberately. Something is in question in what is said, and it is debated through the solutions proposed, represented, and staged. Here the definition of argument meets the definition of rhetoric. Rhetoric is a discourse in which one can hold opposite judgments on the same.

Language, in other words, shall make us see something we have not seen before or understood the scope of. Without language nothing can be created and without shared symbols, we cannot come to an agreement. Thus, language is man's most important vehicle for action in such a way that it constructs our society, our institutions and our image of it. In this chapter, organisation is perceived as persuasive linguistic processes of negotiation. As such they are aimed at modifying and influencing the opinions and standpoints regarding reality of the parties concerned. And it is not difficult to see a commissioner's work as a discursive practice.

The Rhetoric in Relation to its Context

Above we have introduced a social constructive perspective on reforms, especially in connection with rhetoric. Rhetoric is in itself a motivating power. But this needs to be seen in relation to the context of the reform work. The strength of the wind is not just dependent upon its own inner dynamics but also upon the conditions of the environment in which it blows. The temparature of the sea has a decisive influence on its force.

The power of rhetoric can be seen in relation to the person who sends the message and the person who receives it. It is inevitable that the receiver listens and interprets in relation to the context in which he/she finds herself/himself. A clear example of the differences in context is economic abundance as opposed to a recession. A brilliant orator chooses to structure his/her message in relation to the contextual conditions of the receiver.

The idea of context does not oppose the social constructionalist approach of the study. It is not the conditions 'outside' the person but rather one that should be seen as a 'mutually strong perception' about, for example, the economy. Such perceptions can themselves be questioned but if there are too many questions then the society collapses. The other side of the coin is that the mutually strong perceptions also slow down development.

In sum, the concept of rhetoric is fundamental to our frame of reference. Reformatory work as the creator of a regional organisation is thus seen as a rhetoric project. The orator symbolises, educates and creates the relative, diverse, contextual conditions.

The Case Study: the Institutional Landscape and Regional Investigational Work

Historical Background

In the introduction we wrote that the discussion about extended regional self-government has been ongoing during the whole post-war period in Sweden, and that other solutions have been chosen. As in all public organisation the various arguments for a change relate mainly to two general reasons, viz. democracy and efficiency. Thus, it has been maintained over the years that extended regional self-government is an important democratisation, since the citizens in the region thus can exert an influence on their development and future for public as well as privite activities; an extended way of regional thinking gives better conditions for a more effective utilisation of resources, since planning and co-ordination are faciliated, thus creating better possiblities for development in the region. In this way the region would be a strong and clear representative, an argument in itself, growing stronger and stronger, not only in relation to the national level, but above all in the co-operation at regional level that has developed in Europe in the 1990s. As one can see, laudable arguments and reasons. However, they were earlier perceived as too full of consequences since the proposition implies that a number of boundaries, territories, barriers of power and hierarchies have to be forced.

Proposals for a regional division in West Sweden have been shown in two official reports (SOU 1992, p.66, 1995, p.27). The final report of the committee drafting the proposal, Regional Future (SOU 1995, p.27), suggests the shaping of public organisations at a regional level. This means that the division of responsibility between the State and the local authorities will change so that the responsibility for regional development will be transferred from the Government and the county administrative board to the new region. It was suggested that besides West Sweden another region, Scania, should also be formed.

To implement the proposal means institutional and organisational consequences, and that is almost automatically in conflict with established interests. The preliminary selected change towards a new regional unit is therefore not taking place in a vacuum. Within the framework of the various West Swedish social institutions, local authorities, county councils and county administrative boards there already exist different forms of co-operation, but one can state that co-operation takes place within the various social institutions and not cross-sectionally. The formation of a West Sweden region is intended to improve cross-sectional cooperation and 'a West Swedish-thinking'. The concept of a region is therefore an attempt by the reformers to bridge a number of institutional identities that have developed during the post-war period.

The comments made in connection with the proposal of the commission consisted of approximately 500 answers, and many different opinions are indicated from this action. Defenders of the status quo say that the matter has not been analysed and investigated properly and that the result of the proposal is therefore difficult to predict, that the new West Sweden region had not been established properly among the public, and that a referendum a referendum should be organised in order to ascertain their opinion. As the proposed region will take over responsibilities from the state, conflicts that previously would have been between municipalities and the state will now be between municipalities and the region under this proposal, raising other unanswered questions. In particular, to what extent will the county's various parts (smaller municipalities, the country area and the county's peripheral parts) contribute to or participate in the region's development? An explicit fear that many actors express is that the largest city, Göteborg, will dominate.

But the comments also indicate several factors that speak in favour of making up a region in West Sweden, for example the EU's talk of regions and their opportunity to work independently and with cross border contacts. Another important motivating force is the desire from a number of West Swedish politicians for greater independence, and so as a region to have perceived greater leverage against central control, and to be strong enough to match the capital region and new regional formations, such as Scania.

The Swedish Parliament approved the formation of Scania during 1996 but reserved their decision regarding West Sweden. Göran Bengtsson, The County Governor of Göteborg and Bohus counties, made the following comment:

> A large region has been created in South Sweden, Scania, but the demands made on us in West Sweden can be said to be greater than in the south. Down there, they are more agreed upon what constitutes South Sweden and what is the southern Swedish mentality. There are many different opinions and attitudes here in West Sweden that have to be met and united. Naturally there is something that we call 'West Swedish' but it is complex and difficult to put a finger on.[1]

The parliamentary decision and the fact that a number of politicians desire a regional organisation, led the political parties in West Sweden in the autumn of 1996 to constitute the informal West Sweden board, a non-profit association, consisting of 27 West Swedish politicians who have the mandate without prejudice to push the matter of the region forward. The members were strict in saying that they represented their parties – a political initiative – and not their councils or local governments. By doing so they want to constitute 'a West Swedish way of thinking'.

Our interviews with different representatives of different institutions in West Sweden over the years confirm that there exists a division of opinion about what exactly constitutes the regional problem and that the actual problem-descriptions themselves compete. A closer examination of the different reasons for this shows that the particular problem is often included in yet another fundamental problem democracy and/or efficiency issues. A rich symbolic and pictorial language is used when describing one's understanding, due to the lack of a clear definition and logical arguments. Ideologies, half-truths and basic facts are also alternately mixed together.

In a situation like this it is usual to appoint an investigatory committee. And this is what happened. A special investigator was given the

[1] Quotation from the magazine 'Look at West Sweden', Spring 1997, p.10.

task of commencing negotiations during 1996 with representatives of the local councils, county administrative board and county councils and other participants in West Sweden with a view to clarifying the geographic shape of the West Sweden region as well as formulating a basis concerning the localisation of these public regional organisations.

A significant actor is consequently the special commissioner (SP) who has had a number of investigatory tasks associated with the regional question. Besides, as mentioned above, he also received a commission from the political parties and the region of Scania to function as a 'generator' at the instigation of the new regional organisation there.

We will now leave the remaining space in this section to a speech that SP held on October 22, 1996, six months before the Parliament decided on the formation of a new West Sweden region.[2] In his speech SP related various perspectives of the region question – in particular the

2 With a symbolic perspective on reformation one can say that rhetorical sense is an aesthetic side of 'change-talk'. This aesthetic quality can rarely be precisely defined and described. It just is. Probably the most important aspect is form, the order the rhetor imposes on the material – on language, characters, events, details, all of which the rhetor draws from the usually disorderly realm of real life. Take, for example, events in real life; these are not necessarily related by cause and effect or if some are many are not. They do not necessarily lead to conclusions. Organizational change may come to nothing, the new management may not be successful, the economic crisis may not be resolved. Many things happen that are hard to remember or even be aware of. We do not always know which are important and which are trivial. But in purposeful language, as commissions or speeches, you can give give them structure in the form of a plot. Unimportant events will be excluded, causes and effects established, conflicts introduced and resolved. They will be arranged in logical order so that they form a sequence with a beginning, a middle and an end. They may even have suspense, so that we fearfully or gleefully anticipate what happens next.This aesthetical side brings us to yet another proposition: that purposeful language is fictional. The term fiction is commonly used to describe works that tell a story. The elements of a fiction are among other things plot, i.e., what happens in narrative or casually related events that contain a conflict, characterization (simple or complex), theme or central idea in the work, setting (physical world, time in which the action takes place, the social environment), point of view or the author's relationship to the fictional world – the position from which the story is told, and use of symbols (public or private symbols). In fact, all texts are fictional in the sense that the reader sets them apart from the facts pertaining to real life. The fictionality of the text lies in the artistic control the rhetor exercises over the work. This artistic control has the effect of stylizing the material of the work and thus setting the work apart from the context of real life. Even with this fictional element in the text, they have the capacity for being true, true to human experience.

position of the government, region and local authorities attitudes. The speech was heard by many West Swedish county councillors, local politicians and civil servants together with four different county council boards and representatives from various public organisations. Of course, the audience was well versed in the problem of realising a regional reform. This knowledge turned the speech into a combination of images in the speech itself along with images in the minds of the audience. As listeners, therefore we are not just passive receivers of a speech; we also help to create the text.

You wish to see: listen, hearing is a step towards vision:

> It has been proposed that there should be a new county and a regional organisation but this hasn't been completely settled as yet. The Government said what they think, the Parliament has decided in principle but there is a great deal more to be decided such as that which I have received the commission for; the drawing of boundaries and localisation of public activities. In March next year there will be a West Sweden proposition after which the Parliament will make a final decision about the boundaries, localisation and content in this West Sweden region.
>
> In a few days a proposition concerning work division on a regional level between the county administrative board and the county council will be presented and this will then provide the possibility of including the points made in the West Sweden proposition of next year. If you in West Sweden want this. *It is you who have to decide* [our italics, as everywhere else in this chapter]. It is a political process of which there are many opinions. ... I have been there as I have the Government's commission on localisation. There one is much more prepared.
>
> And then ... Stockholm is a long way ahead in this connection ... and this builds strengths. And just imagine if it will be announced that they will be hosting the 2004 Olympics, then there will be a boom the like of which Sweden has never seen before.[3] It is true that there is a special history behind it, but *there are enormous*

[3] At that point, we did not know that the Athenians were to be the lucky ones.

> *attractions in both Stockholm and Scania* [where a connection between Scania and the Copenhagen region is being built].
> It is high time that things got started in West Sweden. Scania has a board comprising of politicians and parties who are prepared to deal with the question. Yesterday evening the first steps were taken to create a West Sweden board and some of those who participated are present here today.

SP has built-in conflicts, crises and resolutions in his speeches, so that opponents are hesitant when the story told is changed. In our case there are some conflicts that are worth mentioning here. One appears in the sense that not everything in the reform has yet been decided, but in the story told it is not the Parliament, nor his mandate that decide, it is the people of West Sweden. This is not a top-down reform!

Another conflict is when SP relates the present region-discussion here in West Sweden to what has already happened in Scania. There you already have a region. And he goes on 'threaten' the audience by saying 'Imagine if Stockholm were to get the Olympic Games in 2004'. That would create a Klondyke-atmosphere there, and where would West Sweden be then? Politicians in West Sweden must make up their minds about the region!

A third conflict is that some local governments are doubtful about the reform. Speaking of characters, the local governments who play an important role in the decision making, make the listener care about the outcome of the story. The local governments are just like fictional characters, interesting and believable, whom the listener cares about. In SP's story they eventually give up their resistance afraid of becoming 'The Remains of Skaraborg'. SP says:

> All of the local authorities of Göteborg and Bohus support the creation of a new region and are prepared to work for it. Älvsborg too. ... Both Älvsborg and Göteborg and Bohus wish to include Skaraborg, partly in order to obtain a counterbalance to the city of Göteborg.
> But what do Skaraborg think about this? They have 17 local authorities of which six wish very decidedly to be included in the new West Sweden region. They are actively committed and it is of

> extreme importance to them. ... But the 11 local authorities that are against in principle would rather see Skaraborg remain as it is today.
> At the same time all 17 local authorities in Skaraborg state that they don't want there to be a *'The Remains of Skaraborg'*. This means that all 17 will have to be included as a whole. None wish a bits and pieces solution. ... My tip is that there will be a greater West Sweden region.

A fourth conflict emerges when one connects the reform with the consequences it will have on occupations in the organisations concerned. Here SP told us that less than five per cent of the employment estimated at fifty thousand are concerned, and later on when he describes his criterion he says that the reform should not move people unnecessarily.

> My commission is concerned with Government activities at county level as well as other regional administration. This is something that the Parliament and Government cannot decide upon. ... I have to show a complete picture before the Parliament can make a decision. This picture consists of the county administrative board, the counties' chief of police, county courts, tax authorities, debt collectors, forestry board, county surveyors, social security, transports, etc..... have I forgotten anything, it is a lot...that has to be divided. ... *I would think that these services employ 50,000, but less than 5 per cent who are included in my task, approximately 2,500 people*. Take for example the county employment committee or the social services, most of their employees are to be found in the local social security offices or employment exchanges, and they are not included in my localisation task.

All common experience demonstrates that amalgamations evoke discussions about financial cuts and redundancies, but this is not mentioned by SP. In building in a conflict in the author's own story, he makes it possible to handle conflict on a fictional or imaginative level, and just as cats always land on their feet, he too manages by means of constructing a winning end.

What else does this speech have that makes it persuasive? Another element is that *SP places the events and the actions in their proper context*. They are held in a situation where there are disputes among the parties concerned, and despite clashes of opinion and disagreements and the disputes must be resolved. And the audience knows this. *SP adopts an appropriate point of view concerning the audience*. They understand the conflicts and they are aware of the politics in both the matter and the situation. This is also persuasive. The speech is formed homogeneously with regard to the political aspect and understood in an *interpretative community*. Another significant, and indeed political action is to declare that he has been given an *implementary task*. It is not a common investigation but an implementary task. SP has a mandate to find a solution.

> At the end of November I'm going to present a proposal regarding boundaries and localisation and my ambition is that it will be accepted by the government and the parliament. It is not a common investigation but more of an *implementing* task.

SP's basis for forming a judgment is generally held by the audience and thus understandings are generalised. We believe that this is also effective from a persuasive point of view. Therefore SP manages, still in his story, to express a trustworthy attitude towards a position, which reduces the image of him as a supporter of the reform, and rather makes him a person who can express the audience's experience of the process of constructing the reform of a region.

> *When you look at the localisation of different organisational activities there are a number of criteria which I actually found when I was in Scania. These criteria or grounds of evaluation are used when I am discussing West Sweden*.
> The first point is *service* to companies, citizens and others. Localisation must not result in bad service to the people. Point number two is the *effectiveness of the authorities*. They must not be made more expensive. It now appears that different grounds of evaluation will compete against each other. If it is an effective authority that you are looking for then most people would say that

all service should be located in the city of Göteborg. But this can be said of a lot of things, that you place everything in one place thus making it more effective even though it might be a bit tight.

Then we have another criterion which is that *we shouldn't move people unnecessarily*. We are not to play musical chairs with the employees ... now there are many people working in different places and we should therefore not move people just out of principle.

The next ground of evaluation is the one which I feel that the Government will think is the most important one and that is that there should be an *intra-regional balance*. In other words, everything should not be located in Göteborg. And this is not a negative ground of evaluation but rather a positive one. In order that there should be a new West Sweden region, with commitment and participation then there must be activity throughout the region. Everything should not be concentrated on Göteborg. People in Mariestad, Skövde and Vänersborg and other places must feel that they can have a say and that they can influence the decision-making powers concerning interesting issues in their own county. This is a very important point.

The final point is that there should be a *long-term structure that promotes growth in the new West Sweden region* – there should be no temporary solution just because it might be necessary today. Based on what I have told you I am now putting together the pieces of the puzzle and I am negotiating with different parties … and will present my proposition at the end of November.'

This talent for judgment shows a consciousness that sense-making is to be found in the degree of trust or mistrust we put in our own and other persons' words. Sir Geoffrey Vickers (1965) considered this balancing quality to be one of the criteria in making good judgment. Also Beiner (1983) in his 'Political Judgment' presents the rhetoric ability as the way in which one convinces oneself and others in a situation where there are no given criteria for a suitable procedure. To convince people demands a clever orator who, through his/her persuasive powers, chooses the argument which the public can accept and make their own. The quotation shows how the Government's special investigator evaluates, argues and relates his work by creating meaning regarding a number of questions that are all in one way or another involved in conflicts.

To inquire into what SP says is thus to learn how he constructs his world. The speech creates an imaginary world, and this world embodies a theory about how his world works – a world view. Rhetors may or may not be aware of this but their views of the real world inevitably influence their construction of the imagery one. World views expressed in the speech are subjective. *The image one sees as a reader of SP's view of the reform process is that it is a negotiated order*, and that he, as he tells his story, has invented and used different bases for forming a judgment. This *makes him a discerning person*, a person who can balance different interests.

The medium of institutional and organisational change is in this context language, both oral and written. Creators of texts use language in a special way. *SP uses language for its denotative and connotative values*. The denotative uses of language give the ability to provide symbols – words – that mean one thing only. Any symbol will do, as long as it represents the referent clearly and exactly, thereby eliminating the emotional, the irrational and subjective sides of meaning. However, institutional and organisational changes are seldom neutral and descriptive, they are always normative. To hide the normative aspect you use the connotative values of language. Connotation is the meaning attached to words in addition to their explicit referent. The connotative meanings of words are subjective, multiple, and sometimes arbitrary. A word such as region, criteria such as efficiency, service, decentralisation, balance, progressive, all have denotative meanings which you will find in textbooks, but they also have a *connotative meaning which indicates flexibility, judgment, modernity*. These are ingredients that are persuasive for the audience, so that the overall purpose of the reform to create an identity for West Sweden will be served.

A phenomenon that we have already mentioned, which is worth mentioning again, is that *examples are effective ways of persuasion*. In addition to offering a world view, commissions and speeches can be true by presenting an experience of reality. The experience may be new or old, unique or shared by many people. Whatever it is, the rhetor uses experiences to put us in the midst of it because *concretising makes it visible*, makes the listener feel it, the result being that we understand it better. Therefore, abstract ideas, such as competition between regions

(Scania and Stockholm), learning from experience, SP saying that he used bases for forming judgement in Scania, justice, the balance between different criteria, become recognisable.

Persuasive storytelling about the reform process is a form that allows the rhetor to handle the different ways in which the actors assess the claims being made in the light of pressing circumstances, historical traditions, new possibilities, social interests, and personal motives.[4] The reform manifests itself through a wide array of symbol-generating mechanisms; one example is persuasive stories where external enemies are created, a new language is invented to describe the situation better, myths are created which encourage quiescence or changes. Reformers are relatively free to construct visions and rhetorical appeals which both disrupt and confirm long-standing interest-based coalitions. Labels such as development, participation, 'Regional Europe', 'The Remains of Skaraborg', etc. may be combined with traditional symbols, such as the flag, to create new political and organisational coalitions. But there are, of course, also other mechanisms such as the utilisation of the mass media in order to produce reform-favouring images, but let us leave that for another article.

Parallel with the work described above of implementing the concept of a region, there are the contextual conditions that promote and encourage towards thc creation of a region. The strength of the reform work is also reflected in a wider power context.

[4] One can see SP's speech as a form of education in a sphere infused with politics, interests and power. According to Czarniawska-Joerges (1990), reforms generally appear to have four main functions. They relate to power, they legitimate – which strengthens one's confidence in those who have the intention to improve. They also instruct and educate the members of the organizations in the new norms and values. Finally, they are entertaining whilst simultaneously threatening, depending on the level at which one finds oneself in the organizational process. Czarniawska-Joerges states that reforms: '...create many opportunities for the collection of new knowledge alternately that it can give rise to many new problems. It is the ability to learn in an unstable situation that decides whether it will be the former or the latter' (1990, p.231). This observation of learning and education are also in line with the ideas of March and Olsen. 'Politics is regarded as education, as a place for discovering, elaborating, and expressing meanings, establishing shared (or opposing) conceptions of experience, values, and the nature of existence. It is symbolic, not in the recent sense of symbols as devices of powerful for confusing the weak, ... but more in the sense of symbols as instruments of interpretative order (March and Olsen 1989, p.48).

No important actor is against the reform as far as we have seen in our study. The elite of the organisations involved support the region and feel that they will have more of a change in tasks than a disappearance. The region question is therefore not a question that can be characterised by the different elites competing with each other. There are no reforms that therefore compete with the regional reform. There is, therefore, no alternative narrative to regional cross-sectional cooperation. On the other hand, alternatives such as the status quo are not a realistic possibility either, since most of those in power have committed themselves to the regional reform.

Further, the regional reform has never been connected with any symbols of disapproval such as a new regional building costing say £20 million. What happens on other political stages also influences the process in a particular way. This influence functions both as an example and as a threat. Examples of the activities taking place on these stages are 'limitless health care' within the county council, regionally funded structure projects within the county administrative boards of West Sweden, and a local authority work organisation busy marketing West Sweden in Europe/Brussels.

In sum, these contextual factors have resulted in the regional question having won everyone's overall approval and they have been included in long-term strategies concerning the West Sweden region. It is a point of reference for all institutions. In spite of this, the Government has prepared a defence by emphasising that regions are being introduced for a trial period. This is a way of both establishing a form – if one does not meet with resistance – and cancelling the project – if one should meet with resistance.

On May 15, 1997, the Parliament decided on the formation of the new region of West Sweden which is comprised of the counties of Göteborg and Bohus, Älvsborg and Skaraborg, but of which the local governments of Habo and Mullsjö are exempt. The new region will commence its activities on January 1, 1998. Göteborg has been proposed as the seat of regional government. The population of the new region is estimated at 1.5 million, which means that West Sweden will be Sweden's second largest region. Stockholm, the capital area, is the largest one.

Simultaneously with this event, the four county councils of the previous system will be amalgamated into one. The new county council has been proposed as the autonomous regional organisation that will deal with the tasks included in the trial activity. This area of activity, i.e. that of a new autonomous and directly elected council and regional organisation will begin on January 1, 1999. In sum, a new institutional organisational structure is consequently in the process of being generated in West Sweden.

In our frame of reference we described reforms as negotiations of symbols, as education, as rhetoric and fiction. We have now contextualised these theoretical concepts in our study and we have shown that they are useful tools in the understanding of the reform process of West Sweden. This paper will suggest that good reform processes imply negotiations between ideas, interests and institutions. Reformers are future-oriented storytellers who write persuasive texts which are read by other people, often in diverse and conflicting ways. *Stories can organise information, transmit understanding, and guide judgment*, thus enabling people to translate impressions of a distant event into a form that allows a listener to grasp its significance. The potential in the reform lies within the addressee's perception of the persuasiveness of the reformers' storytelling.

Persuasive Storytelling About the Reform Process

Many Swedish researchers describe the Swedish public sector as undergoing a reality crisis, consisting of different sorts of crises: economy, efficiency, identity (see for example, Berg and Jonsson 1991). The coexistence of old and new principles creates paradoxes. As a consequence this creates a crisis of imagination. All this has implications for the public sector institutions and their organisational structure, as their tasks are divided between them. In the absence of leading principles that could point to some definitive, univocal answer that would exclude any other, the problem is bound to be disputed and solved 'equivocally': that is, with an answer that is not unique and possible once and for all. *Rhetoric appears forcefully in times of crisis*, for the simple reason that only the lack of directing principle in the settling of questions causes these questions to be relentlessly submitted to controversial answers. And rhetoricians usually appear in times when stable values disappear, when forms break down and new ones appear, coexisting with all the old ones. Their task is, then, to try to *make sense of what is happening* by working out reasoned typologies of structures and finding persuasive imaginations.

In a previous article we have described how our idea about a West Sweden region began to grow (Jensen and Leijon 1996). Our concern was related to the way the ideas were spread, accepted and translated to emerge as a reform. Previous experience of institutional reform work, which was mainly theoretic, was that passive institutional resistance often undermined the reforming process. Things remained as they were, and what resulted was a continuance of investigatory work.

During the past five years we have monitored regional work in West Sweden and we can now see a tendency within reform work which partially refutes previous experience. Institutional resistance does exist as well as sluggishness in the process, but this is not strong enough to undermine the process.

In the introduction we raised a question of whether commissions can create a new institutional order. Our case has demonstrated that the answer is yes. Region as a new mental order is established, and as an administrative mantra, the idea of a region has grown rapidly causing the ideological character to be strengthened. The thoughts surrounding a region transform it into being part of a reform-friendly progressive cultural discourse that has hegemonic tendencies. Therefore, the idea of a West Sweden region has through this consensus *mobilised a power mechanism* in the networks of involved institutions that is now being defined within different organisational structures.

We have pointed out that language plays a key role in establishing these loose networks and in bringing about a possibility of putting them in order. Language makes objective the shared experiences and makes them available to all within the community, thus becoming both the basis and the instrument of the collective stock of knowledge. If a shared vocabulary exists and objectives and values can be translated into one 'language', a variety of different interests can be enrolled in a governing organisational structure. It is through common vocabularies and shared language that loose networks of interests across time and space can be established, and that is, as we see it, the most important role commissionary work can play.

Our analysis is primarily of the *strategic use of language*. We therefore reject the idea that language represents an aspect of reality and we move toward the notion that it functions in various ways that are constitutive of realities. The language of politics is not a neutral medium that conveys ideas. It is rather an *institutionalised structure of meanings* that channels political thought and action in certain directions. Here we have argued that we must attend to the ways symbolic action produces transformation in assumptions, beliefs, practices and affiliations. We have done this by describing 'persuasion about the reform process' as a form. This rhetorical form structures the audience's consciousness and anticipation. The force of an argument is realised when the inferential form articulated in the *symbolic practices* of a social actor enters the concrete historical world populated by rhetorical audiences, marked by *problems and exigencies* – themselves constituted, to some degree, by discourse – and structured by institutions, traditional practices and other constraints.

The consciousness of different actors has thereby been structured by means of their agreement with general concepts regarding the necessity of a region. Thus, the regional discourse tends to reign in the form of an agreement, the conditions of which cannot always be questioned. Furthermore, an imaginary world has thus been created that is experienced as being objective reality.

The rhetoric surrounding a West Sweden region has strengthened the *regional discourse into a closely woven unit*. Therefore, creating a region is not a thing that the actors can simply choose or even deny because now the concept of the region structures what is possible. The investigation and the talk about a West Sweden region are the intellectual power mechanisms that will establish a West Sweden region as a strategic reality and a subject of knowledge. In this way the region becomes the subconscious image that decides the conditions for the field of organisational structures.

If one, for example, reflects on all the books, conferences and political manifestations that contain the word 'region' then it is not difficult to see the *mystifying and subtle elements* in the idea of a West Sweden region. Generally speaking, there is a greater sense of community than is justified. Furthermore, there is an administrative use of language and a number of interesting contradictions in the thought of a region that consists of a group of institutions with a primary goal of making sure that West Sweden is developed as a commercially political unit. What has been achieved at present is perhaps not a genuine form of regionalism – despite the West Swedish flag – but more of a social-economic system or concept for the utilisation of depleted resources. The Swedish debate on the idea of a region has developed into a *rhetoric motor* in a strategy for decentralised political decision-making that is connected to *the art of economic engineering* on the level of social planning.

In sum, to say that a West Sweden region is a strategic construction is to say that a region is created in a process where the region is a product of history and not an independent entity. The West Sweden region is a social construction which is shown in new expressions and it contains a number of varying forces. In this way, one can say that a region is a continuous construction of that which we identify at a particular moment in time.

The implication of a region, in accordance with several other political concepts, is confirmed by history while, at the same time, it is being constituted by it. There is no West Sweden region if it is not defined and codified by means of several organisational structures. In this connection, we have wanted to show that the idea of a *West Sweden region has been constructed with strategic aim and that the reality that it identifies is also used strategically*. Rhetoric can help us to explain this. Persuasion as a means of changing states of mind is shown to be as important in achieving social consensus on policy as in resolving conflicts among experts over technical as well as value issues with public policy implications. A West Sweden region cannot be reduced to an idea, an identity or a reality. That which is reality is rhetoric where presentations and identities are formed and historical conditions founded.

Conclusion

So whatever its form, rhetoric deals with the problematic and the questionable. Manipulation and propaganda proceed as if the problems they were dealing with were solved. Positive or constructive rhetoric exhibits the questions and puts forth arguments for or against the chosen solution. But once uttered, speech enters the service of power. But does this mean that the study of rhetoric simply collapses into a study of power? No, not necessarily. We clearly prefer to chart another course. For us, rhetoric means defining the public sphere itself as an argumentative or a rhetorical field.

If study of political rhetoric merely commits us to consider bombastic language, word tricks and deceptive speech, then we should leave this subject to those who analyse erroneous forms of communication. The practice of political rhetoric is far more than the uses or misuses of language. Political rhetoric is the engagement of motives, principles, thoughts, arguments, an engagement which functions to form attitudes and assist judgment regarding the broad range of civic affairs.

A great deal of the organisational theoretic discourse that presently takes place has become more and more fixated by the contrast between the extent of the demands of cooperation and its actual extent. In this article we have described how these demands have been created. A future question is what impact the demands will actually have on the commercial/industrial political development in West Sweden. A quite striking but proven experience of that which exemplifies the progress of truth is that it looks much greater than it really is. *When you get there there is no there there.* Edelmann (1977) expresses the rhetorical function of political language very well in a subtitle of one of his books: 'Words that Succeed and Policies that Fail'.

Finally, this time it looks as if a reconstruction of the county organisation has resulted successfully in the creation of the West Sweden region. In this chapter we have pointed out that this time the play on words has resulted in something that was unthinkable some ten years ago. But what are the linguistics and internal dynamics that await the symbolic manifestation of the regional organisation? Most of these internal dynamics have not been included in the development which has had an important part in this play on words. Godot is waiting in the wings and will definitely be on stage in 1998 – but that part of the play was not written by Beckett.

References

Baier, V., March, J., and Sætren, H. (1986) 'Implementation and ambiguity.' *Scandinavian Journal of Management*, 179-212.

Beiner, R. (1983) *Political Judgment*. London: Methuen & Co Ltd.

Berg, P.-O. and Jonsson, C. (1991) *Strategisk ledning på politiska marknader*. Lund: Studentlitteratur.

Berger, P. and Luckmann, T. (1967) *The Social Construction of Reality. A Treatise in the Sociology of Knowledge*. New York: Doubleday.

Czarniawska-Joerges, B. (1990) 'Kommunerna i reformernas sagoland.' In N. Brunsson and J.P. Olsen (eds) *Makten att reformera*. Stockholm: Carlssons, 216-231. Published in English as *The reforming organisation*. London: Routledge, 1993.

Edelmann, M. (1964) *The Symbolic Uses of Politics*. Urbana: University of Illinois Press.

Edelmann, M. (1977) *Political Language. Words that Succeed and Policies that Fail*. Chicago: University of Chicago Press.

Jensen, C. and Leijon, S. (1994) 'The West Sweden Region – An Idea Searching for a (Re)form.' In J. Alden and P. Boland (eds) *Regional Development Strategies – A European Perspective*. London: Jessica Kingsley Publishers, 14-37.

March, J. and Olsen, J.P. (1983) 'Organizing political life: what administrative reorganisation tells us about government.' *The American Political Review 77*, 281-296.

March, J., and Olsen, J.P. (1989) *Rediscovering Institutions: The Organisational Basis of Politics*. New York: Free Press.

Perelman, C. (1982) *The Realm of Rhetoric*. Notre Dame, IN: University of Notre Dame Press.

Shotter, J. (1993) *Conversational Realities. Construction Life through Language*. London: Sage.

SOU (1992) *Västsverige – region i utveckling*. 66. Stockholm: Allmänna förlaget.

SOU (1995) *Regional framtid. Regionberedningens slutbetänkande*. 27. Stockholm: Allmänna förlaget.

Vickers, G., (1965) *The Art of Judgment. A Study of Policy Making*. London: Chapman Hall.

PART IV

REGIONAL DEVELOPMENT AND MULTI-LEVEL GOVERNANCE

Over the last few decades, the role of traditional central government regional subsidy programmes has been gradually replaced by bottom-up development bodies and initiatives. The changing structure of the delivery and implementation of regional policy throughout Europe has been assisted and encouraged by the increasing importance of the European Union (EU) system of governance, with the structural funding programmes critical in this process. This section identifies the development of the governance structures in a variety of countries and uses several applicable theories to explain the emerging pattern of change towards a multi-level system of governance.

It appears that, since the inception of the European Regional Development Fund, (ERDF), the role of the European Commission has become increasingly important in the development of the regions within the Objective areas. However, it can be seen that the impact of the Commission's method of stimulating regional development through bottom-up initiatives and programmes has not only affected the assigned areas but also has had direct implications for national regional policy developments throughout the EU. Alongside these developments within the EU there are examples where a similar process of change can be identified outside the European system and thus it may be important to consider where the process of change originates. In other words, has the change towards bottom-up regional policy been brought about by the desire of national governments to empower the regional agents and reduce their own direct role in regional development, and/or has the European model been accepted elsewhere as the most effective and efficient method of regional development?

The relationship between different tiers of Government may be studied from a number of different perspectives. On the *European Level* the so called 'multi-level governance' approach proposes that 'decision-making competencies are shared by actors at different levels rather than monopolised by state executives', and that it is therefore necessary to adopt an 'actor-centred' approach that specifies the role of particular individuals and institutions in the decision making process (Marks *et al.* 1996, p.346).

On the *National Level* parallel arguments can be found in the 'Power-Dependence' approach which was developed to aid understanding of the relationship between central government and sub-central public bodies (Rhodes 1988). Both approaches identify the mutual dependence between different tiers of government based on their respective control of resources which are important for the development and implementation of public policy. The 'policy network' approach is one which adds weight to the debates on 'multi-level governance' and 'power dependence' as it also recognises the importance of a multitude of actors exchanging information, expertise and other resources at both the national and European levels.

At a *Regional Level* the explanation and debate on the approaches which can, and are implemented, is continued. Analyses of the recent suggestions for change in the electoral system evokes the debate that democratic principles and regional government are not necessarily a more beneficial system for the effectiveness and efficiency of regional policy but that the current agents may in fact be superior.

The chapters in this section develop the debates and give a thorough explanation of policy implementation at a number of levels. In Chapter 9, Oddbjørn Bukve evaluates Norwegian regional policy, noting the change from a system where there was a high degree of autonomy for the political bodies at the county level to one where governance rather than government has become increasingly evident. In the course of one year, the county municipalities turned on the issue of managing regional policy incentives, and a political government model was replaced by a regional development agency at 'arms-length' from political control. Further, there was an institutional line of change in the mid 1990s with county municipalities now play a strategic rather than operational role. This chapter notes that within the 'free counties' in Norway there has been a move to cooperation and joint planning, whereas in those areas where there are county municipalities historic political power configurations do not yet allow for the conditions for partnership working.

In Chapter 10, Henrik Halkier considers the consequences of recent radical change from a highly centralised Danish regional policy towards regional governance and empowerment. The result has been an increase in the capacity of the regions to pursue their own agenda with regard to economic development. Analysis of the changing patterns of resource dependency between the various tiers of government, based on the theoretical constructs of policy analysis, network theory and the new institutionalism, allows the author to determine the new overall pattern and consider the consequences on the Danish regions' prioritisation of economic development policies.

Finally, in Chapter 11 Ruth Downes highlights the numerous agencies involved in regional development in Austria and the informal nature of the responsibility for regional policy. This system appears to work through many informal ties between the actors involved, and continued to do so after Austria entered the European Union. Indeed, the only institutional structural change after joining was the regional management system, put in place to help administer the funds on the regional level. The chapter catalogues how the particularly strong consensus base to decision making, the lack of change in the institutional structure, and the overall emphasis in the Austrian system on the EU policy approach has made the partnership principle of funding more easily fulfilled in this economy. The chapter, however, also adds that vertical and horizontal cooperation remains constrained by political rivalry and administrative 'turf wars' - a situation not unique to Austria.

References

Marks, G., Hooghe, L. and Kermit, B. (1996) 'European integration from the 1980s: state-centric v. multi-level governance.' *Journal of Common Market Studies 34*, 3, 341-78.

Rhodes, R.A.W. (1988) *Beyond Westminster and Whitehall - The Sub-central Governments of Britain*. London: Unwin Hyman.

9 Towards the End of a Norwegian Regional Policy Model?

ODDBJØRN BUKVE

Introduction

From 1977, county municipalities in Norway had responsibility for a large proportion of business support measures in regional policy. Politically, the decisions were controlled by the county's standing committee on industry. The report from the Steine Committee (Steine 1995), which was presented in 1995, concluded that the county municipalities no longer would have this responsibility. Instead, the commission recommended the establishment of regional agencies within the Norwegian Industrial and Regional Development Fund (SND). SND is a state body connected to the Ministry of Industry and Energy.

In many county municipalities, this was seen as a serious threat to their influence on regional policy, leading to a weakening of the whole county-municipal institution. The immediate reaction from the counties was a mobilisation against the proposal. Most county municipalities protested against the Steine Committee in their consultation statements, whereas other consultation bodies on the whole supported the proposal.

The county of Nord-Trøndelag opted for another strategy, by negotiating an agreement with SND. A separate SND agency would be established in the county, but the county municipality had the right to select a management board. The agreement implied that the regional agency was given wide powers in relation to the main SND office in Oslo. A decisive factor for the Nord-Trøndelag initiative was admittedly the fear that the two Trøndelag counties would be placed under a joint SND agency in Trondheim, thus leading to the loss of their own office.

The Minister for Industry and Energy, Mr Jens Stoltenberg, quickly perceived the Nord-Trøndelag model as a possible political compromise. The government chose this model, but kept open the geographical area for regional SND agencies. Consequently, a process was started in which a number of county municipalities lost no time in establishing their own agreements with SND in terms of regional agencies based on the Nord-Trøndelag model. The motivation was to avoid the worst alternative: that the county would be subordinated to a SND agency comprising several counties, thus losing the local expertise in addition to the political responsibility. In the course of one year, the county municipalities therefore reversed completely over the issue of managing regional policy incentives. A political government model was replaced by a regional development agency at arm's length from political control. The Norwegian model for regional policy, as we have known it for the past 20 years, has become history.

Problems and Perspectives

The focal point of this chapter is the changing role of the county municipality in regional policy. In the first part, the main features in the development of Norwegian regional policy are discussed. Then the models for regional governance and regional policy in some European countries are looked at briefly, in order to put the Norwegian model in perspective. The key argument is that Norway has been characterised by a strong role for elected bodies at the county level in the implementation of regional policy. In the first place, the county municipalities have had the responsibility for planning processes at the regional level. In the second place, the county municipalities have been in charge of a number of business support policies, both business-oriented incentives as well as support to infrastructure development.

The last part of the chapter focuses on the recent transformation of the organisation of regional policy. It begins with a description of the institutional changes, and continues with a discussion of why the Norwegian model has come under pressure? Why have new ways of organising been launched, and why are they gaining ground? In the last part of the chapter, this question is discussed from various angles, viewing it alternatively as an organisational or functional problem, as a result of conflicts of interest, and lastly as a result of a government level losing its legitimacy.

The Concept of Regional Policy

It is hardly possible to give an unequivocal definition of regional policy. From an analytical point of view, it may be useful to view regional policy as the spatial aspect of all public policy, whether it is integrated in an intended regional policy or not. The advantage of such a wide concept lies, above all, in the fact that it can be applied to evaluate the strength of the intended regional policy. This understanding of regional policy as a sum of sector policies is in Norway frequently referred to as the 'big' regional policy, whereas the intended regional policy is referred to as the 'small' regional policy. The intended regional policy may in next turn be understood as regional planning, as top-down spatial distribution policy, as well as a bottom-up regional policy giving responsibility and scope of action to regional actors.

In this chapter, there is a concentration on the two last meanings of the concept, particularly on the changes in regional policy from a top-down policy to a bottom-up approach.

The Norwegian Model in a Comparative Perspective

The Development of the Norwegian Model

Norwegian regional policy has a history prior to the county municipality. In the first 15 years after World War II, regional policy was primarily a modernisation policy. In the 1960s, however, the strong urbanisation and depopulation of the rural areas became considered as a problem. The challenge was to plan in such a way that a larger share of the growth could be localised outside the central urban areas. In this case we can talk about a redistributive policy. The growth was to be redistributed by means of compensation for particular disadvantages of a localisation in peripheral areas.

DU (the Norwegian Regional Development Fund) was established in 1961. Business loans, together with support for training and increased mobility of labour, were among the policies implemented in the first period. In 1965, the Labour Government pointed out nine growth centres in rural areas. The objective was to prevent centralisation by building attractive centres in the rural areas. But the non-socialist government which came to power after the general election in the same year, perceived the growth centre policy as a centralisation policy. The new government watered down the growth centre idea by launching smaller development areas as a supplementary strategy. The growth centres, however, were allowed to keep their status. In 1968, SIVA (the Norwegian Industrial Development Estate) was established to develop the infrastructure in the new growth centres. New taxation laws provided openings for tax-free allocations for investments in the rural areas.

The policy measures of DU were substantially strengthened through the graded investment grants from 1971. The grading system gave the highest grants to the most peripheral municipalities. The impact area of peripheral development incentives now comprised more than 300 municipalities, that is, more than two thirds of all the municipalities in the country, and an even larger share of the land area. Maximum investment grant was initially 35 per cent, later 40 per cent (limited to the county of Finnmark and the northern part of the county of Troms). Other new policies in the 1970s included regional transport grants, as well as grants to the municipalities for development of infrastructure in low-industry areas.

It was in this period of decentralisation initiatives that the county municipality was established as an independent political level. The county planning, which was initiated in 1973 under the auspices of the county governor, was now transferred to the new government institution. The development department of the county governor, which was in charge of regional policy, was also transferred to the county municipalities. The county municipalities, therefore, had control over both business-oriented policy measures and grants for infrastructure development. Consequently, they controlled both regional planning and implementation of regional policy.

After 1980, a fundamental reorientation in regional policy took place. Redistribution was to be replaced by innovation; a top-down strategy by a bottom-up strategy. New policies were introduced. In 1983-84, the DU grants for capital investments were supplemented with grants for immaterial investments. This concept covered marketing and product development, as well as seed capital for planning of new businesses. Flexible guidelines as to which businesses were to be given priority were introduced, instead of limiting the policy measures to certain industries.

However, at the same time as these changes took place, the actual value of the DU grants decreased from 1977.

Another part of the innovation strategy was a systematic effort to strengthen industrial development initiatives at the municipal level (Bukve 1994). A number of centrally supported pilot projects were initiated, and from 1987 the national authorities gave grants to municipal development funds. These funds were small, and they were primarily meant to help small businesses through their first phase of business development.

The transition towards innovation policy was linked to an idea that Norway was heading for a period of comprehensive changes in the industrial structure, where one could discern the contours of the emerging knowledge society. Innovation had to be linked to increased knowledge and technological development. This line of thought formed the basis for a number of initiatives. One group of initiatives were special entrepreneurship campaigns, as well as courses and scholarships for people who wanted to develop their own business. For example, DU made special efforts to mobilise more women to set up new businesses. A second group of initiatives dealt with programmes for technological development aimed at small and medium-sized businesses. With research councils, ministries, DU, and the Industrial Fund as initiators, a number of programmes of this type were launched in the course of a few years. Arbo (1993) mentions some 20 programmes of this kind. A third group had to do with development of the knowledge infrastructure at the regional level. Supported by the Ministry of Local Government and Labour, a system of regional research foundations and 'knowledge centres' was established. Similarly, the national counselling service for industry was transferred to the county municipalities from 1988.

Throughout this period the county municipalities had responsibility or co-responsibility for a large part of regional policy. Glosvik (1991) has divided the tasks into four. The first task is regional planning. The situation in the 1980s was that the county planning was receiving less attention as an instrument in regional policy. On the other hand, most counties introduced strategic industrial planning as a new planning form around 1990.

The second task is management of a wide range of policy measures. The biggest group is business-oriented policy measures through DU. Around 1990, the county municipalities had decision responsibility for 90 per cent of the cases and 60 per cent of the total grants from DU.

From 1991 a so-called 'local loss responsibility' was introduced, that is, the county municipalities themselves had to carry the economic loss in case of failed projects. Furthermore, the county municipalities allocated means for infrastructure development. At the same time, the development towards more industrially neutral policy measures was carried on, and the county municipalities got more freedom to formulate objectives for their regional-political efforts. From 1993 a system of 'Management by Objectives' has been introduced, and a share of the total grants to each county is allocated on the basis of former results.

The third task is counselling for business and municipalities. Business advice is dealt with by special bodies. These bodies are usually organised as limited companies, foundations, or county-municipal firms. Guidance for the municipalities is particularly aimed at giving advice to municipal development officers.

The fourth task is stimulating bottom-up initiatives. According to Glosvik, this task is about mobilisation and arena building. This task is likely to be organised through projects or programme efforts. In 1992, the total grants over the budget of the Ministry of Local Government and Labour amounted to NOK 58 million. Of this NOK 36 million was managed by the county municipalities which supported 201 projects in all this year (Bukve 1994). The average grant, then, was approx. NOK 180,000, indicating that most projects were small. Important project purposes were local mobilisation and establishment projects, community development, co-operation between schools and industry, network building, strategic industrial planning, and regional industrial projects.

When the unemployment rate rose towards the end of the 1980s, unemployment became just as high in central areas as in the rural areas. The need arose for a general innovation policy aiming at innovation and industrial development in all types of regions. In a new Parliamentary white paper (St. meld. nr. 33 1992-93) it was stated that the task was to draw up an overall regional policy to develop viable regions in all parts of the country. The role of the big cities as knowledge and innovation centres was highlighted. Policies for grants to small and medium-sized businesses would from now on apply to the whole country. Restructuring grants, previously limited to the peripheral regions, could also be used everywhere. The number of municipalities eligible for rural development schemes was reduced. DU was shut down and, with other industrial banks and funds, it became a part of SND (the Industrial and Regional Development Fund) from 1993. Whereas DU, for the whole time since its establishment, had been placed under the Ministry of Local Government and Labour, the new SND became a body under the Ministry of Industry and Energy.

The responsibility for regional policy remained in the Ministry of Local Government and Labour. Since the business-oriented policies were transferred to the Ministry of Industry and Energy, this department has emphasised the development of a more strategic, policy-designing role. The guidelines for the county municipalities' role in regional policy have been changed as well. From 1995, the work has been organised around a programme effort, not around the administration of a range of policy incentive schemes. In doing this, the Ministry wanted to reduce the number of minor projects which were not part of a strategic effort.

Later on, the central role of the county municipalities in regional policy was met with criticism. In 1995, the Steine Committee proposed that the county municipalities were no longer to have the regional responsibility for the SND money. Regional SND agencies have been established. The latest white paper on regional policy, which was presented in March, 1997, suggests a further concentration on policy formulation and programme management as the role of the county municipalities. The county municipalities are not to allocate grants, but instead have a strategic co-ordination role through the work with so-called regional development programmes.

Two different lines of change can be distinguished in the development of Norwegian regional policy: from a top-down policy to a bottom-up approach, and with regard to the institutional dimension. From the 1970s to the mid-1990s, county municipalities had an important role in the implementation of regional policy. During the latter years, however, allocation of regional policy grants again has become a responsibility for regional state agencies, while the county municipalities are intended to play a strategic role through regional development programmes.

Norway from a Comparative European Perspective

Sharpe (1993) points out that the rise of a new government level between national and local government is a common feature of the western European countries. He uses the term 'meso level' to characterise this new element in government. A fully developed meso level is characterised as being an independent political level with democratically elected bodies and a separate administration.

In Norway, the most significant changes are linked to the establishment in 1975 of the county municipality, with a popularly elected county council and a separate administration. However, it is not in the establishment of the county institution itself that we can talk about a specific Norwegian model. The strengthening of the meso level is a general phenomenon, and the form it has taken in Norway can be understood as typical of a northern-European model for regional government (Sharpe 1993). County councils constitute the democratically elected regional level in these countries. Only when going into the organisation of regional policy can the contours of a distinctive Norwegian model be seen emerging.

During the years after the war, the regional level obtained a planning role for economic development. Sharpe considers regional planning as 'an extremely important phase' in the development of the meso. A main task for regional planning was the spatial management of economic growth. The 'crisis of the orthodoxy' in regional planning during the 1970s (Hudson and Lewis 1982) was caused by the fact that there no longer any growth to manage. Regional planning was not a suitable instrument for solving the new problems. The problems for regional planning also affected regional policy strategies in more general terms. When the basic problem no longer is to manage and distribute wealth, but rather to create wealth, policies and strategies are submitted to new tests. The years around 1980 were marked by a reformulation of regional policy. National redistribution policy lost ground. The development moved in two directions which could be perceived both as complementary and contradictory. One direction is about phasing down regional policy *qua* public policy, leaving more of the development to market forces. The United Kingdom under Thatcher has been the most typical example of this strategy. The second strategy deals with replacing a top-down redistribution policy with a bottom-up development policy, giving regions and local communities more responsibility for creating their own development (Stöhr 1990). Policies and incentives have been reorganised with this in mind in many of the European countries, more or less mixed with increased market orientation.

Regional policy is increasingly formed and implemented through regional development bodies outside of traditional government - frequently called RDAs (Regional Development Agencies). Halkier and Danson (1996) look upon the rise of such agencies as an integrated part of the development from a traditional top-down regional policy to the present bottom-up policy. Whereas the top-down policy was oriented towards redistribution, the bottom-up policy is oriented towards self-development and increasing regional competitiveness.

Top-down policy was usually organised within the framework of national ministries or sub-bodies of the national government. Each body was in charge of a limited set of policies. The control of the policy measures in other words was fragmented. Typical policy measures are capital allocations and regulations. On the other hand, bottom-up policy is organised at the regional level, typically through a quasi-autonomous agency which deals with a wide set of policy measures: venture capital, guidance, training, and infrastructure.

One aspect which must be highlighted is the increasing significance that the regional policy of the EU has had for the member countries of the European Union. An ever greater share of regional policy means are being channelled through the EU. In this way programmes and working methods also becoming more homogeneous. Even if historical traditions affect the way in which the various countries adapt to the regional policy of the EU, it becomes increasingly possible to contrast the Norwegian model for regional policy with a common EU model - with some variations.

In the planning, organisation and implementation of the EU programmes, partnership is a key factor. The very concept of partnership is not unambiguous. On the one hand, it is used as a term for co-operation between the EU level, the national level, and lower government levels in the planning and implementation of regional policy. On the other hand, it is used as a term for co-operation between public bodies, private industry, and various types of organisations. The concept is thus flexible enough to encompass many different types of networks and co-operation. Still, it points towards a change in which government through hierarchic authority is replaced by management through mutual adaptation and co-ordination.

The Place of the Meso Level in Regional Policy - Norway versus Europe

The question of the place of the meso level in regional policy is actually twofold. First, it applies to what impact the regional level has on the formulation of regional policy. Second, it has to do with the role played by the regions in the implementation of regional policy.

With regard to the former, some people would say that we are heading towards a Europe of regions. The nation state is about to lose ground, it is said, and in the future Europe dynamic regions will play a key role. At best, this is a qualified truth. In the first place, it is impossible to talk about a uniform regional system in Europe. The regions vary in terms of size, responsibilities, in political and financial autonomy. In the second place, the nation states are active players in forming the place of the regions in the formulation of policy. There is much variation as to how much the nations involve the regional level in relation to the EU level.

However, there can be little doubt that the changes in regional policy strategies have given the European regions a broader place in the initiation and implementation of programmes within the area. The implementation responsibility has been moved from national authorities to regional and local partnership arrangements of various kinds. Consequently, the regions are placed in a network where there is co-operation, on the one hand, with the national level and the EU bodies and, on the other hand, with regional industry, organisations and local communities. This is an important element in the strengthening of the meso which has taken place.

In many ways Norway is a pioneer in this type of process. As early as the mid-seventies, Norway developed a system in which the county municipalities were to have important responsibilities for regional policy, through county planning and administration of a broad range of incentives. The extensions of the county-municipal responsibility which have taken place after 1975 confirm this picture. But the Norwegian model is still special, because so much emphasis has been laid on the county municipalities' political control over regional policy. Political bodies in the county municipality have had ultimate responsibility for county planning and decisions on the use of incentives in regional policy. This differs from the EU, where partnership bodies of various kinds have a far more significant role. The outstanding feature of the Norwegian model is, therefore, neither the increased strength of the regional level, nor any particular choice of strategies. The particular features of the Norwegian model lie in the organisational forms and the emphasis on political control at the regional level.

The Transformation of the Model

Context: The Weakening Periphery Dimension

Towards the late 1980s, the situation concerning the regional problem was once more about to change. In the early part of this decade, the reorganisation of regional policy from a redistributive to a development policy was the most important issue. The main focus in regional policy, however, was still on the difficulties in the rural periphery. The new problem towards the late 1980s was a marked rise in the unemployment rate in urban areas. Structural difficulties in industry now became commonplace. In the regional report of 1989 (St.meld.nr.29 1988-89) this problem is not touched upon. Industrial development was discussed as an issue for the rural periphery.

Four years later this had changed dramatically. According to the regional report of 1993, entitled 'City and land hand in hand - on regional development' (St.meld.nr.33 1992-93), cities were to be developed as motors of the economy. Education, research, and transport systems came into focus for the urban-oriented regional policy. At the same time openings were made for investment grants to small and medium-sized businesses in urban areas also. Thus, there has been a shift of balance in regional policy from a focus on peripheral areas to a broader consideration of regional development in different kind of regions.

The Establishment of SND

In 1992 it was decided to change the organisation of the business support system through the closure of DU and its incorporation into the new Industrial and Regional Development Fund (SND). The Industrial Fund, Small-businesses Fund, and the Industrial Bank were also incorporated into the SND. The reorganisation of the business support apparatus had been an approved strategy for the Labour Party since its 1985 manifesto. Then the party wanted the responsibility for business-oriented regional policies to be transferred from the Ministry of Local Government and Labour to a new and extended Ministry of Industry and Energy (Skrøver Aaraas 1993). The argument behind this was to use the experiences from DU to develop new small businesses in regions marked by major restructuring needs. When the Labour Party came to power in the spring of 1986, the question came on the public agenda for the very first time. The Minister for Local Government and Labour changed his mind on this matter, however, after the regional policy section of the Ministry of Local Government and Labour had applied strong pressure on him. The matter was then put on ice.

In 1988, a study by Statconsult changed the perspective of the discussion by pointing to grey zones between the various industrial funds and the need for co-ordination between them. In the so-called Berge Committee, an internal working group within the Labour Party/TUC which presented its report in March 1991, this perspective on the reorganisation process was adopted. In the spring of 1991, a parliamentary bill on the matter was announced in the revised national budget.

In the consultation phase there was an intense tug-of-war between the Ministry of Local Government and Labour and the Ministry of Industry and Energy. The Labour Party, however, had learnt from its defeat in 1986, and the process was strongly controlled politically. In the final phase the whole case was taken up to cabinet level, and the Prime Minister actively went in for a solution in line with the recommendations from the Berge Committee. In the Norwegian Parliament the Labour Party was supported by the Conservatives. Parliament decided upon the reorganisation in June, 1992, and the merger was effective as from 1st January, 1993.

The decision process in this matter had clear strategic features. It was a matter of defeating the opposition in the Ministry of Local

Government, and it was also important to get the matter settled as quickly as possible before the rural opposition had time to organise a joint reaction. This explains why the government did not wait until the next white paper to launch the reorganisation.

At the same time, the reorganisation meant that SND was left with two regional systems. The nationwide policy measures were to be administered by the regional SND agencies, an organisational construction SND inherited from the Industry Bank. The county municipalities, however, were still to have responsibility for the periphery-oriented policy measures. The issue of organisation at the regional level was an unclarified question after the parliamentary resolution of 1992. In the Berge group, the TUC had advocated an organisation where the county municipalities had no responsibility, whereas the Labour Party was positively disposed towards the county municipalities as management bodies. In the consultation round the opinions diverged significantly. Most county municipalities were in favour of co-ordinating the policy measures, but thought they themselves should have the regional responsibility for the entire SND range of policy measures.

It was implied that the question of regional organisation of SND would be reintroduced and, in December 1994, the Ministry of Local Government and Labour and the Ministry of Industry and Energy appointed a new working group, the so-called Steine Committee, to consider this. According to the mandate, the Committee was to present alternative models for organising the regional apparatus of the SND. The committee majority recommended a model where the county municipality was no longer the regional body of the SND.

The Steine Committee report is a discourse on technical co-ordination. Majority and minority fractions apply the same type of arguments for and against each other's models. The majority refers to the separate regional agency model as marked by a clear distinction between SND and the responsibilities of the county municipalities, and a simplification for the clients when business support measures are co-ordinated in the regional agencies. The county-municipality model, on the other hand, implies a twofold and vague responsibility for business support.

The minority in the committee looks upon the separate agency model as marked by an unfavourable division between development and planning tasks, and in practice two parallel systems, whereas the county-municipality model takes care of the link between planning and implementation of policy measures. Behind this lies, in reality, the question whether it is the policy guidelines from the Ministry of Industry and Energy or the concerns of the Ministry of Local Government and Labour which are to carry most weight when policies are to be implemented.

'Free county' Experiments and Regional Development Programmes

The initiating and developing role on the part of the county municipality in regional policy - the role as a regional development actor, was linked particularly to the many projects the county municipalities had going. However, these projects were fairly small, and it is hard to detect tendencies in what the money had been used for. By and large, the local actors and the county municipalities seemed to adapt to the policy signals given in the budget bills of the Ministry of Local Government and Labour. Grant maximisation strategies seemed to dominate, more than creativeness and innovation.

The need for improving innovative capacity at the regional level began to be felt. For the Ministry of Local Government and Labour there were two sources of inspiration in this work. The first source was the so-called 'free county' experiment, the second was the EU way of doing programme work connected with the activities of the Structural Funds.

Projects with 'free municipalities' and 'free counties' were launched in 1986. The county municipalities of Finnmark, Nordland, Nord-Trøndelag, and Aust-Agder obtained status as free counties. The free county municipalities got control over policy measures for regional and labour-market policies in a lump sum. Furthermore, co-operation was established between the county municipality and the national services in the county (Amdam 1996). This applied to the services of agriculture, fisheries, and labour market. The project period was terminated in 1991, but on account of two prolongations, the projects in the counties of Nordland and Aust-Agder kept going until the end of 1995.

The freedom to use the lump sum money was limited, because the national regulations on the whole would apply as before. Besides, the new means that the free counties were given, so-called rural-development grants, were quickly turned into a general grant that other counties could benefit from also. It is not the experiments with new forms of incentives that have been important in the free counties. It is at the organisational level that the most important changes have taken place. Amdam (1996), who has assessed the free county projects in Nordland and Aust-Agder, sums up in the following way:

> Perhaps the biggest improvement lies in the fact that the free county participants have developed a joint planning which works .... Close partnerships have been developed between the county municipality and the national services in the free counties. There is one challenge area in particular that I would have liked the free county projects to have further developed and obtained experience with; partnership and networks between private and public actors. (Amdam 1996, p.10f.)

The free county projects changed in character from being experiments with new incentives to new types of interaction at the county level. The 'free counties' developed some of the co-operation which was never achieved through county planning. It must be added that all counties have experienced a development of a certain amount of co-operation between the agricultural offices in the county and the county municipalities, linked to co-operation on the allocation of rural development grants. The finances for such grants are allocated from the budget of the Ministry of Agriculture, but they are to be jointly managed by the agriculture sector and the county municipalities.

A programme organisation of industrial development in the counties was introduced in 1995. From that year, the Ministry of Local Government and Labour reorganised its policy programmes. Under the heading 'regional programmes for industrial development', three categories of measures are included. These are investments in physical infrastructure, in knowledge-oriented infrastructure, and industrial development through major regional projects of initiatives and co-operation. For these areas the county municipalities are to draw up programme documents as a basis for the use of the funds. The Ministry must approve the programmes. The programme work is clearly inspired by the SPD work in the EU. For 1995 and 1996, the programme work did not include the business-oriented incentives. However, from 1997 an opening was made for the programmes to include business-oriented measures corresponding to 20 per cent of the total SND means in the region.

The County Municipalities Under Pressure

A final question concerns how the changes in the role of the county municipalities in regional policy can be explained. This will be discussed on the basis of functional perspectives, strategic perspectives, and explanations with the emphasis on legitimacy.

Functional Perspectives

A functional perspective on the role of the county municipalities in regional policy will have its basis in the fact that this role satisfies certain functional demands on the political system. In this perspective one can explain the role of the regions in regional planning with the need to co-ordinate between public sectors. Regional policy and regional planning may be looked upon as mechanisms for co-ordination in a specialised, function-divided organisation. The functional division of work still exists, but, in addition, a generalist, cross-sectoral administration (Fesler 1949) is introduced to co-ordinate between the functional policy sectors within an area.

In the functional perspective one can see regional administration of industrial policy as a way of reducing overload at the national level, and as a strategy for adapting the implementation of policies to local needs. The assumption is that the regional bodies have greater knowledge of local problems.

Evaluations of county planning are critical to the way this planning has met the tasks of co-ordination. In a number of countries regional planning has been discontinued because it was perceived as of little relevance to solving the problems of growth. In Norway county planning has held its ground in spite of these criticisms. This may be an indication that regional co-ordination in Norway is not only a matter of a genuine functional demand, but that co-ordination has a particularly important role on the rhetorical level. Co-ordination is considered important because it is associated with rationality and functionality.

In the past 20 years, regional policy has changed from policies for redistribution to policies for development, and from resource-oriented strategies to market-oriented strategies. Admittedly, there have been conflicts concerning some elements in the adjustments, but by and large they have taken place without major conflicts. They have been presented as - and perceived as - functional adaptations to changes in the environment.

One exception, however, was the organisation of the regional apparatus of the SND. In the functional perspective regional decentralisation can be understood as a way to reduce overload in central bodies and as an adaptation of policy implementation to local needs. However, these points are not underlined by the majority in the Steine Committee in their argument for a separate regional apparatus of the SND. The need for reducing overload, to be sure, is recognised by supporting the establishment of separate SND agencies. It is the minority in the committee, however, which emphasises the adaptation of national policy implementation to regional plans and target areas.

The functionality highlighted by the Steine committee majority is about simplification for the clients. Support is a commodity which it should be easy for the businesses to shop for. This argument may seem credible. On the other hand, it has weaknesses because it fails to discuss the relationship between objectives, policies and organisation. In other words, the Steine Committee avoids discussing in relation to what objectives the policies and organisational forms are to be functional. In the evaluation of Norwegian regional policy by Mønnesland, Hervik and Dale (1993), this problem has been explicitly underlined:

> Generally, one can maintain that the more objectives a single policy affects, the greater the need is to co-ordinate the policy measures to one and the same institution. If the policy affects only one objective, there may be less reasons for co-ordination. SND is obviously an institution which will be in accordance with the main principle that whenever there is a case of many policy measures concerning industrial development as one of the objectives, there exists a need for co-ordination. Nevertheless, it is still important

> that also the other purpose, aiming at development of the periphery, is taken care of in this co-ordination body. Otherwise co-ordination will easily mean that an earlier objective is not taken care of, and even if it can solve the co-ordination for the remaining objective, this is not the type of co-ordination that planning theory advocates. (p.139)

These kind of deliberations about the relationship between general industrial policy and peripheral development are not discussed by the Steine Committee. In this case the functional language seems to cover the underlying problem issues. Can the power perspective, then, tell us more about the pressure on the position of the county municipalities in regional policy?

Strategic Perspectives

The problem of analysing the power struggles in public policy is that they seldom leave verbal traces. The reason is that they frequently form part of complicated processes between the use of power and persuasion. March and Olsen thus write that:

> Democratic procedures of discourse seek systematically to subordinate authenticity in the expression of personal feelings, intentions and motives to a ritualized politeness that mimics a community of shared commitments, values and affection. The hypocrisy is not a flaw but a gamble that sentiments can be shaped by conventions of expression. (March and Olsen 1995, p.85)

The discourse linked to conflict between interests and values is most legitimate in political bodies, but it does not contain the same degree of legitimacy when it comes to implementation or choice of alternatives to attain objectives agreed upon. In such cases possible power struggles will be camouflaged by a functional discourse.

There are two types of power struggles which seem to be central in the discussion of role of the county municipality in regional policy. The first is linked to the conflict between the industrial and the periphery policy segments, concerning the control of policies and institutions for regional development. The second is linked to a political conflict between parties which to a varying degree prefer a decentralised development of society.

In the 1960s, a periphery policy segment started to break away from the industrial segment in Norwegian government. These two segments have developed in highly different ways. In the early post war years, the industrial segment was oriented towards the development of big industry based on the country's own raw-material resources. From the 1960s, this segment has to a larger degree concentrated on the development of knowledge industries based on technological research and innovation (Wicken 1993). Tore Grønlie (1993) has shown that the industrial activism of the state from the late 1950s was linked to an active power centre of top civil servants in a circle around the minister. He refers to a ministry of two cultures, one traditional management culture and one activist culture on the side of the formal structures. This activist culture had its connections to big industry, not to the many small and medium-sized businesses. The Ministry of Industry and Energy throughout the whole period has been marked by a close link to the large enterprises.

The periphery policy segment from the start was linked to another culture. It was connected to the Ministry of Local Government and Labour, and it has developed a working method of good contacts with clients all over the country. In this segment casework and detailed administration has been more important than in the general industrial policy.

The question of a co-ordination of industrial policy and rural development policy first arose under the Conservative Government in the early 1980s. But the Minister for Local Government and Labour opposed any changes. In the next instance it was the Labour Party which took up the thread, which has been mentioned already. The timing was probably not a coincidence. With the strength the periphery policy segment had attained in the 1970s, there simply had to be a reaction on the part of the function-based sectors which felt their rationale weakened.

The discourse on co-ordination has been marked by functional arguments, as shown in the discussion above of the Steine Committee. However, it is evident that the type of co-ordination chosen will have institutional impacts, and civil servants on either side have mobilised for certain solutions. Thus the civil servants in the Ministry of Local Government and Labour had their arguments heard around 1985-86, but were caught off their guard in the next round. For the Ministry of Industry and Energy, the organisations in industry have been their chief supporters. Both LO (the Norwegian TUC) and NHO (the Norwegian Federation of Businesses and Industry) have mobilised for a co-ordination of the industrial policy under the Ministry of Industry and Energy. LO played an important role when the Labour Party in 1990 went for a united SND instead of a separate peripheral development body.

Those county municipalities which had control over regional policy measures have all supported separate arrangements for the periphery development policy. Such arrangements, however, have not been equally important to county municipalities which previously did not have control over any industrial policy measures. What may be lost is relevant for these standpoints.

Changes in the conflict pattern between political parties have made it easier for the industrial policy segment to strengthen its influence. The centre parties and the Socialist Left Party may be considered more in favour of decentralisation than Labour and the Conservatives. After the EU referendum in the early 1970s, these parties made good progress, and the Labour Party had to meet them high up in their own half. This is a key explanation for the decentralist upswing in the 1970s.

However, the Labour Party has always had to balance the rural wing of the party and those who were linked to cities and big industry. Towards the late 1980s, when the political opposition was so divided that they were incapable of forming a competing government alternative, this also changed the Labour Party's working conditions. The party could find solutions alternatively with the Conservative Party and the centre parties. The rural wing of the party lost ground, and the party could accept more easily solutions on the conditions of the industrial policy segment.

Thus, there are elements of both a bureaucratic maximisation and a changed balance of political strength in the increased pressure on the county municipality as actor in regional policy. This explanation, however, is not the only one. How vulnerable an institution is, also depends on how the institution is perceived. This will be dealt with in the final comments.

Leadership and Legitimacy at the Regional Level

The Norwegian county municipalities have enjoyed a greater autonomy than the regional level in other European countries. This autonomy can be linked to their responsibility for important policy areas. It can also be linked to the fact that county politics after 1975 quickly developed into being an independent political arena with little overlapping to the local level. Studies in the early 1980s showed that the activity of county politicians in local politics was decreasing. They did have political experience from the municipal level, but the coupling between offices at both levels of local government seemed to disappear. The county politicians also identified themselves with the county municipality and their party, not the municipality they hailed from. The autonomous role of the county municipality is thus linked to what Page (1991) has referred to as a high degree of legal localism, but a low degree of political localism.

One question which arises is if the county municipalities actually have any strategic alliance partners in the region. This seems not to be the case in relation to the dominant actors in industry. Generally speaking, partnership between public bodies and private industry is based on the fact that in this type of economic system, decisions concerning investment and location belong to the private sphere, whereas the public sphere decides on the rules of the game. It is a question of mutual dependency, with the result than new initiatives have to be triggered off by a mutual adaptation between public rules and incentives on one side and private initiative on the other. This evidently sets limits for public policy as well. The public sector must pay attention to what conditions are needed to make the businesses willing to invest. In this economic system capital thus takes precedence. Moving or withholding investments is a threat to any regime.

The relations of the county municipalities to industry seem to have been client relations to individual businesses rather than partnership. We have seen that the major industrial organisations have been sceptical to the role of the county municipalities in regional policy. The place held by LO and NHO in relation to the county-municipal activities in regional policy has also been marginal. They have played no role whatsoever in county planning. In the bodies where decisions on support to businesses have been made, the politicians have been in the majority, and for a period there were no representatives for industry at all. There has been no regional corporatism with a corresponding influence for the industrial organisations as they have had through the corporative organisation at the national level and the close networks between the Ministry of Industry and Energy and big business.

Neither have the municipalities been strategic partners for the development of the county municipality. By and large the municipalities have feared that the county municipality would develop into a super-municipality, at the same time as they have been concerned that the localisation decisions of the county would not have any adverse effects on themselves. Interaction is developed only to a limited degree.

The relations to the state administration in the regions have been relatively detached as well, even if the free county projects appear to have improved their co-operation. It is rather the case that a strengthened state administration at the regional level has entered into competition with the county municipality in recent years.

Paradoxically, we can conclude that the Norwegian county municipalities have had a strong and autonomous role in regional policy, but that this autonomy has also become their weakness. The county municipalities can to a limited degree govern through hierarchical command lines - through government. In their work with the major service sectors, such as hospitals and secondary schools, they are also to a large degree dependent on central government decisions. Furthermore, in regional policy the task is not hierarchic management, but to set other social forces in motion through interaction. The challenge lies in developing governance more than government. However, there are many indications that the county municipalities do not have the necessary alliance partners and legitimacy in the surrounding landscape (Torsteinsen 1997). Whenever power struggles arise, the county municipality is put under pressure.

Perhaps it is necessary to focus on the county leadership to understand this development. Have county leaders been too much involved in fire fighting in the money-consuming service sectors, more than they have been strategic leaders with the ability to set the course and promote common visions for regional development? Have the ambitions for autonomy turned into a weakness? For the time being, this must stand as an hypothesis rather than a final conclusion. At any rate, there is an element of irony in the fact that the role of Norwegian county municipalities in regional policy is now under pressure, at the same time as Europe puts more and more focus on the regions when looking into the next millennium.

References

Amdam, J. (1996) *Frå samordning til samhandling. Sluttevaluering av frifylkeforsøka i Aust-Agder og Nordland*. Volda: Møreforsking rapport 20.

Arbo, P. (1993) *Teknologi- og kompetanseorientert støtte*. Tromsø: NORUT Samfunnsforskning.

Bukve, O. (1994) *Lokal utviklingspolitikk. Kommunen som næringspolitisk aktør*. Oslo: Samlaget.

Fesler, J. (1949) *Area and Administration*. Alabama: University of Alabama Press.

Glosvik, Ø. (1991) 'Rolleendringar for fylkeskommunen.' In O. Bukve *et al* (eds) *Kommunestruktur og tiltaksarbeid*. Sogndal: Vestlandsforsking rapport 19/91, 81-115.

Grønlie, T. (1993) 'Industriforvaltningen - et styringsredskap?' In T. Nordby (ed) *Arbeiderpartiet og planstyret 1945-1965*. Oslo: Universitets-forlaget, 121-141.

Halkier, H. and Danson, M. (1996) *Regional Development Agencies in Western Europe. A Survey of Key Characteristics and Trends*. European Research Unit, Aalborg University, European Studies Series of Occasional Papers, 15.

Hudson, R. and Lewis, J.R. (1982) 'Regional Planning in Europe. Introductory Remarks.' In R. Hudson and J.R. Lewis (ed) *Regional Planning in Europe*. London: Pion, 1-6.

March, J.G. and Olsen, J.P. (1995) *Democratic Governance*. New York: Free Press.

Mønnesland, J., Hervik, A. and Dale, K. (1993) *Bedriftsrettet distriktsstøtte. Evaluering av Distriktenes Utbyggingsfonds virkemidler*. Molde: Møreforskning/ NIBR/SNF.

Page, E. (1991) *Localism and centralism in Europe*. New York: Oxford University Press.

Sharpe, L.J. (1993) 'The European Meso: An Appraisal.' In L.J. Sharpe (ed) *The Rise of Meso Government in Europe*. London: Sage, 1-39.

Skrøver Aaraas, O. (1993) *Opprettelsen av Statens Nærings- og distriktsutviklingsfond*. Thesis in Political Science, University of Oslo.

Steine (1995) *SNDs regionale forvaltningsapparat - rapport fra arbeidsgruppen*. Oslo: Statens nærings- og distriktsutviklingsfond.

St. meld. nr. 29 (1988-89) *Politikk for regional utvikling*. Oslo: Kommunal- og arbeidsdepartementet.

St. meld. nr. 33 (1992-93) *By og land hand i hand. Om regional utvikling*. Oslo: Kommunal- og arbeidsdepartementet.

Stöhr, W. (ed) (1990) *Global Challenge and Local Response*. London: Mansell.

Torsteinsen, H. (1998) 'Heves kontrakten? Elitenes holdninger til fylkeskommunen.' In Baldersheim (ed) *Kan fylkeskommunen fornyast?* Oslo: Det Norske Samlaget, 176-214.

Wicken, O. (1993) 'Teknologer og industriutvikling.' In T. Nordby (ed) *Arbeiderpartiet og planstyret 1945-1965*. Oslo: Universitetsforlaget, 159-171.

10 The Regionalisation of Danish Regional Policy: Governance and Resource Dependencies in Transition

HENRIK HALKIER

Since the beginning of the 1990s, Danish regional policy has changed dramatically. As of January 1991, all central government incentive schemes were terminated, and since then the main components of spatial economic policy have been a host of regional and local initiatives supplemented by EU structural funds. Denmark would in other words seem to be an extreme example of the overall trend in European regional policy, namely the shift away from national programmes towards regional and supra-national schemes.

This paper investigates the implications of the transformation of regional policy from the perspective of political decentralisation by trying to establish to what extent recent changes have increased the capacity of Danish regions to pursue their own agenda with regard to development. On the one hand subnational actors have clearly become more involved in local/regional economic policy than ever before, but on the other hand these initiatives take place in the context European programmes and in a national context that hitherto has been dominated by a strong unitary state tradition and a staunchly liberal approach to industrial intervention. The capacity of Danish regions to pursue their own development priorities, in other words, could turn out to be heavily circumscribed.

The aim of this paper is to examine the transformation of regional policy in Denmark from the perspective of political decentralisation in order to establish to what extent recent changes have increased the capacity of Danish regions to pursue their own agendas with regard to economic development. This is done by analysing the way in which this process of rapid and profound policy change has affected the patterns of resource dependency between the various tiers of government.

The text is divided into three parts. The following section provides a brief outline of the analytical framework, based primarily on contributions from traditions within policy analysis, network theory and the new institutionalism. The main body of the text examines the changing face of spatial economic policy in Denmark, dealing in turn with the development of policies and initiatives emanating from the national, European and regional levels respectively, and assessing their implications for the different levels of government involved. Finally, the interaction of the three tiers of spatial economic policy within a multi-level governance framework is assessed in order to establish the new overall pattern of resource dependencies and the consequences of decentralisation for the capacity of Danish regions to pursue their own priorities in economic development.

The text reports results from ongoing research on Danish regional policy in a European perspective, and the methodologies employed in the empirical studies stem from policy analysis and historical-institutional studies, i.e. interpretation of documentary sources and a series of interviews with key administrators and decision-makers.

The Analytical Approach

The relationship between different tiers of government has been studied from a variety of spatial perspectives, and thus it will be possible to draw upon inspiration from a range of existing, and not entirely unrelated, bodies of literature.

On the *European level* Gary Marks and his co-proponents of the so-called 'multi-level governance' approach (Marks *et al.* 1996 and Marks 1996b) have argued that 'decision-making competencies are shared by actors at different levels rather than monopolised by state executives' (Marks *et al.* 1996, p.346), and that it is therefore necessary to adopt an 'actor-centred' approach that specifies the role of particular individuals and institutions in the decision-making process. On the *national level* parallel arguments can be found in the 'Power-Dependence' approach developed by Rob Rhodes as an alternative way of understanding the relationship between central government on the one hand and sub-central public bodies on the other (Rhodes 1998). Rhodes stressed the mutual dependency of different tiers of government based on their respective control of resources that are of importance to the development and implementation of public policy, and like in Marks' polemic against the state-centric approach, he refused to give priority to one particular type of resources - constitutional or legal authority - at the expense of, for example, informational or organisational sources of influence. Finally, the recent growth in studies focusing on *policy networks* (Jordan and Schubert 1992; van Waarden 1992; Hanf and O'Toole 1992; and Rhodes and Marsh 1992) has also led to the recognition that 'policy-making includes a large number of public and private actors' exchanging 'information, expertise, trust and other policy resources' (Jordan and Schubert 1992 p.11f), and although the approach was originally developed to deal with policy sectors within national policies, it can clearly also be applied to policy networks with an international dimension such as, for example, the European Structural Funds.[1]

The three traditions clearly move along parallel lines by focusing on institutions and their mutual resource dependencies in a historical context. The analytical framework of this text shares this general perspective and incorporates ideas especially from Rhodes and the literature on policy networks within a neo-institutionalist perspective inspired by earlier studies of networks, institutions and policy-making in spatial economic policy.[2] As can be seen from Table 10.1, three levels of analysis are involved in the study of organisations and policy-making, looking respectively at the individual government organisation, its relationship with other actors, and the way in which the whole area of activity is being coordinated.[3]

For each organisation three dimensions are seen as crucial, namely the domain it occupies, the strategies pursued in relation to its environment, and the resources at its disposal. *Domain* is central to most organisations because their *raison d'être* is to perform certain tasks and operate in a particular geographical setting, and the multi-tier and

1 Examples of this are Conzelmann (1995) and Heinelt and Smith (1996).

2 Notably Halkier and Damborg (1997), and Halkier (1996). As argued in the former, the seminal work of Rhodes can be further developed by drawing upon contributions to burgeoning literature on networks, notably Thorelli (1986), Gustaffson and Seemann (1985), van Waarden (1992), and Heinelt and Smith (1996).

3 For a detailed version of the following argument, see Halkier and Damborg (1997).

territorial nature of political governance in Western Europe ensures that domain-oriented conflicts can enter the policy process at many points. The *strategies* of an organisation are an obvious object of study, being the general guidelines according to which resources are employed to influence its environment. Many authors have stressed the significance of positioning strategies, i.e. how an organisation attempts to conduct its relations with other organisations (Rhodes 1998; van Waarden 1992; Gustaffson and Seemann 1985), but in order to understand the scope for conflict the potentially diverging strategies in relation to the target group for a particular policy must be taken into account as well because, for instance, their goals or policy instruments are perceived as being incompatible. *Resources* are the means by which an organisation maintains itself and influences its surroundings. Commanding resources is intimately linked to the potential for exercising power,[4] either by employing them as policy instruments vis-à-vis private actors or as means of linking up with other organisations to achieve specific goals, and therefore establishing the position of each organisation in this respect is a crucial, but by no means uncomplicated, task. The text follows a typology developed in an earlier study of policy instruments in that it distinguishes between four basic resources: authority, information, finance and organisation (Halkier 1996, p.57ff). Apart from any intrinsic theoretical advantage this may have, stressing the similarities between policy instruments and inter-organisational relations also underlines the fact that establishing for example networks or new organisations may be a substitute for direct policy implementation (or vice versa) because the basic resources involved are the same.

The inter-organisational relationship between public bodies will be studied from two perspectives: the way the bargaining process is conducted and the resulting exchange of resources. The written and unwritten rules governing the exchange are placed under the heading of *bargaining*, i.e. the way interaction is formally institutionalised and guided by informal conventions of conduct. The *exchange* dimension denotes the outcome of concrete processes of bargaining, in other words what types of resources are involved, in what directions they flow, and the resulting overall balance. Obviously assessing the exchanges taking place will give

[4] For a discussion of resources, power and policy instruments, see Halkier (1996, p.47-62).

important information about the nature of the underlying mutual dependencies and the success or otherwise of the strategies adopted by individual organisations.

The multi-organisational dimension refers to the way in which activities are *integrated* and coordinated, i.e. relations of power and dominance between public bodies and tiers of government in a particular field of public policy.

The conceptual framework summarised in Table 10.1 should be able to capture key aspects of the relationship between different tiers of government in the process of policy-making, both with regard to conflicts and inter-dependencies, and this claim will, hopefully, be borne out by the ensuing empirical analysis of the changing role of the Danish regions in spatial economic policy and the ongoing process of Europeanisation.

Table 10.1 Organisations and policy-making - an analytical framework

Level of analysis	*Dimensions*	*Sub-dimensions*
Organisational	Domain	Territory
		Function
	Strategies	Policies
		Positioning
	Resources	Authority
		Finance
		Information
		Organisation
Inter-organisational	Bargaining	
	Exchange	
Multi-organisational	Integration	

Source: Adapted from Halkier and Damborg (1997)

Regional Policy and the Danish Regions

Given the high level of inter-tier collaboration in the field of regional policy, the picture drawn is bound to be a complex one. In the following, the analysis is organised according to the tier of government from which a particular programme originates, i.e. a combination of spatial coverage and political institutions. In practice this means that programmes initiated by central government applying only to Denmark will be discussed under the heading of national policies, the supra-national Structural Funds of the EU are discussed under the heading of European policies although they are implemented through specific national and regional programmes, and initiatives developed by regional authorities for their particular locality is covered under the heading of regionally-based policies. For each of these three levels, the analysis begins with an outline of the development of policies from the 1970s to the late 1990s, followed by an assessment of the changing patterns of resource dependencies between various actors and tiers of government with regard to this particular set of programmes and initiatives.

National Policies

It has become generally accepted that recent decades have marked a profound change of paradigm in regional policy in the affluent parts of Western Europe (Stöhr 1989; Albrechts and Swyngedouw 1989; Martin and Townroe 1992; Bachtler 1993; and Halkier and Danson 1997): the traditional central government programmes providing financial subsidies to boost investment in designated problem areas have become less important, and instead more emphasis has been given to European and regional programmes. The development of national-level regional policies in Denmark could be interpreted as a particular radical version of this change because all central government regional grant schemes were abolished as of January 1st 1991.

Overall responsibility for regional policy rests with national authorities and is subject to national legislation, and from the late 1950s till the early 1980s the proclaimed objective of regional policy was to promote equality between different parts of Denmark with regard to economic welfare, especially between the urban centres and the rural peripheries. From the mid-1980s the case for a national regional policy was, however, primarily put in economic terms, its *raison d'être* seen as mobilisation of indigenous regional resources in support of the general attempt to improve the international competitiveness of Danish firms (Bogason 1982; Gaardmand 1988; Bogason and Jensen 1991; Erhvervsministeriet 1995).

Direct subsidies to individual firms were the mainstay of central government regional policy from 1958 till 1990, and the administration of the grant schemes was firmly centralised and did not involve input from the regional level.[5] The first decade saw a gradual introduction of an array of schemes targeting primarily individual firms (soft loans, investment grants) but also local authorities (soft loans for construction of industrial property). From 1967 support was restricted to designated problem areas, but since the beginning of the 1980s coverage has been gradually reduced, partly because of pressure from the European Commission, and currently designated areas comprise only around 20 per cent of the total population.[6]

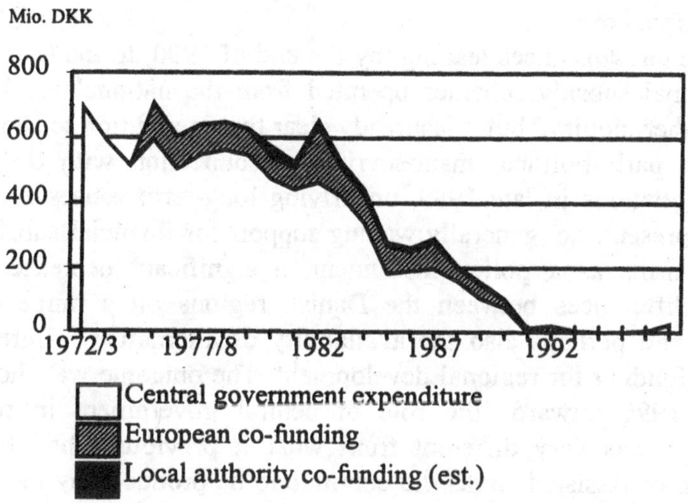

Source: Annual reports of the Regional Development Directorate 1981-88, Danish Government Accounts 1989-95. *Note:* 1981-88 figures are commitments, 1989-95 figures expenditure.

Figure 10.1 National policy programmes (expenditure by source, 1995 prices)

5 A detailed analysis is given in Bogason (1982).

6 Direktoratet for Egnsudvikling (1980-87), Industri- og Handelsstyrelsen (1988-91), Erhvervsfremmestyrelsen (1992-96). Overviews are provided by Bogason (1982), Gaardmand (1988) and Industriministeriet (1990).

As can be seen in Figure 10.1, the dominant trend in central government expenditure on regional policy would appear to have been one of decline at least since the late 1970s. Until the mid-1980s accounting conventions did, however, artificially inflate the figures,[7] and thus in expenditure terms the turning point must be located much later, i.e. around the year 1988. Figure 10.1 also shows that national-level regional subsidy schemes were supported by both subnational and European means. While the involvement of local authorities was limited in financial terms,[8] the European contribution was more sizeable. Some of the latter was simply counted as a general reimbursement of Danish government expenditure, but most of it was used to establish a soft-loan programme parallel to the existing national one.

The circumstances leading, by the end of 1990, to the termination of all regional subsidy schemes operated from the national level are in need of further inquiry,[9] but it is already clear that in addition to short-term factors like party-political manoeuvring in connection with the yearly budget negotiations in late 1989, underlying long-term causes must also have been present, i.e. generally waning support for financial subsidies to individual firms as a policy instrument, a significant decrease in the economic differences between the Danish regions on a range of key indicators, and perhaps also the availability of alternative - European - sources of funding for regional development. The outcome was, however, that from 1991 onwards the role of central government in regional development was very different from what it previously had been. A Danish map of Assisted Areas did continue to be produced by the Danish Agency for Trade and Industry (DATI) into which the Regional Development Directorate had been incorporated, and its approval by the European Commission allowed central government to give financial support to individual firms in problem regions when providing matching

7 Central government accounts do not take repayment of loans into account but focus on direct public outlays, and in the early years soft loans was the main policy instrument. If the financial advantage experienced by the firms receiving support is calculated, what looks as a massive 59 per cent fall in real terms from 1982 to 1985 actually turns out to make little difference (Yuill *et al.* 1992, Table 5.3).

8 Central government loans towards bespoke industrial property only covered 75% of the investment while the remaining 25 per cent was financed by the local authority in which the development took place.

9 For a preliminary analysis, see Halkier 1998, p.24ff.

funding in connection with Structural Fund programmes (Yuill *et al.* 1998; Erhvervsfremmestyrelsen 1996), but in addition to various functions in relation to European programmes and regional initiatives the most important generic task of central government has been to continue to ensure access to business and technological services also in disadvantaged regions.[10] The existing national network of regionally based Technology Information Centres (TICs) has sometimes been heralded as a new form of national-level regional policy (For example Erhvervsministeriet 1995), but as there is no preferential treatment built into the TIC system (see Bogason and Jensen 1991; Jensen 1994), this would merely seem to represent a deconcentration of the delivery of national business services. Furthermore, a flexible system of 'fire-fighting' has gradually been put in place, and since 1996 the so-called Notification Pool has provided funding for new targeted initiatives in, for example, business advice in localities threatened by major industrial closures (Arbejdsministeriet 1997; cf. Susanne Johansen, personal interview 19.6.97). With such a narrow policy profile it is hardly surprising that total expenditure on national initiatives for regional economic development has turned out to be limited after 1991, and thus it seems reasonable to conclude that the transition to the new policy regime involved a significant reduction in the direct attempts of central government to influence the distribution of economic activity across the face of the nation.

Table 10.2 sums up the changing input of resources from the three levels of government implicated in national programmes for regional economic development, and it is of course immediately evident that the situation changed profoundly with the abolition of traditional grant schemes in the early 1990s. In the original set-up, national policies were largely a self-contained entity, financed and administered by central government. Given the generally relative low level of expenditure on national-level regional programmes in Denmark compared to other European countries (Yuill *et al.* 1996, Table 5.6), it would be reasonable to assume that the continuation of national programmes cannot have been contingent on co-funding from other tiers of government, and that European regulations had a limited direct impact on its operation. With the introduction of a new approach central government abandoned its direct role as redistributor of private economic activity between the regions.

10 A clear programmatic statement can be found in Erhvervsministeriet 1995.

Apart from a minor fire-fighting role in connection with major industrial closures, it adopted a position in which the central elements were overseeing and coordinating the policies of subnational actors and participation in the regional programmes of the Structural Funds, i.e. a situation in which central government depends on other tiers of government if it should decide to seek to deliberately influence the spatial distribution of economic activity.

Table 10.2 National policies for regional development in Denmark: resources and levels of government

Input	*Authority*	*Finance*	*Information*	*Organisation*
European	Increasing influence on designated areas and grant levels	Some co-funding from mid-1980s till early 1990s		
National	Latent since 1991 Consensus changing	Self-financing, from 1991 potential	Statistical surveys maintained	DATI maintained
Regional		Limited co-funding till 1991		

European Policies

Regional policy acquired a new dimension with the establishment of the European Regional Development Fund (ERDF), and although it is clear that the operation of the Structural Funds differs between the member states of the EU (Conzelmann 1995; Heinelt 1996; Bachtler and Taylor 1997), the basic features of the development of its operation in Denmark do of course reflect the general direction in which these European programmes have moved, with the changes introduced by the 1988 reforms as a major watershed (Staeck 1996; Wishlade 1996).

From 1975 until 1988 regional policy on the European level was essentially a mechanism for redistribution between the member states, operating through a system of national quotas employed either as an outright reimbursement of expenditure on national policy programmes (cf. the discussion in the preceding section) or as co-funding of major improvements of the regional and local infrastructure. Only from the mid-1980s did the Structural Funds come to play a significant role in Denmark, because in the early years most of the European funds for regional development were spent on Greenland (Erhvervsministeriet 1995, p.19ff). The Arctic dependency did, however, leave the EU in 1985, and from this point in time quite substantial sums became available for development projects in the continental parts of the kingdom. The Danish expenditure pattern was in line with that in other relatively prosperous member states, and only from the mid-1980s did more innovative types of projects start to emerge, for example more advanced forms of infrastructure such as sector-based industrial parks or comprehensive regionally-based development programmes such as NordTek in North Jutland.[11] Central government played an important role in the administration of the Structural Funds prior to the 1988 reform with the Regional Development Directorate responsible for ERDF matters, and although regional authorities were given the opportunity to indicate their preferences with regard to applications from their own area, the final decision rested with the Directorate (Direktoratet for Egnsudvikling 1984, p.12). All in all this certainly suggests that the ERDF began its operation in Denmark as an extension to national policies rather than a separate programme with a distinct identity.

The origins of the 1988 reform has been associated with European high politics (Hooghe 1996; Hooghe and Keating 1994), and as the major national concerns with regard to European policies have been agriculture and fisheries rather than regional development, it is reasonable to assume that the Danish input into an area of policy in which other member states have far greater interests at stake will have been fairly limited. In the following, the development of the Structural Funds therefore will be treated as a change in the external environment to which Danish actors responded. The reform changed the functioning of the Structural Funds quite substantially by introducing a multi-year programme-based approach to regional policy and adopting partnership between the Commission, national government and subnational actors as a basic principle. Under the

11 The development of ERDF prior to the 1988 reforms can be followed in some detail in the Annual Reports of the Directorate.

new rules Denmark was allocated two Objective 2 programmes, targeting areas of industrial decline in North Jutland and Storstrøm respectively, and one Objective 5b programme covering rural areas on a number of small and medium-sized islands. However, it also benefited from some of the spatially targeted Community Initiatives, notably Interreg and Pesca. In the second round of programming, starting in 1994, the designated areas were expanded significantly and now covered 15.3 per cent of the Danish population while the budget allocation of European monies nearly doubled (Yuill *et al.* 1992, p.64; 1996, p.78). Also the profile of Structural Funds projects in Denmark changed: in the programming periods which started in 1994, support for so-called 'knowledge projects' - supporting capacity-building in firms with regard to, for example, research or marketing - was planned at 41 per cent, while infrastructure projects and direct financial subsidies accounted for only 31 per cent and 26 per cent respectively of budgeted public expenditure (Erhvervsministeriet 1995, Table 3.3).

The introduction of the partnership principle has often been heralded as a measure that advanced the role of regional actors in the policy process (Hooghe and Keating 1994; Bullmann 1996; Keating and Loughlin 1997), but as the role of a particular tier of government may well differ in the various phases of the policy process (Heinelt 1996; Marks 1996a), a more detailed analysis capable of distinguishing between planning and implementation is needed (Halkier 1997; Damborg 1998). In the planning stages of Structural Funds programmes the role of central government is primarily concerned with negotiating area designations and the proposed development strategies with the Commission ensuring that strategic priorities are in accordance with basic principles of national policy, especially the current preference for framework measures. The lead in the actual programme formulation is to be found at the subnational level with regional government organising a process of consultation with local government and private sector 'social partners', developing new policy initiatives and producing the draft version of the development programme for the region. Also in the implementation phase the role of central government has gradually become a limited one: although DATI provides matching funding for subsidies to individual firms and undertakes a formal appraisal of applications especially with regard to issues of legality, the crucial early and substantive stages of project evaluation in which the economic, technical and organisational prospects of an application are assessed are now firmly situated on the regional level.

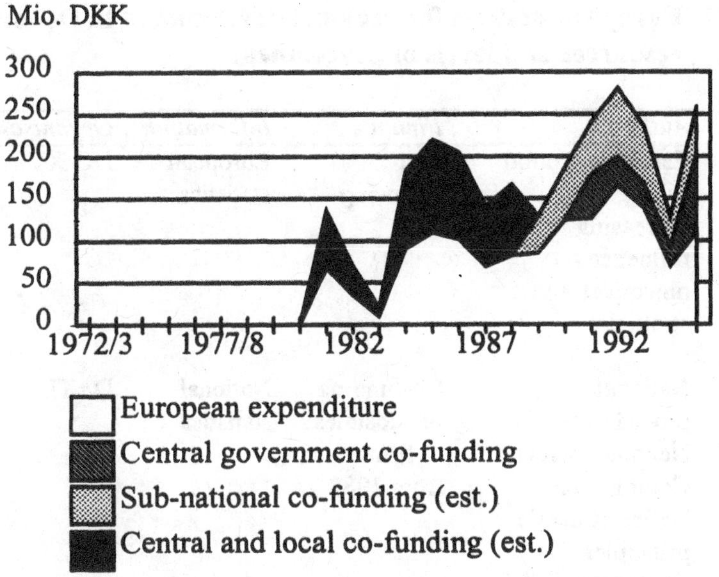

Sources: Direktoratet for Egnsudvikling (1980-87), Industri- og Handelsstyrelsen (1988), Finansministeriet (1989-95). No data available for the period 1975-80, for all co-funding 1981-87, for national co-funding 1989-90, and for regional/local co-funding 1989-95. Pre-1988 estimates are based on the assumption that ERDF fund 50 per cent of total project expenditure, and post-1988 estimate on the assumption that regional/local authority co-funding on average amounts to 50 per cent of ERDF outlays.

Figure 10.2 European policy programmes (expenditure by source, 1995 prices)

The partnership principle is also evident in the way in which ERDF programmes are funded, with sizeable contributions from both central government and subnational public bodies, as illustrated by Figure 10.2. Although the structure of co-funding varies between different types of projects, making national and/or regional/local co-funding a precondition for approval of Structural Funds programmes deliberately creates a mutual resource dependency between the three tiers of government involved.

Table 10.3 European policies for regional development in Denmark: resources and levels of government

Input	*Authority*	*Finance*	*Information*	*Organisation*
European	Establish ground rules Increasing influence on objectives and strategies	Part-financing	European statistics	DG XVI
National	National procedures Negotiate with Commission Define strategic principles Decreasing role in approval of individual projects	Co-funding of subsidies to firms from 1988	National statistics	DATI
Regional	Increasing since 1988: * strategic planning * processing of applications * recommendation of projects	Co-funding of infra-structure and framework measures	Regional statistics Knowledge of firms	Regional programme administrations

Table 10.3 sums up the changing input of resources from the three levels of government implicated in European programmes for regional economic development, and it is of course immediately evident that the situation changed profoundly with the 1988 reforms of the Structural Funds. In the early years the ERDF essentially functioned as a mechanism of redistribution between EC member states that supported the existing regional policies of national governments, the transition to the new partnership-based approach certainly made a major difference in the case of Denmark. While the European Commission and the nation state still establish the basic spatial and financial delimitation of Structural Funds activities, substantive issues are primarily dealt with by subnational

institutions, although central government maintains a general role with regard to process management, legality and basic policy principles. Two conclusions can be drawn on the basis of this. First, that the European measures never constituted a self-contained programme of spatial economic policy, and that it even in its present form is crucially depending upon national and regional levels of government for access to a wide range of resources. Second, the internal division of labour between the national and regional levels now places Denmark among the most decentralised countries in the EU with regard to Structural Funds programming.[12] All in all the Danish approach to administration of the Structural Funds can perhaps best be described as having evolved towards a state of 'controlled decentralisation' within a multi-level governance setting.

Regionally-based Policies

Also the field of subnational development policies must be analysed in terms of 'before' and 'after', although the boundary between the two is not as clear-cut as was the case with national and European regional policies. Since the mid-1980s regional and local authorities have become increasingly involved in efforts to stimulate growth in their locality,[13] but as economic development is not one of the statutory functions of subnational government in Denmark, such initiatives operated in a grey zone until this type of activities were formally legalised and regulated by central government through an act of parliament in 1992.

Bottom-up initiatives in economic development began with the setting up of public-private partnerships in the form of Development Committees in the 1930s and 1950s, aimed at attracting firms from outside to locate in the area by means of promotion and advice and, from the late 1950s, trying to attract support from the new national policy schemes. The importance of the Development Committees did, however, wane as local and regional government gradually became more active in economic development (Bogason 1982; Industriministeriet 1987; Erhvervsministeriet 1995). The political motivation for this economic activism at the

12 For a comparative European perspective, see Heinelt (1996).

13 The sometimes competitive relationship between regional and local tiers of government with regard to the policy domain of economic development has been analyzed elsewhere (Damborg and Halkier 1996), but will not be discussed as a separate issue here.

subnational level seems to have been fuelled by practical experience with the decentralised administration of labour market policies in a period of high levels of unemployment in combination with the dominance of a liberal discourse of economic management on the national level in the 1980s (Industriministeriet 1987; Jørgensen and Lind 1988) - plus, of course, in the 1990s the policy void created by the termination of central government schemes and the example set by the decentralised management of Structural Funds projects and programmes. The net result was a conspicuous increase in the level of subnational initiatives, and from the early 1990s all regional and the majority of local governments were engaged in activities aiming to stimulate indigenous economic activity, promote local employment, and secure a higher level of taxable income. The new emphasis on indigenous growth in the 1980s also involved a notable shift with regard to policy instruments: more or less specialised advisory services came to dominate - supplying information on for example markets, technology and general management issues - supplemented by provision of various forms of technological and organisational infrastructure such as incubator units, test facilities and collective marketing efforts (Damborg and Halkier 1998a; Erhvervsministeriet 1995; Industriministeriet 1987). Reliable statistics have only been obtained from 1994 onwards, but the level of expenditure has been relative stable and a yearly average of 185 mio. DKK in the period 1994-97 certainly establishes the regional level as a major player in spatial economic policy.[14] The extent to which co-funding of Structural Funds projects is included in this grand total is unclear,[15] but the availability of funds from the European level has undoubtedly in many ways played a catalytic role by prompting sub-regional actors to engage in economic development activities.[16] The degree of dependency created by this, however, would seem to be moderate because the Danish Structural

[14] Calculated on the basis of the aggregate regional government accounts. Despite number of caveats, these figures are still believed to present a reasonably accurate picture of the current situation (cf. Amtsrådsforeningen 1997, p.4f). Thanks are due to Janet Samuel of the Association of County Councils in Denmark for providing access to the figures.

[15] It is interesting to observe that the three regions in which we find the highest per-capita expenditure on economic development by regional government - Bornholm, North Jutland and Storstrøm - are traditional peripheral areas with a major involvement in European programmes.

[16] Cf. the discussion in Damborg and Halkier (1998b).

Funds programmes rely on the generation and development of projects by subnational actors, and - with the possible exception of small units of local government - European co-funding in most cases could be substituted by regionally generated tax revenues, for example, if regional or local government decided to give priority to this area of public policy. Although these sub-national policies aimed at improving the competitiveness of local firms originate in regional problems, on the aggregate national level, their spatial effects cancel out each other and hence:

> these ... activities probably no longer contribute to the evening out of regional discrepancies, but rather to contribute to *national* economic development. (Oscarsson 1989, p.50)

A decentralised form of industrial policy is, of course, very much in line with the current thinking of central government, but also represents a change of objectives that potentially has very different consequences for individual regions, depending on their economic and institutional strengths and weaknesses.

The role of central government as a regulator of regional and local development initiatives has evolved gradually. While it was always crystal clear what subnational government was *not* allowed to do, namely grant financial subsidies to individual firms, what they actually could do remained unclear until 1992 when a new parliamentary act designated *collective* business services - i.e. measures targeting all or a group of firms within its area - as the field in which regional and local authorities could engage (Lov 383, 20.5.92.). The other central plank in central government regulation has been attempts to bring about a higher degree of coordination amongst actors on the subnational level. Since the beginning of the 1990s, in most of the regions, bottom-up development activities have involved a large number of relatively small organisations, including both regional and local government organisations, a host of quangos and a wide range of public-private partnerships (Damborg and Halkier 1998a and 1998b). This complex institutional pattern would seem to have been brought about by a number of factors - political preference for collective framework measures, the uncertain legal position, the need to project a business-like image - but it has nonetheless given rise to concerns about duplication and waste of public resources. Central government has launched several schemes aiming to induce subnational actors to coordinate their activities such as the production of joint Regional Development Plans and the setting up of so-called Business Centres as permanent forums for discussion between development bodies in a particular geographical area.

The attempts by central government to promote coordination have relied exclusively on voluntary organisational measures backed by limited financial incentives. If this exercise in networking and institution building should eventually lead to the creation of 'one-stop-shop' development agencies, it is already clear that only to a limited extent will these coincide with the current boundaries of regional government, as most of the Business Centres consist of local government groupings within a particular region (Industriministeriet 1987 and 1992; Erhvervsministeriet 1995; cf. Susanne Johansen, personal interview 16.6.98.).

Table 10.4 Regionally-based policies for regional development: resources and levels of government in Denmark

Input	*Authority*	*Finance*	*Information*	*Organisation*
European		Co-funding of some initiatives		
National	Regulation of policy instruments Since early 1990s encouragement of cooperation	Limited co-funding for cooperation		DATI
Regional	Since late 1980s: * institution building * strategic priorities	Since late 1980s a large aggregate divided between many actors	Increasing knowledge of firms	Since late 1980s many small actors * regional/ local * quangos * public-private partnerships

Table 10.4 sums up the changing input of resources from the three levels of government implicated in regionally-based programmes for economic development, and again it is noticeable that the situation has

changed profoundly since the end of the 1980s. From playing, at best, a marginal role through place promotion, bottom-up development has become a growth industry in its own right with a large number of regional and local actors involved, and with important links to actors on the national and European level. On the one hand, central government regulation has established the legal framework for regional and local development initiatives, thereby preventing the introduction of financial or other subsidies to individual firms as policy instruments. It is therefore hardly surprising that sub-national activities have been dominated by especially advisory services and various forms of organisational infrastructure. On the other hand, funding from the European Structural Funds has undoubtedly acted as a catalyst for the development of a burgeoning bottom-up economic development scene by enlarging the financial scope for regional and local action. Having been brought into existence, the long-term dependency of especially regional, but also local, government on external funding does, however, seem to be moderate, and subnational actors should therefore have the capacity to continue to pursue their own priorities with regard to spatial economic policy within the regulatory framework established by the national and European tiers of government.

Conclusions and Perspectives

From the late 1980s spatial economic policy in Denmark changed beyond recognition, starting as an ideal-typical version of traditional top-down policy regime and emerging in the early 1990s as an almost radical version of the new bottom-up approach to regional development. How did these changes affect the relative influence of the three tiers of government involved?

As illustrated by Table 10.5, summing up the key features of the policy regimes before and after the changes taking place around 1990, there can be little doubt that the roles have been recast dramatically, with regard to the domains occupied by the three levels of government, by the strategies pursued and by the resource dependencies involved. In the traditional regime central government enjoyed a *de facto* monopoly on regional policy, managing the only economic policy programme entailing systematic spatial discrimination and effectively controlling the necessary

Table 10.5 Levels of government and the changing regimes of regional policy in Denmark

Level	*Traditional (till the late 1980s)*	*New (from the early 1990s)*
European	From mid-1970s regulation of national area designation and grant levels	Only programme of spatial discrimination Significant source of finance
National	Only programme of spatial discrimination Control of all key policy resources	Regulation of EU and regional programmes Some co-funding of European programmes
Regional	Limited co-funding of national programmes	Subnational industrial policy Many small actors control key resources in regional and EU programmes

resources, including political authority based on cross-party consensus and the means of implementation in terms of finance, information and organisation. The new policy regime differs markedly, first because central government has effectively opted out of policy implementation, and second because the activities of the three levels have become intertwined in a complex system of multi-level governance with asymmetrical resources dependencies. Currently European programmes are unique in discriminating systematically between localities in their policies, while subnational actors control informational and organisational resources that are critical to policy implementation, and the most important role of central government is to attempt to regulate initiatives emanating from the two other levels. The new regional policy regime, in other words, involves a separation of the roles formerly concentrated on the national level: the authority to instigate spatial discrimination is now exercised via the European level while regional and local actors effectively control the sharp end of the implementation process, and the critical contribution of central government would appear to be to promote and regulate the new dominant policy paradigm with its emphasis on indigenous development and industrial-policy type measures.

Taken together these changes have indisputably increased the capacity of regional actors to influence strategic decisions with regard to economic development initiatives. Under the traditional regime they were excluded from the policy process altogether, now these actors are capable of designing programmes, setting up institutions and shaping individual projects. Of course bottom-up activities still depend on external resources, primarily central government regulation and to some extent funding from European programmes, but given the relatively broad nature of both the former and the latter, targeting the needs of the individual locality should certainly be possible. What this means in terms of the spatial distribution of economic development would, however, be good now. Contrary to traditional central government policies, which involved highly visible financial transfers from prosperous to less prosperous regions, the spread of economic development activities to relatively well-off regions will intensify inter-regional competition, and the fate of weaker localities therefore will depend on much less tangible qualities, such as the will and capacity to mobilise resources in order to create an environment conducive to innovation and growth.

All in all, the preceding discussion suggests that the medium-term outlook for spatial economic policy in Denmark appears to be stable, at least compared with the turbulence of the previous decade. As in Europe at large, the organisational and informational resources with which subnational actors are associated would seem to be particularly critical in a period where not just the quantity but also the quality of investment is seen as crucial to regional development, and the enhanced position of subnational actors would seem to be more than a fickle whim of political fashion. Moreover, in terms of politics central government has played an important role in furthering decentralisation in the domain of spatial economic policy, and the framework-oriented approach to industrial policy continues to enjoy broad political support. The endurance of the new policy paradigm will certainly be tested in the coming years when the enlargement of the EU towards the east results in a major reform of the Structural Funds. In these circumstances, the continuation of the current levels of support in the relatively prosperous North Western member states is highly unlikely, and this of course could lead to the resurrection of traditional forms of central government regional policy.

In Denmark, however, with limited regional disparities and increasing international competition, the political will to target resources to address geographical imbalances at the expense of competitiveness must be in doubt. Further, the consensual preference for framework-types of policy instruments rather than financial subsidies would probably suggest that - apart from doing nothing - continuation of a programme-based national programmes along the lines of the Structural Funds could be the least unlikely option. Such an approach could be presented as a regional form of industrial policy, and by leaving the coordination within the regions to regional-based actors and by merely providing some measure of additional funding, central government would avoid becoming too heavily entangled in territorial politics and inter-organisational strategies on the sub-national level. For the time being, at least, the new and decentralised approach to spatial economic policy is unlikely to be abandoned.

Acknowledgements

This text is partly based on work undertaken as part of a comparative research project conducted in conjunction with the European Policies Research Centre, University of Strathclyde, Glasgow. Earlier versions of the argument have benefited from suggestions from workshop participants in Helsinki, Frankfurt/Oder, Aalborg and Grenaa, and from the lucid and sceptical comments of Staffan Zetterholm and Charlotte Damborg of Aalborg University's European Research Unit, and Sven Illeris of Roskilde University. Full responsibility for the final version of the text rests, as ever, with the author.

References

Albrechts, L. and Swyngedouw, E. (1989) 'The challenges for regional policy under a flexible regime of accumulation.' In L. Albrechts *et al.* (eds): *Regional Policy at the Crossroads - European Perspectives*. London: Jessica Kingsley Publishers, 67-89.

Amtsrådsforeningen (1997) 'Erhvervsfremme i amterne - en oversigt.' København: Amtsrådsforeningen.

Arbejdsministeriet (1997) 'Bekendtgørelse om en varslingspulje.' 72, 28.1.97.

Bachtler, J. (1993) 'Regional policy in the 1990s - the European perspective.' In R.T. Harrison and M.Hart (eds) *Spatial Policy in a Divided Nation*. London: Jessica Kingsley Publishers, 254-69.

Bachtler, J. and Taylor, S. (1997) 'EU regional development strategies: comparisons and contrasts among Objective 2 Programmes.' In J. Bachtler and I. Turok (eds) *The Coherence of EU Regional Policy. Contrasting Perspectives on the Structural Funds*. London: Jessica Kingsley Publishers, 219-45.

Bogason, P. (1982) 'Denmark: the regional development council.' In D. Yuill (ed) *Regional Development Agencies in Europe*. Farnborough: Gower, 107-28.

Bogason, P. and Jensen, L. (1991) 'Statens ansvar for regional udvikling i Danmark.' *NordREFO 3*, 51-82.

Bullmann, U. (1996) 'The politics of the third level.' *Regional & Federal Studies 6*, 2, 3-19.

Conzelmann, T. (1995) 'Networking and the politics of EU regional policy: lessons from North Rhine-Westphalia, Nord-Pas de Calais and North West England.' *Regional & Federal Studies 5*, 2, 134-72.

Damborg, C. (1998) 'The North Jutland Objective 2 Programme: coordination and evaluation.' *IQ-NET Occasional Paper* 2.

Damborg, C. and Halkier, H. (1998a) 'RDAs in Denmark - towards a Danish approach to bottom-up regional policy?' In H. Halkier, M. Danson and C. Damborg (eds) *Regional Development Agencies in Europe*. London: Jessica Kingsley Publishers, 80-99.

Damborg, C. and Halkier, H. (1998b) 'Development bodies, networking and business promotion in North Jutland.' *European Studies Series of Occasional Papers, European Research Unit, Aalborg University* 28.

Direktoratet for Egnsudvikling (1980-87) *Orientering og årsberetninger, 1980-87*. Silkeborg: Direktoratet for Egnsudvikling.

Erhvervsfremmestyrelsen (1992-96) *Årsberetning, 1992-96*. København: Erhvervsfremmestyrelsen.

Erhvervsfremmestyrelsen (1996) 'Rapport om afgrænsning af støtteberettigede områder.' Silkeborg: Erhvervsfremmestyrelsen.

Erhvervsministeriet (1995) 'Regionalpolitisk Redegørelse 1995.' København: Erhvervsministeriet.

Finansministeriet (1988-96) *Statsregnskabet*. København: Finansministeriet.

Gaardmand, Arne (1988) 'Jobbet til manden eller manden til jobbet? Om dansk regionalpolitik 1945-85.' In NordREFO (ed) *Om regionalpolitikken som politikområde*. Helsinki: NordREFO, 67-108.

Gustaffson, J. and Seemann, J. (1985) *Små Institutioner i Store Systemer - Tilpasning og Påvirkning*. Aalborg: Aalborg UP.

Halkier, H. (1996) 'Institutions, power and regional policy.' *European Studies Series of Occasional Papers, European Research Unit, Aalborg University* 16.

Halkier, H. (1997) 'The North Jutland Objective 2 Programme: institutions and implementation.' *IQ-NET Occasional Paper* 1.

Halkier, H. (1998) 'Danish regions and the Europeanization of regional policy.' *European Studies Series of Occasional Papers, European Research Unit, Aalborg University* 27.

Halkier, H. and Damborg, C. (1997) 'Networks, development agencies and intelligent regions - towards a framework for empirical analysis.' *European Studies Series of Occasional Papers, European Research Unit, Aalborg University* 22.

Halkier, H. and Danson, M. (1997) 'Regional development agencies in Europe: a survey of key characteristics and trends.' *European Urban and Regional Studies 4*, 3, 243-56.

Hanf, K. and O'Toole, L.J.jr (1992) 'Revisiting old friends: networks, implementation structures and the management of inter-organizational relations.' *European Journal of Political Research 21*, 1-2, 163-80.

Heinelt, H. (1996) 'Conclusions.' In H. Heinelt and R. Smith (eds) *Policy Networks and European Structural Funds*. Aldershot: Avebury, 294-321.

Heinelt, H. and Smith, R. (1996) 'Introduction.' In H. Heinelt and R. Smith (eds) *Policy Networks and European Structural Funds.* Aldershot: Avebury, 1-8.

Hooghe, L. (1996) 'Building a Europe with the regions: the changing role of the European Commission.' In L. Hooghe (ed) *Cohesion Policy and European Integration. Building Multi-level Governance.* Oxford: Oxford UP, 89-126.

Hooghe, L. and Keating, M. (1994) 'The politics of European Union regional policy.' *Journal of European Public Policy 1,* 3, 369-92.

Industri- og Handelsstyrelsen (1988-91) *Årsberetninger 1988-91.* København: Industri- og Handelsstyrelsen.

Industriministeriet (1987) 'Lokal erhvervspolitik - debatoplæg om forholdet mellem statslige og lokale initiativer.' *Arbejdsnotat* 7.

Industriministeriet (1990) 'Regional erhvervspolitik i Danmark - Rapport afgivet af arbejdsgruppen vedrørende regionalpolitik.' København: Industriministeriet.

Industriministeriet (1992) 'Pejlemærker for fremtidens erhvervspolitik.' København: Industriministeriet.

Jensen, L. (1994) 'Ændringer i dansk opfattelse af statens ansvar i 80erne og 90erne.' *NordREFO 3,* 89-112.

Jordan, G. and Schubert, K. (1992) 'A preliminary ordering of policy network labels.' *European Journal of Political Research 21,* 1-2, 7-27.

Jørgensen, H. and Lind, J. (1987) 'Decentralized welfare capitalism: the case of employment and industrial policies.' *Acta Sociologica 30,* 3-4, 313-37.

Keating, M. and Loughlin, J. (1997) 'Introduction.' In M. Keating and J. Loughlin (eds) *The Political Economy of Regionalism.* London: Frank Cass, 1-13.

Lov om kommuners og amtskommuners deltagelse i erhvervsudviklings-aktiviteter, 383, 20.5.92.

Marks, G. (1996a) 'Exploring and explaining variation in EU cohesion policy.' In L. Hooghe (ed) *Cohesion Policy and European Integration. Building Multi-level Governance.* Oxford: Oxford UP, 388-422.

Marks, G. (1996b) 'An actor-centred approach to multi-level governance.' *Regional & Federal Studies 6,* 2, 20-38.

Marks, G., Hooghe, L. and Blank, K. (1996) 'European integration from the 1980s: state-centric v. multi-level governance.' *Journal of Common Market Studies 34,* 3, 341-78.

Martin, R. and Townroe, P. (1992) 'Changing trends and pressures in regional development.' In P. Townroe and R. Martin (eds) *Regional Development in the 1990s - The British Isles in Transition.* London: Jessica Kingsley Publishers, 13-24.

Oscarsson, G. (1989) 'Regional policies in the Nordic countries - origin, development and future. In NordREFO/OECD (ed) *The Long-term Future of Regional Policy - A Nordic View.* Copenhagen: NordREFO, 41-58.

Rhodes, R.A.W. (1988) *Beyond Westminster and Whitehall - The Sub-central Governments of Britain.* London: Unwin Hyman.

Rhodes, R.A.W. and D.Marsh (1992) 'New directions in the study of policy networks.' *European Journal of Political Research 21,* 1-2, 181-95.

Staeck, N. (1996) The European Structural Funds - their history and impact. In H. Heinelt and R. Smith (eds) *Policy Networks and European Structural Funds.* Aldershot: Avebury, 46-73.

Stöhr, W. (1989) 'Regional policy at the crossroads: an overview.' In L. Albrechts *et al.* (eds) *Regional Policy at the Crossroads - European Perspectives*. London: Jessica Kingsley Publishers, 191-97.

Thorelli, H.B. (1986) 'Networks: between markets and hierarchies.' *Strategic Management Journal 7*, 37-51.

Waarden, F. van (1992) 'Dimensions and types of policy networks.' *European Journal of Political Research 21*, 1-2, 29-52.

Wishlade, F. (1996) 'EU Cohesion policy: facts, figures and issues.' In L. Hooghe (ed) *Cohesion Policy and European Integration. Building Multi-level Governance*. Oxford: Oxford UP, 27-58.

Yuill, D. *et al.* (1992) *European Regional Incentives 1992-93, 12th Edition*. London: Bowker-Saur.

Yuill, D. *et al.* (1996) *European Regional Incentives 1996-97, 16th Edition*. London: Bowker Saur.

Yuill, D. *et al.* (1998) *European Regional Incentives, 17th Edition*. London: Bowker Saur.

Personal interview

Susanne Johansen, senior civil servant, DATI, Silkeborg, 19.6.97 and 16.6.98.

11 EU and National Regional Policies in Austria

RUTH DOWNES

Introduction

Austria joined the European Union at the start of 1995, together with Finland and Sweden. The subsequent implementation of the Structural Funds, the European Union's regional policy instrument, was to have a particular impact within the country. Over the period 1995-99, the country received ECU 1.6 billion in Structural Fund support, nearly half of which comprised agricultural support through Objectives 5a and 5b. Just over 40 per cent of the Austrian population was designated as eligible for assistance under all three of the Structural Fund objectives.[1]

The impact of Structural Fund intervention in Austria has been considerable, and not just in financial terms. It is inevitably an exacting task to integrate a new and externally determined policy within an existing policy and administrative system which may operate under quite different principles. This has proved to be particularly true in the Austrian setting. The aim of this chapter is to highlight key areas where the impact has been greatest and examine, in particular, the institutional ramifications of Structural Fund intervention in the country. Two areas in particular will be discussed. First, the considerable differences in approach between Austrian and EU regional policy and development and second, the particular difficulties which have been encountered in the implementation of the Structural Funds due to the peculiarities of the Austrian institutional framework. The chapter concludes with consideration of future directions in the light of a second round of Structural Fund finance.

[1] 3.5 per cent of the population in Objective 1, 8.2 per cent in Objective 2 and 29.1 per cent in Objective 5b.

Austrian Regional Policy

Nature of Regional Policy

Traditionally, Austrian national regional policy has had a low political profile for several reasons including the small size of the country, the lack of serious regional disparities, the high level of labour mobility and commuting, and the fact that the services industry (and tourism in particular) has, in the past, compensated to a great extent for agricultural decline. As a result, the priorities and objectives of Austrian regional policy have tended to be more implicit than explicit, although significant shifts in emphasis can still be seen. The current Regional Planning Report (Österreichische Raumordningskonferenz 1993) of the co-ordinating body for regional policy and development outlines three factors which underpin the current Austrian approach to regional support:

- regional economic policy should comprise of more than regional subsides to business, in particular the critical role of improving locational quality has been underestimated previously;
- regional enterprise support must be broader than investment subsidies, and assistance to overcome information barriers or advice in the creation of networks should be considered equally important; and,
- regional investment assistance should not aim solely to attract inward investment but should also support endogenous development.

It has been clearly recognised in Austria that many types of regional disparity exist which cannot be addressed purely through investment in infrastructure and inward company migration - an approach prevalent in the 1960s and 1970s. Economic growth problems related to geographical characteristics, deficiencies in the knowledge base or the innovative capacity of areas require different policy approaches, many of which are longer-term in nature and aimed at changing mentalities and locational preconditions. Austrian regional development policy, therefore, has evolved more into a 'dynamic structural policy' which focuses on the endogenous potential of regions and their integration into regional, national and international networks.

It is actually extremely difficult to isolate a clear regional policy in Austria as is possible in many other western European countries. Regional policy is viewed very broadly, almost more as the spatial element of all other policy areas. Only a very limited number of aid schemes operate which would be classed as traditional regional policy instruments. Many federal schemes in other policy areas, for example technology or the labour market, are available nationally but have a regional dimension through, for example, higher award rates in assisted areas. Below federal level, each of the nine *Länder* has an individual regional development plan, autonomously implemented by the districts, aimed at economic development in its specific area. These plans and *Land* level action are important to overall spatial planning in Austria and, within the federal structure of the country, are often perceived as 'regional policy'. It is not, however, regional policy in a social equity sense as it does not concentrate on underdeveloped areas or attempt to counteract regional disparities - although some *Land* measures do contain spatially differentiated components.

While this broader approach may be valid in terms of achieving integrated regional development, it is important to understand that there is little coordination of the regional elements of other policy areas under the umbrella of regional policy. The Federal Chancellery is nominally responsible for the coordination of this policy area and ÖROK (*Österreichische Raumordnungskonferenz* - Austrian Spatial Planning Conference), the co-ordinating body for regional development, acts as a forum for all those involved in the regional development field (see below). A recent ÖROK publication states that: 'regional economic policy is a very differentiated policy area for the improvement of locational quality ... regional economic policy in Austria must be characterised as a fragmented system within which neither spatial planning nor regional policy have direct access to all the measures of relevance to the policy area' (Österreichische Raumordningskonferenz 1998). In short, it is difficult to isolate 'regional policy' as it is operated within Austria.

Institutional Structures in Austria

The fact that regional policy is not a clearly defined policy area is further reflected in its allocation of institutional responsibility. The constitution does not specify a clear allocation of responsibility for regional policy to either the federal government or the *Länder*. In practice, there is an informal allocation between different bodies at federal, *Land* and local levels of both legislative competence and administrative jurisdiction of public activities affecting regional development and spatial planning.

The broad view of regional policy and the involvement of a range of sectoral schemes to provide a greater and more flexible range of support possibilities also increases the number of actors involved in the administration and implementation of policy. At least five Ministries, as well as a number of other organisations, have regional policy competencies at federal level, together with a range of agencies at *Land* level. This broad spread of institutional competence necessitates a brief look at the main features of the public assistance structures in Austria because their complexity, and the degree of their involvement in the field of regional policy, lies at the heart of the institutional difficulties encountered in the implementation of the Structural Funds.

There is a strong tradition of consensus-based decision-making and coalition politics in Austria which also gives powerful voice to social partners. The distinctive political system has exerted considerable influence on the nature of the institutional structures. The current so-called 'red-black' coalition of the two main parties - the Social Democratic party (red) and the Austrian People's Party (black) - has been in power since 1986. The red-black political split is not just seen in the governing coalition but is reflected right through the public administration system (and indeed often wider than that) with Ministries adhering politically broadly to one party or the other. Many development and funding agencies are managed by two individuals - one black and one red - while key assistance funds often have both black and red representation on their management boards. The result has been the division of many policy areas between black and red organisations, often leading to overlapping or duplicated responsibilities. While this system is now beginning to loosen, it still exerts considerable influence. The overall result is a complex and opaque structure which, in reality, often works principally on the basis of informal links between individuals.

Figure 11.1 shows an overview of the main organisations involved in the provision of business support in Austria at federal level only. This is by no means the complete picture but helps serve to illustrate the complexity. The use of devolved agencies, boards and funds, as well as special banks, in the administration of aid schemes is another characteristic

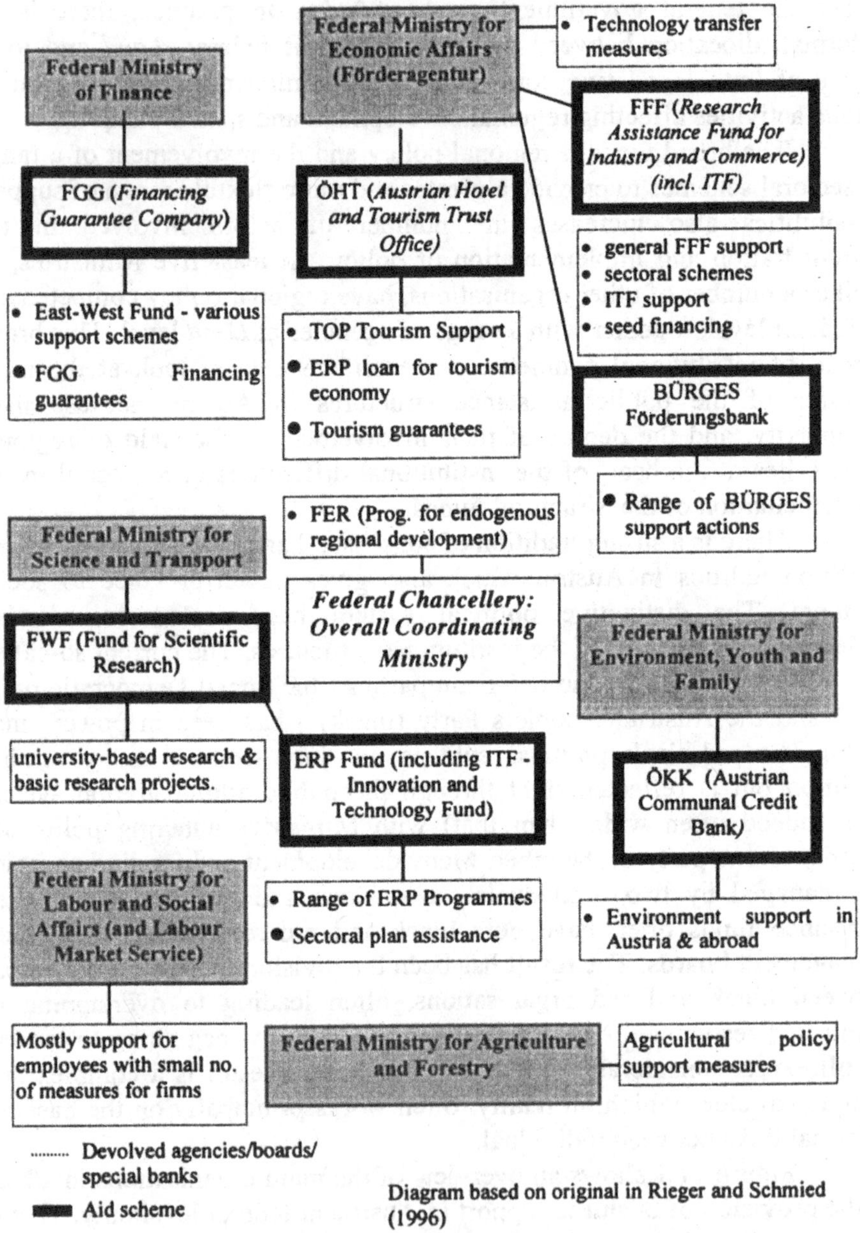

Figure 11.1 Institutional overview of Austrian business support at federal level

of the Austrian institutional system. Each individual aid scheme has its own so-called *Richtlinie*, or regulatory guideline, which outlines the scheme's objectives, eligibility criteria, administrative procedures and so on. Each Richtlinie is linked to a budget specific to that scheme.

This situation is broadly mirrored at *Land* level (see Figure 11.2) where the *Land* governments are divided into individual departments, each of which administer their own schemes, all with dedicated *Richtlinien*. One of the most important developments of recent years has been the introduction in the majority of *Länder* of semi-independent economic development agencies. Competencies falling under the jurisdiction of such agencies generally include investment attraction, project management and operation of industrial parks, consultancy and locational marketing. In contrast to the general situation at federal level, one advantage of these agencies is the possibility to bundle different forms of support under the administration of a single institution. Overall, Austria has one of the highest number of individual aid schemes in Western Europe. In 1994, for example, over 60 federal and 130 *Land* schemes were notified to the EFTA Surveillance Authority, over half the total submitted by the three new member states.

There are some coordination structures in place within this complex picture - including in the regional development field. The Federal Chancellery is responsible for the coordination of measures in all policy areas at federal level and has a separate department for regional policy. It also represents the country in international arena in the field of regional policy and has a central role *vis-à-vis* the Structural Funds. ÖROK, created in 1971, is based in the Federal Chancellery and acts as a forum for cooperation between all the different actors at various levels in the regional policy field. Decisions reached within ÖROK are recommendations only and do not have legal force. However, given that many of the key policy-makers and planners in the field are represented with ÖROK, the general direction of recommendations is usually reflected in subsequent policy decisions.

Overall, there appears to be a rather ambiguous attitude within Austria to the complexity of the institutional system, both within regional development policy and more generally. The overlap, duplication and lack of transparency, the almost inevitable by-products of such complexity, are viewed as negative, but the wide range of support options and the consensus-based model are also seen to have certain advantages. The

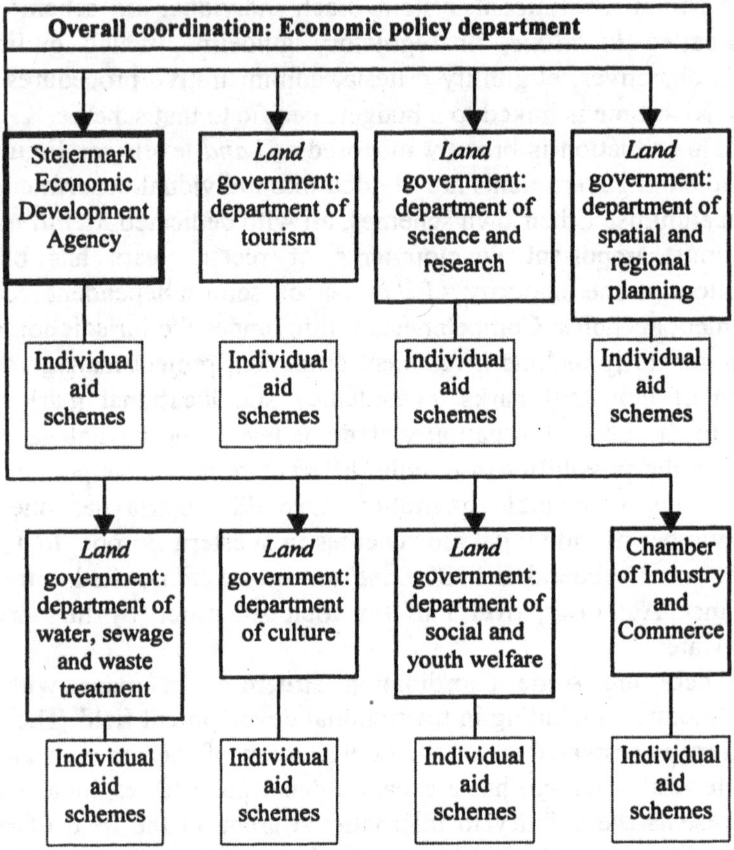

Figure 11.2 Implementation agencies (Steiermark) Objective 2 programme (ERDF part)

effective system of informal links between individuals working with government has developed over a number of years and is the key to the functioning of such a complicated structure. Austria is also a relatively small country and so the policy circles are not overly large. Thus, although the complexity may seem very difficult to an outsider (and certainly has caused problems within the European Commission), within Austria it is widely accepted as being the way the country has traditionally operated. This does not, however, negate the need for reform and this also is recognised within the country.

Impact of the Structural Funds

Against this background, the Structural Funds have revolutionised regional policy in Austria, significantly upgrading its profile in political and financial terms. The Funds were much publicised and debated before accession to the European Union and, in some ways, promoted as a form of compensation for Austria being a net contributor to the EU. The required designation of assisted areas gave the policy new prominence and the additionality requirement linked to the significant supplementary inflow of resources meant that budgets were secured for regional development purposes at a time when cuts were being made across the board. This, in turn, led to several sectoral policies being included more explicitly under the regional policy banner.

The difficulties which began to emerge as the implementation of the Structural Funds progressed are rooted in incompatibilities between the Austrian and EU approaches. The first Structural Fund programming period in a country inevitably involves a steep learning curve and each of the new member states has experienced considerable difficulties. In the Austrian case, it was the two areas outlined earlier where these difficulties were highlighted the most: the philosophy of regional development and the nature of the institutional system.

Incompatibilities in Approach

The strategic approach of Austrian and EU regional policy differs considerably. The EU's multi-annual programming approach, based on a structured plan with clearly established aims and objectives, is not readily integrated with the rather nebulous Austrian regional policy, focused on the stimulation of dynamic structural change. This incompatibility is not seen in all areas - the partnership principle, for example, is more easily fulfilled in a country with a tradition of strong consensus-based decision-making and the overall emphases of EU policy (e.g. SMEs, R&D, environment) are broadly reflected in the Austrian support system. Certain other Structural Fund-related requirements, however, did show up the differences more clearly. Two examples of this are assisted area designation and monitoring and evaluation.

The approach to assisted area designation in Austria in the 1990s has been more one of identifying regional problems than problem regions. Indeed, in 1991, the country had no legally binding assisted areas map, although the map from the previous year was broadly used by those requiring it. Exact definition of assisted areas is considered by many (although not all) Austrian policy makers, in regional and other fields, to reduce flexibility and create islands which are cut off from neighbouring areas by different rates of award. The complex matrix of award rates imposed by DG IV, the European Commission Competition Policy Directorate, has certainly increased the complexity of the aid system in the country and many fear has led to unhealthy competition between regions. Strict assisted areas maps may also present a barrier to regional cooperation, even when there is a clear reason for neighbouring areas to work together. Other policy makers, for example in the technology policy field, fear that such strict designated areas actually hinder the stimulation of innovation by isolating disadvantaged areas, where innovative potential may be lower, from surrounding areas. The Austrian national map at the start of the 1990s, for example, contained so-called Z-areas, which often included regional urban centres, where particularly innovative projects could be assisted, which would generate spread effects into neighbouring more disadvantaged areas. These areas were disallowed under competition policy regulations by the Commission in 1994.

The creation of a monitoring and evaluation system in Austria was a second area which highlighted differences in regional policy approach between the country and the EU. Historically, there has been no real evaluation culture in Austria, either in general terms or within the specific field of regional policy. The diversity of regional policy competence makes the accumulation of information and data across the whole system of regional economic development very difficult. Perhaps more importantly in terms of strategic approach, areas of increasing importance to Austrian regional development, such as the stimulation of endogenous potential or the creation of regional partnerships, are much more difficult to evaluate effectively. The hard, quantitative indicators required by the Commission often fail to reflect the real development effects in the region, or require considerable background explanation before they can be properly interpreted. There is a potential danger that, within the time and administrative pressures of Structural Fund implementation, preference will be given to projects which are more easily quantified, such as large scale investment projects. This would stand in contrast to the regional policy direction advocated by the Austrian Federal Chancellery.

In spite of the difficulties which have been encountered in the establishment of a monitoring system, it is worth noting that the process has not been entirely negative. In theory, the requirement to establish more structured data on project output is considered broadly beneficial by many within Austria. The Structural Fund requirement has led to the creation of the relatively comprehensive monitoring system which centralises data from all the individual Structural Fund programmes across the country and offers a comparable coverage not available in all member states. A more positive perception of evaluation as a method of improving strategic direction rather than purely as a system of control is also slowly taking hold - although many individual funding agencies and some programme managers still view the collection of monitoring data as a burden with little return.

Incompatibilities in Institutional Structure

Incompatibilities between the Austrian system and Structural Fund requirements have also been particularly evident with regard to the institutional structures. In considering how to implement the Structural Funds following EU accession, the decision was made in Austria to use the existing national policy structures. This is not unusual and was also the approach adopted, for example, by the Finnish government - and indeed most 'older' member states during the first programming period. This method of implementation was selected in Austria for a number of reasons. These included the conviction that the creation of brand new structures would have been virtually impossible for reasons both of time and resources - particularly given the uncertain future of the Structural Funds after 1999. Many of the Austrian Objective areas, particularly Objective 2, were also too small to justify the establishment of new administrative structures at regional level. Further, given the additional financial resources available through the Structural Funds, there was political pressure from many quarters to include as many relevant agencies as possible. Thus, with few exceptions, no new structures were created: while some organisations received new competencies, these often tended to mirror existing areas of responsibility.

The Federal Chancellery, became responsible for the coordination of the Structural Funds in Austria and dialogue with the Commission. The overarching Austria-wide coordination lies with ÖROK while the financial coordination of each of the three Structural Funds is undertaken by three individual federal 'fund-corresponding' Ministries (*fond-korrespondierende Ministerien*). The management of individual Structural Funds programmes is carried out at *Land* level and coordinated by a specific *Land* government department which is responsible for overseeing the implementation of the particular programme and compiling the required monitoring data.

The only new institutional structure introduced by the Structural Funds is the regional management system, put in place to help administer and implement the Funds at regional level. While regional managers or consultants had operated in conjunction with national regional policy prior to EU accession, the comprehensive coverage introduced in line with the Structural Funds was a new development. Over 30 regional managers were put in place to aid the implementation process in Objective 1, 2 and 5b regions.

The exact remit of the regional managers has often been rather ambiguous and considerable variation exists in terms of the motivation, experience and sphere of activity between individual managers. The Federal Chancellery has described the following areas of competence as falling under the regional manager remit:

- transfer of information into the region, including innovative project ideas, information on financial support and specific consultancies;
- lobbying for, and information dissemination about, the region;
- assisting cooperation and coordination within the region, including tasks such as improving contacts and information flows between

regional actors, stimulating joint participation in projects, consensus building, bringing cooperation partners together; and,

- providing initial consultancy, ie. acting as a first point of contact for regional firms and helping them identify possible partners, funding sources etc.

The regional managers are not designed to act as competitors for other regional development organisations in the region, but rather to help stimulate cooperation between them for the overall benefit of the region. The identification and stimulation of good projects in the region and the support of these projects through to the implementation stage is less often included in official descriptions of the regional manager role - although a number are already working in this direction. Again, some disagreement exists about the extent to which regional managers could and should carry out this more in-depth type of regional development role.

While the choice to use existing institutional structures in the implementation of the Structural Funds appears logical, the nature of the Austrian system described above has made carrying out this decision in practice significantly more difficult. The very wide division of competence in the regional policy field resulted in the involvement of an enormously high number of funding organisations and schemes in the implementation of the Funds. In total, over 160 federal and *Land* aid schemes are being co-financed under Structural Fund programmes. In the Styrian Objective 2 programme alone, for example, 19 funding agencies and 46 aid schemes have been used. Further, the relatively informal functioning of institutional links and decision-making structures is not ideally suited to accommodate the complex requirements of EU aid. Indeed, the *ex ante* appraisal of the Objective 2 programmes commented that 'it will be very difficult to combine the promotion rules and limits of the EU Commission with the traditional Austrian promotion system' (Hesina *et al.* 1995).

A significantly increased administrative burden for the funding agencies involved in the distribution of the Structural Fund monies has been the first ramification of this choice. Award decisions are taken by individual funding agencies (at federal or *Land* level) responsible for the particular incentive schemes (*Richtlinien*) included in the Single Programming Document (SPD). The very high number of organisations and aid schemes involved has made this a complex and fragmented process. For many schemes, the demands of administering the EU aid have proved disproportional to the often very small co-financing budget. The way in which the Structural Fund monies have been allocated to schemes has often meant a concentration of resources in a relatively small number of schemes with the remainder spread very thinly over a much larger number. In the Objective 2 programmes, for example, up to 45 per cent of the total budget can be accounted for in only 6-7 schemes. On the basis of current experience, some funding agencies administering small co-financing budgets will almost certainly withdraw from the SPD in the next round of Structural Fund support.

A second ramification of the use of existing structures has been the absence of clear strategic direction in the process of Structural Fund implementation. Although SPDs exist for each Objective area, the practical reality has been that no real strategic overview has been maintained. Funding agencies make award decisions on the basis of their own internal criteria, with EU co-financing generally being awarded to a project if it is located in a Structural Fund designated area. There are rarely additional criteria for co-funded projects, although in a small number of cases, funding agencies do not co-finance every eligible project but attempt to target EU money on particularly high quality projects. For the vast majority of funding agencies, the SPD is of little or no relevance and the strategic direction set out in it is effectively sidelined. The flexibility to change the strategic direction is also limited by the implementation through such a large number of different schemes as shifting budgets between individual schemes is a complex and difficult operation.

Impact of Structural Funds at Different Institutional Levels

Major institutional incompatibilities, such as those outlined above, have caused tension and conflict for the implementation of the Structural Funds in Austria. However, this only provides part of the picture. More detailed analysis of the differentiated impact of Structural Fund intervention on the various tiers of government administration also identifies certain positive effects of the implementation process.

At federal level, the higher policy profile of regional development has led to the explicit incorporation of specific regional components within the activities of a range of Ministries. Caution must, however, be used in the evaluation of this trend which has been characterised as a 'profession of faith' which is not deeply rooted. The incorporation of regional components is also almost certainly motivated to a greater or lesser extent by the desire to access additional finance. However, seen from another angle, this trend does provide a starting point on which to build in the future and regional policy has certainly been placed much more firmly on the political agenda.

The Structural Funds have also increased the formal fora for coordination between federal Ministries - although arguably the impetus for coordination has had a greater positive impact at *Land* level. The institutional divisions between Ministries still exist and have not been greatly affected, for example, by Commission demands to integrate ERDF and ESF spending. Achieving effective coordination and/or simplification between individual Ministries is extremely difficult, as demonstrated by recent attempts to reform technology policy structures at federal level.

At *Land* level, perhaps the biggest impact of Structural Fund intervention has been to encourage coordination and cooperation between different regional development actors - even including departments within the same *Land* government which previously operated largely independently of one another. The impetus came principally from the requirement to produce multi-annual, coordinated regional development plans in the form of SPDs and the formation of programme groups to undertake this task. These groups comprised representatives of the federal Ministries, the *Länder*, the social partners and municipality representatives, bringing under one umbrella representatives from the three main tiers of government. Although they have generally been superseded in the implementation stage by internal *Land* coordination meetings, the initial work of the programme groups meant that participants learnt about the activities of other areas and were obliged to operate outside their normally relatively narrow areas of competence. While the SPDs themselves may, in this programming round at least, have subsequently proved of little relevance to the actual implementation, as shown earlier, the coordination initiated by their preparation could have longer-term beneficial effects.

The need for *Land* governments to initiate coordination with the federal level authorities has also been an important development. Contacts had clearly existed previously, although often narrowed to the administration of jointly co-financed federal-*Land* schemes. Coordination through fora such as the programme groups, and more strategically-oriented discussions, was less common and this development could make an important longer-term contribution to establishing more network-based and less hierarchical structures.

Some moves towards a simplification of structures are also evident at *Land* level. The Styrian system of economic development assistance, for example, has combined several *Richtlinien* into one, and similar initiative can be seen elsewhere. Perhaps of greater importance are new attitudes emerging in the run-up to the second round of Structural Fund finance in 2000-2006. Clearly, the continued current uncertainty relating to the reform of the Structural Funds under Agenda 2000 and the exact borders of the designated areas makes definite planning difficult. However, in several *Länder* the current programme managers have already initiated a process of thinking and planning. A common aim appears to be the definition of much clearer strategic aims and objectives and a simplification of the implementation procedures. This would principally be achieved through the involvement of a much reduced number of aid schemes and agencies, chosen to reflect more closely the strategic aims of the programme.

This activity not only points to the fact that the programme managers have learned from the mistakes and trials of the first programming period. It also suggests, however tentatively, that the advantages to be gained from a more integrated, programme based approach to regional development are being recognised. 'The qualitative demands made of the Austrian administration by the European Commission have resulted in a positive pressure to increase the strategic consistency of national regional policy' (Schwarz 1996). There is increasing effort, for example, to link the preparatory strategic planning and thinking for the next Structural Fund round with existing economic plans (*Leitbilder*) in the *Länder*. The aim is to find common strategic aims and thus more effectively target all available resources to meeting those aims. There is also some evidence of broader, more multi-disciplinary thinking with initially separate projects (such as the Regional Innovation Strategy initiative in Lower Austria) now feeding explicitly into the thinking for the new potential Structural Fund programme. Benchmarking and drawing on wider European experience is also widespread.

Finally, at regional level, although not a completely new phenomenon, the regional management system has helped to promote a more bottom-up approach to local development. This structure could be an important instrument in the future for the stimulation of cooperation at local level and endogenous regional growth. There is potential, for example, for expanding their activities in areas such as the active encouragement of cooperation, based on in-depth knowledge of regional firms and their circumstances, the provision of advice on the pre-selection of projects and the promotion of strategically important or innovative projects.

The current system, however, is not well integrated with other regional development initiatives, and sometimes not even within the Structural Fund system itself. Much currently rests on the motivation and vision of the individual concerned and continued uncertainty about the exact role of the regional managers has hindered their ability to contribute effectively to the overall process of regional development. There is on-going debate about the future remit of regional managers but an increased role would require a clearer definition of objectives, an accepted integration of their activities into planning and implementation structures and a recognition of the associated resource implications.

Towards the Future

The process of planning and preparation for Austria's second Structural Fund programming period is already gearing up. Discussions based on the experience of the last five years will examine new options for strategic direction and implementation of the Funds. Key components of the debate include how best to balance the priorities of Austrian regional development policy with the principles of the Structural Funds, as well as institutional issues, in an attempt to avoid some of the difficulties encountered in this first round.

In this regard, it is interesting to note that the actual progress of implementation in Austria was relatively good and the absorption of finance broadly on target. This is principally because the channelling of Structural Fund resources through existing structures has meant that application procedures for individual funding applicants have remained unchanged. Although the administrative burden for funding agencies themselves increased, the actual process of distributing the monies has been relatively smooth.

It is here that an interesting inherent contradiction can be observed. On the one hand, the Austrian policy rhetoric and discussion favours endogenous, dynamic regional development focusing on 'soft' factors, regional cooperation etc. but, on the other, the most important financial instruments used for regional development purposes in the co-financing of the Structural Funds comprise primarily investment-oriented business aid schemes. It may, in fact, be the choice to rely on such schemes as key sources of co-financing which restricts the working out of the Austrian 'vision' for regional policy more than any of the Commission imposed conditions. Clearly there is also another side to the coin; the Commission's demands (as well as domestic political pressure) to use all the money within the programming period arguably also favours an emphasis on business investment schemes which can use up large amounts of money relatively quickly. More innovative schemes, focusing for example of the promotion of cooperation or regional partnership, can prove either too slow or too cheap to develop.

Interviews with national policy-makers in Austria show that there is some feeling that the opportunity to push forward beneficial institutional reform on the back of Structural Fund implementation was lost in the first programming period. Underlying reasons for this were the time pressure associated with completing the programming plans and the significant additional administration and paperwork required by scheme notification and EU regulation compliance. Ultimately, the pressures and immediacy of smaller administrative requirements took precedence.

> An early wide-ranging 'clean-up' and restructuring of the Austrian system of assistance would, without doubt, be of considerable value. However, this would require the full attention of the funding agencies which are taken up with more time-consuming and currently more pressing questions, although of less importance in terms of their substance. This means that there is no time left for changes which are more important overall but which are not subject to time deadlines and constraints. (Zwerenz 1996)

It must also be remembered that the 1995-99 programming period was Austria's first contact with the Structural Funds and thus a sharp learning curve was to be expected. Experience from 'older' Member States shows that it takes considerable time to integrate and balance the Structural Fund requirements with the national system, using the positive aspects to best advantage and mitigating the problems as far as possible. The challenge within Austria in the run-up to the next programming period is to identify those areas where reform is most desirable and to achieve this change as effectively as possible.

In the institutional arena in particular it is clear that the universally recognised benefits of greater coordination and cooperation will take longer than a single five-year programming period really to take hold and it will be important to build on the important initial steps which have been taken in this direction. Vertical and horizontal cooperation remains constrained by political rivalry and administrative 'turf wars' - not a situation unique to Austria. However, effective regional and local development (both within and beyond the Structural Funds) increasingly emphasises the need for integrated approaches, mobilising different actors and government levels to work together. The Structural Funds have provided an important external impetus in this area not just in Austria - the 'integrated regional government offices' in England and Finland, regional conferences in Germany and area partnerships in Ireland are just a few examples from other European countries. There is considerable potential within Austria for progress in this area to continue and, if effective structures can be found, a real opportunity exists for the Structural Fund approach to improve the Austrian structures without overriding them.

Greater explicit strategic planning and prior consideration of the real objectives to be reached through the use of Structural Fund finance will help not only the implementation but also the visibility of EU support and its integration into wider economic and regional policy. It has been demonstrated above that this process has already been initiated by a number of programme managers. There is now the chance to identify ways to use the Structural Funds to co-finance innovative or riskier strategic initiatives related directly to new specified programme objectives. Agenda 2000 encourages 'the greater use of other forms of assistance than grants' in order to 'increase the multiplier effect of structural resources'. This has the potential to overcome some of the more philosophical differences in approach to regional development and to use the Structural Funds to support more dynamic and innovative projects rather than simply business investment. Clearly, however, this requires more careful planning and consideration in the preparation of programming objectives and implementation structures as well as, more widely, perhaps a different approach to the time pressure of financial absorption.

The first Structural Fund programming period has shown up strengths and weaknesses in both the Austrian and EU systems where the mutual consideration of the other's approach could be useful. The current preparations and negotiations for the 2000-2006 period are a forum for identifying the areas where positive change can be made. Improvements in all aspects of programming in other Member States have happened through such a process of incremental change and adjustment. It is important that the sometimes painful experiences of this programming period in Austria should reap future benefits for the country.

References

Hesina, W. *et al.* (1995) *Ex-ante Appraisal of the Austrian Objective 2 Regional Development Plans.* Seibersdorf: Austrian Research Centre Seibersdorf.

Österreichische Raumordnungskonferenz (1991) *Österreichische Raum-ordnungskonzept 1991.* Vienna: ÖROK.

Österreichische Raumordnungskonferenz (1993) *Siebenter Raumordnungs-bericht.* Vienna: ÖROK.

Österreichische Raumordnungskonferenz (1998) *Raumordnung in Öster-reich.* Vienna: ÖROK.

Rieger, H. and Schmied, C. (1996) *Handbuch EU-Konformer Förderungen.* Vienna: Ueberreuter.

Schwarz, W. (1996) *EU Regionalförderung in Niederösterreich - eine neue Qualität unserer Regionalpolitik.* AMR Info. 26.

Zwerenz, G. (1996) 'Wirtschaftsförderung - EU-konforme Durchführung und viel neuer Verwaltungsaufwand.' *Wirtschaftspolitische Blätter*, 3-4, Vienna.

Further Reading

Bachtler, J., Downes, R. and Michie, R. (1997) *The Interim Evaluation of Objective 2 Programmes.* IQ Net Thematic Paper, Series 2, No. 1, European Policies Research Centre, Glasgow.

Bachtler, J. and Michie, R. (1997) *The Evolution of Objective 2 Programmes and Future Prospects.* IQ Net Thematic Paper, Series 3, No. 1, European Policies Research Centre, Glasgow.

Downes, R. and Bachtler, J. (1997) *EU Structural Funds and Business Aid in Austria.* Regional and Industrial Policy Research Series, European Policies Research Centre, Glasgow.

Downes, R. and Bachtler, J. (1998) 'Komplexitätsreduktion - regionale Wirtschaftsförderung in Österreich.' *RAUM 30.* Vienna: Österreichische Institut für Raumplanung.

Gruber, M. (1997) 'Perspectives on EU Regional Policy from a New Member State: Austria.' In J. Bachtler and I. Turok (eds) *The Coherence of EU Structural Policies:*

Contrasting Perspectives on European Regional Development. London: Jessica Kingsley.

Kearney, C., Bachtler, J. and Taylor, S. (1996) *Monitoring and Evaluation in Objective 2 Programmes: Progress and Challenges.* IQ Net Thematic Paper, Series 1, No. 4, European Policies Research Centre, Glasgow.

Mayerhofer, P. (1995) Österreichs Regionalförderung nach dem EU-Beitritt. *WIFO Monatsberichte* 5/95.

Michie, R. and Bachtler, J. (1996) *Managing the Structural Funds: Institutionalising Good Practice.* IQ Net Thematic Paper, Series 1, No. 1, European Policies Research Centre, Glasgow.

PART V

PERSPECTIVE

12 Institutional Change, Governance and Regional Development: Problems and Perspectives

GRETA CAMERON, MIKE DANSON AND HENRIK HALKIER

The chapters in this book have clearly demonstrated that economic development in a particular region is no longer the exclusive responsibility of one public body, i.e. central government or a regional development agency. Instead many organisations, often sponsored by different levels of government, are involved in a complex network of policy-making institutions that constitute a new form of governance of regional development. This situation strongly suggests that, although our understanding of the activities of individual agencies still leaves a good deal to be desired (Halkier, Danson and Damborg 1998), the study of inter-organisational relations is rightly becoming a major field of research.

The research results presented, of course, do add to our knowledge about governance and institutional change in regional development, but it is perhaps even more important that by questioning central assumptions in the existing literature, they point towards new directions for future research.

In the introduction to this volume we stressed that two aspects which are central to regional governance, institutional change and regional development in particular would benefit from further examination. These concern, on the one hand, how institutions affect change, and on the other, what the consequences are of qualitative rather than evolutionary changes on regional development strategies and policies.

A critical conclusion to the previous publication 'Regional Development Agencies in Europe' (Halkier, Danson and Damborg 1998) was that the institutions at the core of economic programmes for regions - regional development agencies, themselves have been transforming to reflect and promote these changes. In particular, they have been evolving into coordinators and catalysts of economic development, compared with their perceived traditional role of exclusive, direct deliverers of policies and strategies. This has been brought about by ongoing changes in the structures of governance at the regional level which have altered the position of the economic development agencies vis-à-vis their political sponsors and concomitantly increased the level of decentralisation, both within nations and regions. This book has complemented and built upon those conclusions by exploring a comparative selection of forms and structures established for regional development across Europe. Further, by incorporating a multidisciplinary approach to the analysis of the case studies, it has improved our understanding of the dimensions of the causes and consequences of these changes.

The contributions to this volume have focused on three aspects of inter-organisational relations in regional policy that would seem to be particularly significant:

- institutional cooperation, including partnerships between public and sometimes private actors established to implement joint programmes and strategies;
- horizontal aspects of governance and inter-organisational relations at the regional level;
- vertical aspects of multi-level governance and the interplay between different tiers of government.

It is hardly surprising that institutionalised cooperation has become an important feature of regional development in recent years. With a vastly increased number of organisations active in this field of public policy, formalised cooperation makes the institutional environment of individual organisations less unpredictable, and development partnerships are therefore often shrouded in rhetoric about 'the need to bring key actors together', 'exploit synergies' and 'be able to cope with larger projects by pooling resources' under the unifying banner of shared territorial interest. Especially over the last decade, the range and number of organisations which have become involved with working in partnership has increased dramatically. This has progressed to the extent that many organisations achieve their objectives by collaborating closely with other organisations. This new institutional arrangement of operating has been partially driven by the declining financial support of national governments and the resulting growth of indigenous and bottom-up policies. Examples of this change can be identified throughout the case studies presented here. It is possible also to identify the gradual relative move towards a dependency on support derived from the European Union (EU). This change is significant in that European funding is focused on releasing finance through partnerships, while the EU also increasingly determines the criteria for regional economic development initiatives in other ways than the carrot of pecuniary rewards alone.

Thus, while it cannot be denied that functional advantages and territorial politics play an important part in the rise of formalised partnerships (Halkier and Damborg; Jud and Steiner, for instance, in this volume), at the same time other factors would also seem to be at work. In many cases European or national levels of government have created strong incentives for regional actors to enter into various forms of partnership because access to additional resources from, for example, the European Structural Funds (Halkier and Damborg; Kafakalas and Thoidou, in this volume) or central government (Wong; Jensen and Leijon, in this volume) depend on this adoption of certain organisational formats.

At the institutional or micro level the debate centres around two main themes: the motives and interests of each partner's involvement and the post-establishment consequences of joining the new institutional arrangements of partnership. Such differences in the motives and interests can be considered to be dependent on the status of organisations (whether public or private) and the tiers of government which affect them. Those differences could lead to diverging economic interests, time perspectives, and territorial politics, all of which may impact on the level of compatibility and thus usefulness of the resultant strategies. The methods in place to access European structural funds, and hence the need to embrace the partnership approach to economic development, can have profound impacts on the participating institutions. Thus it may be that the levels of power, conflict and trust inherently involved in working in partnership may be imposed upon an organisation rather than embraced openly as simple extensions of their own cultural approach to development. The arrangements adopted, therefore, may find difficulty in realising the potential benefits of the partnership.

The pragmatic reasons for entering into partnership arrangements also suggest that in practice formalised cooperation in regional development may work more or less smoothly, but that *making* it work may entail a significant effort. As demonstrated by the Styrian case (Jud and Steiner, in this volume), consensus and inter-organisational trust can be built through a deliberate process; they are not 'cultural' assets that some regions like the so-called Third Italy happen to have and which forever will elude other regions. It is, however, also clear that the chances of succeeding in building this form of 'social capital' would still seem to depend on prevailing political traditions. It is perhaps not a coincidence that examples of relatively successful consensus building can be found in countries with a corporatist and collaborative political tradition (e.g. Austria and Scandinavia) while more awkward relations between public and private actors are in evidence in countries dominated by more liberal traditions such as England. Even then, as Downes argues in her chapter, despite the partnership principle of funding being more easily fulfilled in the Austrian economy, vertical and horizontal cooperation remains constrained by political rivalry and administrative 'turf wars'. The other contributions to this volume confirm that this is not a situation unique to Austria.

It may well be that in a medium- or long-term perspective the proliferation of institutionalised partnerships and other forms of inter-organisational collaboration will in itself contribute to the creation of new forms of consensus with regard to regional development. First and foremost the various pressures for isomorphic change would seem gradually to make organisations within a region more similar to one another. Add to this the presence of organisations that are neither public nor private in the traditional sense of the words and the emergence of a 'development profession' sharing a common educational background and careers that straddle traditional sectoral boundaries, and the prospects of a more widely shared consensus about aims and methods in regional policy would seem to be a very real one indeed. It is, however, important to note that the trends towards organisational isomorphism and strategic convergence may eventually undermine some important assumptions underlying current modes of operation within regional policy. The traditional rationale of regional development agencies (Danson, Halkier and Damborg 1998) as semi-autonomous organisations capable of setting their own agenda is clearly being challenged when development bodies operate in a web of formalised interaction. But, paradoxically, the official rationale for partnership and networking may itself be eroded because when organisations become more and more alike, they are less capable of making a distinct contribution to collaborative projects. Hence what was originally a useful pooling of different resources can easily become a recipe for inter-organisational competition (Halkier and Damborg, in this volume), and that could destabilise the organisational set-up surrounding economic development within the region.

Following the establishment of the partnership, and consequent on these arrangements, there may well be secondary effects within each organisation from adopting this form of working. In the short term, there may be such benefits as increased funding and resources in general, for example through enhanced access to information and improved human capital. However, one of the many research interests explored in this volume has concerned how these new links will influence and affect the organisations engaged.

A key question which follows on from this is whether the model of partnership should be universally or whether it is particularly suited to certain environments and organisations. What can be determined is that working in partnership has a variety of effects on those organisations involved, and in some cases those effects may be unfavourable. For example and as determined above, applying DiMaggio and Powell's (1983) theoretical construct of institutional isomorphic change in a non-competitive environment affords one such approach. So, a case can be forwarded which suggests that regional development agencies may compromise their advantages, efficiency and effectiveness in economic development by acting in partnership.

Future research in this area could consider whether the 'encouragement' of partnership through financial gain is the most sustainable institutional arrangement for regional economic development in all circumstances and environments. The experience in the Greek region of Macedonia, for instance (Kafakalas and Thoidou, in this volume) with the gradual establishment of RDAs in the promotion of regional intelligence - through the construction of 'institutional thickness' and artificial administrative bodies - as a method of increasing the competitiveness of enterprises in the region, is somewhat mixed. So, encouraged by the European Union through the arrangements to access the Structural Funds, leaves the question unresolved - can the promotion of 'artificial' regional development through the building of intelligence and/or institutions, by financial inducement, continue after the funding is depleted.

As the European Union reduces its involvement in certain regions with its expansion into the former centrally planned economies, this method of working will come under the focus of local policymakers more clearly. Concentrating on the essential value added of this approach even further, as this arrangement becomes more popular, can new types of partnership be constructed solely on a need for synergies of a non-financial nature? It would appear that Bukve (this volume) has identified a move within Norway, which is not incorporated into the European Union, towards experiences similar to EU member states, where bottom-up policies and reduced political control are now evident. Perhaps it is only a matter of time until Norway progresses towards more formalised partnership working, yet not based on the monetary or bureaucratic controls of the EU.

On a meso level, the last two decades have seen an expansion in the reliance on joint actions between institutions and different tiers of government. One of the terms most used to explain the increase in this is the level of 'institutional thickness'. It is generally considered that the greater the density of organisations the more a region is capable of promoting regional economic development, with the potential to encourage enterprise development and learning. However, the studies on Denmark and Macedonia reported here, extend the belief that there is a certain optimum level of institutional thickness. They suggest that when the number of organisations becomes prolific and bottom-up initiatives explode, the result is weakness rather than strength for the regional economy. The landscape becomes crowded and competitive through duplication of effort and policies. One advantage, of course, may be the level of choice available to the consumer. Whereas industrial districts, for example Emilia Romagna, consider one of their strengths to be the very density of institutions in their respective localities, the area of North

Jutland is experiencing a growth in institutions which is skewed towards competition rather than coordination, with difficulties in establishing trust and a sense of purpose between public and private partners. As argued in the case of West Sweden also, the differences may be due to North Jutland being a new and artificial administrative region with a heterogenous economic structure.

Undoubtedly, the enlargement of the European Union will cause pressure on the regional level to provide institutions for economic development, perhaps exacerbating this problem. Parallels can be drawn between the micro and meso level at this point. As noted above, the 'encouragement' of partnership working through financial criteria has resulted in a significant number of partnerships being formed. The research question arises of whether more such partnerships will develop over time as the opportunity presents itself and, concomittantly, whether the inducement of financial gain will mean the creation of an uncoordinated mixture of organisations duplicating effort and roles in a supposedly non-competitive environment.

Further comparisons may be considered between countries. Whereas urban regime theory - where public and private actors have a perceived common purpose and thus there is strong business participation in urban coalition building - is supported in the United States, the position in Europe appears to be less of cooperation. Investigation into two English regions has shown that unlike the organic nature hypothesised by regime theory, partnership development is very much a mechanistic arrangement to meet the requirements of an external funding framework. In Denmark, in order to gain funding from Europe, competition rather than coordination is the norm and it appears that there are a large number of organisations at the regional level which are public and competing. A main difference, then, is that in the absence of any key significant resources from the private sector, local partnerships in Europe are very much led by the public sector under a 'semi-coercive framework' from central government.

At the macro level the relationship between regionally based initiatives and the emerging European System of governance in Western Europe is examined through the experiences of several countries. An interesting aspect of the cases given is the comparison that can be made between the Norwegian experience and that of those economies within the European Union system of regional development. It appears from the cases that Norway is following a similar path as the European system. That is, one where autonomy for the political bodies at the county/regional level is reducing and being replaced by a structure of governance and 'arms length' involvement. Further, Norway's regional economy depends on the mutual dependence between private and public organisations. This cooperation is based on the system whereby decisions concerning investment and localisation belong to the private sphere whereas the public sphere decides on the rules of the game. Although the organisations are not formally working together as yet, they are unquestionably building a situation where the underlying criteria to partake in partnership is fulfilled, namely mutual dependence.

The European Union and national governments are trying to create sufficient institutional capacity and thickness to build successful regional economies, increasingly as clusters (Danson and Whittam 1998), within which networks and partnerships can operate. Where there is an internal coherence and identity, this promises the potential for success, but in some cases the region has not been defined nor developed sufficiently. Thus institutions may operate in a vacuum or in spatial areas that do not match with the functional regions, making networking and partnership problematic. In some instances such as West Sweden and England, governments have been creating 'artificial' regions without promoting consensus building, with regional assemblies established where members are not democratically elected to their positions. Elsewhere, and particularly in Spain, there are problems of asymmetrical developments, with Catalonia and the Basque Country, for instance, progressing and desiring autonomy more readily than the rest of the country. Moreover, other cases some regions may not be recognised within an economy, including the stateless nations across Europe. All of those inequalities obviously provide difficulty in partnership building and suggest a non-uniform approach to regional economic development.

The cases outlined in this book highlight the differences between the economies in Europe in historical, political, economic, cultural, and organisational terms. Throughout the chapters it is evident that the rising importance of partnership is having various impacts on communities across the continent, with associated effects on their regional development agencies. The impacts have been shown to be of a broadly positive or negative nature and in some cases both are present in varying degrees. It may be that one of the independent variables, such as historical factors, is the key to a successful region. For example, one may propose that if regions know 'who' they are, they may do better in terms of potential to take on processes of development than 'created' regions who have no knowledge (or history) of 'who' they are. There may also be a certain mix of public and private influences which determines potential for success. It has been argued here also that actor strategies, such as 'persuasive storytelling', may have a much greater role in supporting or creating a viable and prosperous region than has been noted previously. It appears that there are many more avenues for research on the role which partnership working has in reducing, depleting or indeed accentuating the differences and inequalities between regions than have been explored in the literature.

Following the wave of research in the 1980s on industrial districts and the recent attention paid to clusters as the prefered route to promoting successful regional economic growth strategies (see Danson and Whittam 1989 and 1999 for details), there is a greater appreciation of the role of cultural and other invisible factors in development processes at the sub-national level. By analogy and directly, this work does suggest that the partnership model will operate more favourably in some circumstances, and particularly where there is a pre-disposition towards consensual politics, trust and cooperation. An expansion of the realisation that partnerships and networks may not be universially applicable as the model approach to regional economic development could be expected to follow in the coming years.

Nevertheless, research on arrangements for new patterns of institutional change, governance and regional development and their effects is in the early stages of development. As outlined and developed in this book, there are many issues surrounding the model at the organisational, regional, national and European levels and therefore further research of both a comparative and historical nature would increase the ability to identify where partnership is most liable to be sustainable and successful.

This necessitates a return to the methods and academic disciplines applied to the research of governance and institutions in regional development, and underline that the study of bottom-up regional policy today requires that the traditional reliance on methods from economics and geography is supplemented by, for example, organisational and institutional studies, politics and administration, and history and discourse analysis. The changing nature of regional policy does in other words lead to an expansion of the disciplinary boundaries within which regional studies traditionally operate.

Through the judicious use of such a range of approaches, this book goes some way to explaining the changing structure within regional development, from one where organisations work alongside each other to one where cooperation and working in partnership is becoming the norm. Whether exogenous factors such as the European Union, financial resources, and 'persuasive storytelling' encourage a sustainable positive change or whether endogenous factors within an economy are the key, will only be determined in time.

References

Danson, M., Halkier, H. and Damborg, C. (1998) 'Regional development agencies in Europe - an introduction and framework for analysis.' In H. Halkier, M. Danson and C. Damborg (eds) *Regional Development Agencies in Europe*. London: Jessica Kingsley Publishers, 13-25.

Danson, M. and Whittam, G. (1998) 'Networks, innovations and industrial districts: the case of Scotland'. In M. Steiner (ed) *Clusters and Regional Specialisation*. London: Pion, 192-210.

Danson, M. and Whittam, G. (1999) 'Clustering, innovation and trust: the essentials of a clusters strategy for Scotland.' In *Innovation Networks and Localities*. M. Fischer, L. Suarez-Villa and M. Steiner (eds) Springer-Verlag, forthcoming.

DiMaggio, P.J. and Powell, W. (1983) 'The iron cage revisited: institutional isomorphism and collective rationality in organizational fields.' *American Sociological Review 48*, 147-60.

Halkier, H., Danson, M. and Damborg, C. (eds) (1998) *Regional Development Agencies in Europe*. London: Jessica Kingsley Publishers.

Halkier, H., Danson, M. and Damborg, C. (1998) 'Regional development agencies in the new Europe - patterns, issues and prospects.' In H. Halkier, M. Danson and C. Damborg (eds) *Regional Development Agencies in Europe*. London: Jessica Kingsley Publishers, 343-57.

Index